TRUMPOCALYPSE

Also by David Frum

Trumpocracy: The Corruption of the American Republic

Patriots: A Novel

Why Romney Lost (And What the GOP Can Do About It)

Comeback: Conservatism That Can Win Again

The Right Man: An Inside Account of the Bush White House

An End to Evil: How to Win the War on Terror (with Richard Perle)

*How We Got Here: The 70's, The Decade That Brought
You Modern Life (For Better or Worse)*

*What's Right: The New Conservative Majority
and the Remaking of America*

Dead Right

TRUMPOCALYPSE

RESTORING
AMERICAN DEMOCRACY

DAVID FRUM

HARPER

An Imprint of HarperCollins*Publishers*

HarperCollins books may be purchased for educational, business, or sales promotional use. For information, please email the Special Markets Department at SPsales@harpercollins.com.

FIRST EDITION

Library of Congress Cataloging-in-Publication Data
Names: Frum, David, author.
Title: Trumpocalypse : restoring American democracy / David Frum.
Other titles: Restoring American democracy
Description: First edition. | New York, NY : Harper, [2020] | Includes index. | Summary: "A huge swath of Americans see the rest of the country building a future that doesn't have a place for them. It's no wonder they'd rather burn it all down. But the fire can be stopped by Americans who act now to protect their country and its democracy"— Provided by publisher.
Identifiers: LCCN 2020003406 (print) | LCCN 2020003407 (ebook) | ISBN 9780062978417 (hardcover) | ISBN 9780062978431 (ebook)
Subjects: LCSH: United States—Politics and government—2017- | Trump, Donald, 1946- | Democracy—United States—History—21st century. | Political culture—United States—History—21st century.
Classification: LCC E912 .F775 2020 (print) | LCC E912 (ebook) | DDC 973.933—dc23
LC record available at https://lccn.loc.gov/2020003406
LC ebook record available at https://lccn.loc.gov/2020003407

20 21 22 23 24 LSC 10 9 8 7 6 5 4 3 2 1

To the conservatives, Republicans, and libertarians of "Never Trump."
As sung in the old American hymn:
"When all were false, I found thee true."

Contents

TRUMPOCALYPSE

Introduction

I write in mid-March 2020 under virtual house arrest. A deadly pandemic sweeps the nation and the planet. A fierce global recession is gathering.

President Donald J. Trump did not start the pandemic, of course. But at every step of the way, Trump has acted as if guided by one rule: "How can I make this trauma worse?"

Trump ignored warnings about pandemics ahead from the very first day he entered office. He dismantled the White House pandemic unit. Later, he refused to use off-the-shelf testing technology that could have saved many lives. Through January, February, and into March 2020, he denied the crisis, lest rising numbers of victims lower the stock market and his poll numbers. His personal unconcern spread the infection to guests at Mar-a-Lago, to thousands of American air travelers forced to wait hours to clear customs among visibly ill fellow passengers.

When the crisis could be denied no further, his first thought was to game the stock market a little longer. His second thought was to bail out casinos and hotels—including his own.

Since his bankruptcies at the end of the 1980s, Trump has contrived schemes and scams to keep his creditors at bay for the next twenty-four hours. That is how he has managed the coronavirus crisis. Each day he devised some new fantasy in the hope of lulling his supporters and boosting financial indexes. Through ten squandered weeks, Trump's digital friends on television, radio, and social media parroted back to him the lies he tweeted at them. There was never any plan. There was only a frantic surge of empty words to continue the flimflam one day longer. He and his propagandists fogged the air with excuses: the virus was a hoax by Democrats and the media, a sinister plot to capsize the economy and deny the magnificent accomplishments of the Trump presidency.

"I don't take responsibility at all." Those words of Donald Trump at a March 13, 2020, press conference are likely to be history's epitaph on his presidency.

At each of the nation's many trials, the person who had sought the presidency also acquired responsibility for decisions and their consequences. As prepresidential Donald Trump himself tweeted on November 8, 2013: leadership means, "whatever happens, you're responsible. If it doesn't happen, you're responsible." Trump dictated those words. He never lived by them. Having preened for three years about the growing economy he inherited, he felt grievously wronged to be held to account for the calamities that struck in his fourth year. The rooster who took credit for the sunrise was outraged to be blamed for the sunset.

As the sick roll lengthened, as the economy collapsed, Trump moaned in ever louder self-pity. It was all so unfair to him! The moaning was echoed and amplified by Trump's allies in media.

"The attempt to deflect and blame the media and Democrats from Trish Regan, Sean Hannity, Laura Ingraham, Lou Dobbs, Jesse Watters, and Greg Gutfeld instead of addressing the coronavirus is really irresponsible and hazardous to our viewers," an unnamed producer at Fox News told CNN's Brian Stelter. The producer could have added Jeanine Pirro, the *Fox & Friends* crew, and so many others, hosts and guests, as well as the radio personality Rush Limbaugh, who argued on air that health professionals were exaggerating the risks of coronavirus in order to stop Trump's primary-season rallies. These pro-Trump talkers were serving Trump as he demanded to be served, and as they had so devotedly served him before. Trump insisted there was nothing to worry about, the virus was only the common flu, that the number of cases would soon drop to zero, that he had imposed airtight containment, that there was nothing to worry about. His allies seconded his message. His supporters believed it.

Trump responds to challenge by directing rage at some designated enemy. Hence his attempt to rebrand coronavirus as "the Chinese virus," so that there would be some target of hatred more satisfying than a microorganism. Tens of millions of Americans responded instinctually to Trump's incitement against the media, against the cities, against China. Even if plague and recession topple Trump from the presidency, that core Trump base will remain, alienated and resentful. An Arkansas pastor told the *Washington Post* in the first week of March that half his congregants would lick the floor to prove the virus harmless.

If they would risk their lives for Trump, they will certainly risk the stability of American democracy. They brought the Trumpocalypse upon the country, and a post-Trumpocalypse country will have to find a way either to reconcile them to democracy—or to protect democracy from them.

Trumpism was among other things an "affinity fraud": a scam that exploits the trust of people who feel something in common with the fraudster. Until mid-March, millions of American conservatives, millions of evangelical churchgoers, millions of trusting Fox viewers, were deceived that they would betray their ideals and their president if they took precautions to protect themselves and their loved ones. An NBC/*Wall Street Journal* poll of March 11–13 found that Democrats were twice as likely as Republicans to cancel gatherings and postpone travel; three times as likely as Republicans to avoid bars and restaurants.

Yet even as the Trump base harmed itself, the rest of American society demonstrated its enduring resilience. While the president blathered lethal fantasies, the free American media shared lifesaving information. While the Trump-led federal government dithered incompetently, state governments and civil society filled the void. Lady Gaga dispensed better health advice to her social media followers than the president of the United States did to his.

You will know, reader, the success of this social response. I can only hope for the best and prepare for the worst.

The body of this book was written in a time of prosperity. You will notice premonitions of trouble ahead, especially the impending consequences of Trump's trade wars. But I did not foresee trouble arriving so soon, on such a grim scale. That trouble will wreck the Trump presidency and very likely inflict damage on Trump's political party. The United States will shortly be swinging on a social and political pendulum far, far away from Trump and Trumpism.

That swing, the book did foresee. In its second half, I speculate about a new era of reform following the Trump era. But there is an important difference between the reforms I urge in *Trumpocalypse* and the reforms promised by the politicians most likely to head the US government after the election of 2020.

The incoming politicians' promised reforms are progressive, with a lowercase *p*. Those incoming politicians vow to redistribute income, expand the social insurance system, loosen immigration enforcement, direct more public funds to colleges and universities, and raise taxes on wealthier people and businesses.

The reforms I address in this book, however, are mostly Progressive with a capital *P*. My proposed reforms would enhance the efficiency of government, improve the integrity of elections, and strengthen the national state. They are, to a great extent, reforms of the process of government, whose benefits will accrue over years and decades—not immediate responses to the crisis of the moment.

In politics, the urgent will usually overwhelm the important. That is natural, inevitable, even to some extent desirable. But the reason that the United States was so vulnerable to a demagogue like Trump was precisely because a long backlog of the "important" has again and again been overwhelmed by the "urgent."

If the United States had a more representative voting system, Trump would never have been elected president in the first place.

If the United States had a more professional public sector, Trump would not have been able to impose his corrupt practices so easily.

If the US Senate functioned something more like a democratic legislature, the public sector would in its turn function more professionally.

If the American population were less riven along ethnocultural lines, then the US Senate would function more like a democratic legislature.

The spectacular debacles that enrage and terrify voters often trace back to technicalities that bore those voters. But Americans will not prevent the debacles until they fix the technicalities.

Trump walked through an unlocked door. We can do a better job policing the walkway to the door. But we would need less policing if the door were more secure. That's this book's grand theme—and I would plead with you to consider this theme as relevant in the hard days ahead as it was when those hard days existed only in my anxieties.

Now I feel another anxiety.

Trump's negligence and fecklessness are inflicting unimagined grief and suffering on the United States. The disease will strike harder in the Blue-voting cities than the Red-voting empty spaces, and many in the Blue zone may blame the Red for the miseries ahead. In the next political chapter, there will be little patience for those earnest anthropological expeditions into MAGA-land that once engaged so much media energy. How do you listen to people if you blame their votes for killing your mother before her time?

I don't know, in this mood, whether I will get much hearing for my pleas for reconciliation and nation building as a response to Trump. Yet post-Trump, reconciliation and nation building will be needed even more than they were needed pre-Trump.

The modern world is too big and too dangerous for the unaided individual. If we have learned nothing else from recent experience, we must learn this. But where will that aid come from? For Americans, the options are only two: nation or tribe. Across the Atlantic, there beckons a third ideal, bigger than either: "Europe." For reasons of history, geography, and culture, no plausible supranationalism exists on this side of the ocean. If Americans do not identify as Americans, they will identify more narrowly and acrimoniously, not more universally and humanely.

Americans must start from where they are, build from what they have, to repair the damage Trump inflicted on the country, to amend the wrongs that, under Trump, they inflicted on each other.

Late into Election Night 2016, I was locked up inside a television studio. I telephoned home a few minutes after the results were certain. I spoke first to my youngest child, then only fifteen. She still remembers what I said to her that night: "I am so sorry. We failed you." I came of age inside the conservative movement of the twentieth century. In the twenty-first, that movement has delivered much more harm than good, from the Iraq War to the financial crisis to the Trump presidency. Underneath it all, there remain ideals in which I still believe. Yet I cannot deny the tally. It is long past time to correct course.

> I had a dream, which was not all a dream.
> The bright sun was extinguish'd, and the stars
> Did wander darkling in the eternal space,
> Rayless, and pathless, and the icy earth
> Swung blind and blackening in the moonless air;
> Morn came and went—and came, and brought no day,
> And men forgot their passions in the dread
> Of this their desolation; and all hearts
> Were chill'd into a selfish prayer for light:

Lord Byron wrote those lines in 1816, after a volcanic explosion in what is now Indonesia dimmed sunshine, chilled temperatures, and killed crops all over the world. Like the people in the poem, we too are praying for light in these lethal days of spring 2020. But when I first read the poem as a teenager, and when I return to it now, I could not, cannot, understand why Byron dismissed that prayer as selfish. We do not pray light for ourselves only, but for everyone. And we do more than pray for it. We work for it. And although as I write, we are working in physical isolation, the miraculous technology of our era allows us to join minds even when our bodies are separated.

This book is dedicated to the many people who are working for the return of light, and most especially to those who share my background in conservative and Republican politics. We have both a special duty—and a special perspective. We owe more; and we also, I believe, are positioned to do more.

The Trumpocalypse of the title is now a Trumpocalypse in reality. We often use the word *apocalypse* to mean something destructive: nuclear apocalypse, climate apocalypse. But the word "apocalypse" originally and literally means an uncovering, a revelation. For the Jews and Christians who introduced the concept into our religious traditions, an "apocalypse" was not the end. It was a beginning. It would inaugurate a new and better order in which justice would triumph at last over injustice. So those ancient prophets yearned. So let it be.

Part I

THE RECKONING

CHAPTER ONE

The Smash-Up

Whether President Trump wins or loses reelection, the forces that brought him to power—and sustained him there as he violated laws and trashed norms—will not magically vanish after an electoral defeat, especially not if the vote is close. An ex-president Trump will tell his supporters that he was defeated by voter fraud or the deep state or maybe by a Never Trump stab in the back. The vast pseudo-information media that sustained Trump in office will gleefully amplify this bitter message. The voices of the pseudo-information media may resonate even louder after Trump's presidency, because that media will not be burdened by the imperative to exonerate or distract from today's latest Trump outrage or scandal. Trump may serve them out of office even better as a source of resentment and a symbol of betrayal than he ever did in office.

Should Trump win, he and his supporters will feel vindicated and empowered. They will violate more laws and trash more norms—a very dangerous outcome.

Should Trump win the Electoral College without a popular-vote mandate, such a win will look even less legitimate to Trump's opponents than his 2016 victory. That, too, will be a dangerous outcome. Through the first Trump term, Trump opponents poured their energies into electoral politics. They registered and voted in record numbers. If that effort proves futile—if Trump wins a second Electoral College victory despite being rejected by the vote of the American people—what happens? Do, say, 70 million Americans quietly agree that their votes matter less than the, say, 65 million people favored by the Electoral College system? Or do they decide that the political system is broken and unfair, and express their dissent by protests in the streets?

The flashpoints of American politics may spark hot and bright in the years ahead.

Flashpoint: As in the Obama years, so in the Trump years, the benefits of economic growth flowed fastest to the big cities, to the knowledge centers, to educated elites. Typical families did not see much benefit from Trump's tax cut. As of mid-2019, Trump's tariffs had devoured all but $100 of the $930 tax cut received by the average American household.

There was no manufacturing renaissance under Trump. The United States added about five hundred thousand manufacturing jobs between January 2017 and the summer of 2019, a slightly slower rate of growth than between June 2010 and December 2016.[1] Manufacturing's share of US GDP slightly declined in the Trump years as compared to Obama's second term.[2] Nor is the outlook brighter ahead. The Trump tax cut utterly failed to produce the promised surge in business investment.[3] In the fall of 2019, manufacturing output began to contract.[4]

Sooner or later, the economic expansion that began in the summer of 2010 will end. But if Trump has left office before the next recession arrives, he will also bequeath the myth of a Trump "good old days" to haunt and taunt those who must clean up after him. Restoring democracy becomes harder when voters credit bygone autocrats with vanished prosperity and blame responsible liberals for the subsequent austerity.

Flashpoint: The gaps between city and country are widening fast. "Rural America is the new inner city," the *Wall Street Journal* proclaimed in May 2017.

In terms of poverty, college attainment, teenage births, divorce, death rates from heart disease and cancer, reliance on federal disability insurance and male labor-force participation, rural counties now rank the worst among the four major U.S. population groupings (the others are big cities, suburbs and medium or small metro areas).[5]

No progress was made in Trump's first two years in bringing broadband Internet to the 39 percent of rural Americans who lacked it. Net farm income peaked in 2013 at $136 billion. By the end of 2018, it had tumbled to about $60 billion.[6] The $28 billion of subsidies Trump poured into the farm belt to compensate it for his trade war is more than *double* the aid given to the auto industry in 2009.[7] The auto money was repaid. The farm money never will be.

In 2008, Democratic-held districts in the House of Representatives produced an average of $35.7 million worth of goods and services. By 2018, Blue-seat output had increased to an average of $48.5 million. Over that same period, the output of Red-seat districts *declined*, from an average of $33.2 million to an average of $32.6 million.[8]

By the end of 2019, 10 percent more people were at work in big cities than had worked there in 2007, before the Great Recession. One percent *fewer* people were working in nonmetro areas in 2019 than in 2007. Over the economic expansion from 2010 through 2019, the cities created jobs at a pace three times faster than the nonmetro areas—*with no noticeable difference in the rate of nonmetro job creation between last three years of the Obama administration and the first three years of the Trump administration.*[9]

Flashpoint: The American sexes live increasingly apart from—and alienated from—each other. About 60 percent of Americans under age thirty-five live without a spouse or partner. People under thirty-five are more likely to live with a parent than with a partner, an outcome not seen since the nineteenth century.[10] It's not only the young. The middle-aged also live increasingly apart. Almost one-third of middle-aged Americans, aged thirty-five to fifty-four, live without a partner.[11] As their lives diverge, as sexual joy recedes, men and women also vote increasingly differently.

By 2019, only 29 percent of American women believed Trump respects women equally to men. While minority women feel especially disrespected, so do 59 percent of white women.[12]

In 2019, men were thirteen points more likely to approve President Trump than women—by far the widest presidential approval gender gap ever recorded. Offered a choice between a government that taxed more and offered more in services, or taxed less and offered less, women and men diverged in 2019 by twenty-two points, again the widest gap ever recorded.[13]

Meanwhile, the Republican Party spoke to the cultural grievances of American men. In 2016, 64 percent of Republican voters complained that society had become "too soft and feminine." Forty-three percent of Republicans agreed that society often punishes men just for being men.[14]

Flashpoint: Trumpism drew its strength from older Americans, especially the baby boom generation. Until the year 2000, Americans over the age of sixty-five did not regularly vote notably differently from those younger than them. But as the country has become more diverse—and with the rise of Fox News after 1996 and Facebook after 2006—older Americans have been radicalized. Over-sixty-fives voted for Trump over Clinton fifty-eight to thirty-nine in 2016. Over-sixty-fives are much less likely to care about climate change than younger Americans—and radically more likely to describe immigration as "a threat to our way of life."[15]

People over sixty-five are less able to recognize fake news when they see it, more likely to be influenced by it after they see it, and vastly more likely to share it on Facebook.[16] And very soon, there will be a lot more of them. America's elderly population will grow fast. People born in the peak year of the baby boom, 1958, turn sixty-five in 2023. By 2030, almost one in five Americans, 19 percent, will be older than sixty-five.[17] (Barring some sad accident, I will be one of them.)

Flashpoint: American media culture in the 2020s not only reports on polarization—but enflames it. Americans still get more news from television than from any other source. By far the most-watched form of television news is local news, relied upon by 37 percent of Americans.[18] That market is dominated by the lavishly pro-Trump Sinclair Broadcast Group, 193 stations in 100 markets reaching 40 percent of the American television market.

The second most important television news type is cable, a medium of course dominated by Fox News, now reinforced by the new Fox-on-meth One American News Network (OANN).

Next to television in importance are social media. About four in ten Americans say they get news from Facebook. About two in ten also get news from YouTube.[19] Facebook and YouTube are the most important conduits for alt-Right and pro-Trump disinformation. Together, Fox News and the right-wing Daily Wire accounted for about 10 percent of the top ten thousand news stories on Facebook in the first quarter of 2019.[20] The single biggest advertiser on Facebook in the summer of 2019, after the Trump campaign itself, was the *Epoch Times*, a far-right source of pro-Trump conspiracy theories and false news.[21]

Meanwhile, Twitter is in danger of becoming the Fox News of the Left, policed by pile-ons by angry Twitter mobs. The middle retreats from the public square or hesitates to speak when there. Among self-described moderates, a big majority—57 percent—feel that the current climate of political correctness forbids them to say aloud things they believe.[22]

Flashpoint: In an increasingly diverse society, Trump has pitted group against group: by race, by religion, by culture. On election night 2012, Fox host Bill O'Reilly lamented, "Obama wins because it's not a traditional America anymore. The white establishment is the minority. People want things."[23] When Trump promised, "We'd all be saying Merry Christmas again," he was not promising a revival of Christian faith. No American president has ever cared less about

Christian faith than Donald Trump. What he cared about was reasserting cultural dominance.

In 2016, fewer than half of Americans identified themselves as both white and Christian.[24] This change is much less due to the immigration of nonwhite, non-Christians than to disaffiliation from Christianity by people whose parents and grandparents were white and Christian. Almost 40 percent of people under age thirty in 2016 professed "no religion."

Despite the favorable economy, Trump's approval rating among black voters tumbled to an amazing 6 percent in midsummer 2019 polls.[25] By then, 80 percent of black voters described Trump as racist.[26]

Should Donald Trump be defeated in 2020, whether he leaves the White House under his own motor power or is hustled out by the White House ushers, Trumpism will not be so easily removed from American national life. Trump himself will rave and rage on Twitter and TV after a political defeat. He will sabotage anyone who tries to lead the Republican Party in a more hygienic post-Trump direction. He will muster all the suspicion and resentment of his former supporters; he will headline a campaign of disinformation and provocation on TV, radio, and social media. What do you imagine Fox News and your father-in-law's Facebook feed will look like post-Trump? What kind of institution will the post-Trump Republican Party be?

Trump transferred a brutal style of politics from right-wing media culture into electoral politics. Unless decisively repudiated in 2020, that style will outlast Trump. Next time, perhaps, it will be tried by a politician with a stronger work ethic, sharper intellect, and fewer personality complexes.

If Trump could have governed his mouth and closed his Twitter account, he might have managed a reasonably popular presidency—at least for a couple of years. Through 2017, 2018, and the early part of 2019, surveys showed Americans were more satisfied with their finances than at any time since the late 1990s.[27] For a more normal president, such good news would almost have guaranteed reelection. Yet even before the economy began to soften in the second half of 2019, even before the Ukraine scandal and the Kurdish sellout, Trump remained stuck as a minority president, the only president never once to reach even 50 percent approval in any reputable poll.[28]

Trump's popularity sagged under the weight of his misbehavior in office. Trump's single best month in the *Washington Post*/ABC poll was recorded in July 2019: 44 percent. Even in his peak month in that poll series, nearly two-thirds of registered voters described Trump's behavior as "unpresidential." Only 29 percent described it as "fitting and proper." Among voters who approved of Trump's performance, still only one in eight described him as "unpresidential."[29] Trump kept assuring himself that all was going well, that every bump in the road was the work of unfair media:

> @newtgingrich just stated that there has been no president since Abraham Lincoln who has been treated worse or more unfairly by the media than your favorite President, me! At the same time there has been no president who has accomplished more in his first two years in office![30]
>
> —January 19, 2019

> Nothing funny about tired Saturday Night Live on Fake News NBC! Question is, how do the Networks get away with these total Republican hit jobs without retribution? Likewise for many other shows? Very unfair and should be looked into. This is the real Collusion![31]
>
> —February 17, 2019

> 93% Approval Rating in the Republican Party. 52% Approval Rating overall! Not bad considering I get the most unfair (BAD) press in the history of presidential politics! And don't forget the Witch Hunt![32]
>
> —February 24, 2019

If the totally Corrupt Media was less corrupt, I would be up by 15 points in the polls based on our tremendous success with the economy, maybe Best Ever! If the Corrupt Media was actually fair, I would be up by 25 points. Nevertheless, despite the Fake News, we're doing great![33]

—June 5, 2019

Trump meant to sound tough. He sounded pitiful. Successful demagogues recognize the hostility of their chosen enemies as a valuable resource for themselves. They foment hatred to position themselves as the victims of hatred. V. S. Naipaul astutely said of Eva Perón: "Even when the money ran out, Peronism could offer hate as hope."[34]

But Trump lacked the emotional toughness of Evita. Trump desperately craved the elite admiration that a more astute demagogue would have despised and refused. Trump could have made political capital out of being the first president since Ronald Reagan not to have attended Yale or Harvard. But no. Instead of seizing the opportunity to identify more closely with his supporters, Trump revealed himself, as journalist Jonathan Chait bitingly observed, as a snob who secretly despised his supporters. Chait spotted an especially revealing moment at a Trump rally in West Virginia in 2018.

We're the smart ones, remember. I say it all the time. You hear the elite. They're not elite, we're elite. You're smarter than they are, you have more money than they do, you have better jobs than they do, you're the elite. So let them have the word *elite*. You're the super elite. That's what it is.

I always hate—I always hate when they say, well the elite decided not to go to something I'm doing, right, the elite. I said, "Well, I have a lot more money than they do. I have a much better education than they have. I'm smarter than they are. I have many much more beautiful homes than they do. I have a better apartment at the top of Fifth Avenue." Why the hell are they the elite? Tell me.[35]

Trump wanted to be thought aristocratic, glamorous, the epitome of his favorite word: *class*. It hurt him when *Vogue* declined to feature his wife Melania or daughter Ivanka on its cover. It hurt him so much that the White House actually released a statement complaining about the non-cover.

> [Melania Trump's] role as first lady of the United States and all that she does is much more important than some superficial photo shoot and cover. This just further demonstrates how biased the fashion magazine industry is, and shows how insecure and small-minded Anna Wintour really is. Unfortunately, Mrs. Trump is used to this kind of divisive behavior.[36]

Trump's supporters loved it that he shared their rage against that world. A Trump supporter spoke for many, praising Trump's all-points combativeness.

> We Right-thinking people have tried dignity. There could not have been a man of more quiet dignity than George W. Bush as he suffered the outrageous lies and politically motivated hatreds that undermined his presidency. We tried statesmanship. Could there be another human being on this earth who so desperately prized "collegiality" as John McCain? We tried propriety—has there been a nicer human being ever than Mitt Romney? And the results were always the same.
>
> This is because, while we were playing by the rules of dignity, collegiality and propriety, the Left has been, for the past 60 years, engaged in a knife fight where the only rules are those of Saul Alinsky and the Chicago mob. . . .
>
> With Donald Trump, this all has come to an end. Donald Trump is America's first wartime president in the Culture War.[37]

But a wartime president needs a wartime plan. Trump had none. Trump's supporters repurposed for him a compliment Abraham

Lincoln had paid General Grant: "He fights." But Trump did not fight. He whined and complained. If Trump and his followers aspired to cultural transformation, they needed a politics to lead the way—a politics that could gain assent from doubters and respect from opponents. They never developed that politics. Maybe they would have failed even if they tried, but they never tried.

My *Atlantic* colleague Adam Serwer wrote an essay in 2018 whose title has become one of the iconic phrases of the Trump era, "The Cruelty Is the Point." The subtitle of the article argued the case in a single sharp statement of condemnation: "President Trump and His Supporters Find Community by Rejoicing in the Suffering of Those They Hate and Fear."[38]

President Trump was and is a very cruel man, no doubt about that. He delights in demeaning and humiliating everyone about him, including his nearest intimates. He insults, he jeers, he taunts, he teases. But the worst cruelties of his administration did not originate in sadism. They originate in the interplay of the following facts about Trump's method of government:

1. Trump does not know and does not care how government works. Even when told, he ignores or dismisses unwanted information.
2. Trump's policies therefore tend to fail in spectacularly visible ways.
3. Trump reacts to failure by reasserting personal control.
4. Trump proves his control by choosing the option that sounds toughest.

This is how we arrived at the policy of family separation at the border. It was not an original component of Trump's immigration policy. It resulted from Trump's frustration at the failure of his immigration policy.

The first year of Trump's presidency, 2017, saw the steepest decline in unauthorized border crossing since the Great Recession of 2008 to 2010.

It's uncertain exactly *why* this happened, but it's a good guess that potential border crossers interpreted Trump's election as a warning of an impending immigration crackdown. Maybe Trump would tighten enforcement at the border. Maybe he would crack down on the employment of illegal labor inside the United States. Unauthorized border crossing is both hazardous and expensive. Potential border crossers will hesitate to risk life and money if the border seems to be hardening.

But the border crossers soon figured out Trump's election had changed little. Yes, Trump was doing more arrests, more deportations, more refusals of unaccompanied minors—but in every case, the increase over Obama enforcement, while real, was undramatic. In Obama's last fiscal year, the United States altogether deported 226,119 people. In Trump's first, that figure rose to 256,085.[39]

More relevantly, Trump and the Republican Congress did little in their first two years to discourage the employment of illegal labor. As reporting by the *Washington Post* revealed, Trump's resorts remained substantial employers of illegal labor deep into 2019.

And so, the immigration lull of 2017 turned into an immigration surge in 2018 and the first half of 2019. By the spring of 2019, unauthorized border crossers were arriving at a rate of one hundred thousand *a month*, a pace not seen since the economic boom of the late 1990s.

Trump looked weak and foolish. And if there is one thing that Trump cannot abide, it is looking weak and foolish. He roared and shouted and demanded that something be done. But what?

Trump's signature immigration idea was "the wall."

The wall concept was vintage Trump. It sounded tough. It pinned the blame for a US problem (employers hiring illegal workers) on an outside enemy ("when Mexico sends its people, they're not sending their best"). It rested on bogus economics. ("Mexico will pay for it.")

And as a policy, it was vaporware. Through his two first and most powerful years as president, Trump forgot about the wall. The Republican majority in Congress ignored it.

Then, as the border crossing resumed in 2018, the wall revealed itself as classically Trump in the most important way of all: it was utterly disconnected from the reality of the problems the United States was facing here and now.

The border crossers arriving in 2018 arrived via Mexico, but not from Mexico. They came from Central America, South Asia, and—in ever surging numbers—West Africa.

The 2018–2019 border crossers were not exactly illegal either. More and more were presenting themselves as asylum seekers, a recognized status in US immigration law. Asylum seekers are not seeking to slip across the border in a way that a wall might stop. They *wanted* to encounter an official, so they could file their claim and receive the papers that would allow them to remain and work in the United States, pending an asylum hearing.

As the numbers climbed, Trump seethed and raged. With immigration as with everything else, Trump thought all he needed to do was show up and be Trump and the problem would solve itself. ("So easy!") With immigration, that fantasy seemed to hold for Trump's first twelve months in office. Then the fantasy crashed into reality. The order went out: Do something! Do something *tough*!

Early in 2017, the El Paso, Texas, border section had begun experimenting with detaining all border crossers, including asylum seekers. US rules forbid detaining adults and children together, so the new zero-tolerance policy implied separating children from parents. It's still not clear whether anybody in El Paso recognized in advance that zero tolerance must lead to family separation. Nobody seems to have thought very hard about any aspect of the new policy, including questions like "How are the children to be cared for in custody?" and "How are the families to be reunited afterward?" But what the El Paso office did notice was that border crossings in their section by family units soon dropped precipitously.[40]

This very unscientific piece of information began to circulate first through the immigration bureaucracy, then up into the Trump White House as proof. The hazy evidence from El Paso hardened into a data point: family separation can reduce unauthorized border crossings by 64 percent. The experiments began to scale up.

When Trump began to demand "Do something *tough!*", here was something "tough" right at hand. In spring 2018, zero tolerance was applied all across the southwestern border.

And again, nobody seems to have thought very hard about what would happen next. The policy in the El Paso section had involved only a few dozen families. One child was separately detained in May 2017. Another one was separated in June 2017. Seven were separated in July 2017; ten in August 2017.

But the promise of deterrence by separation rapidly proved false. Instead of tumbling as promised in response to the new zero-tolerance policy, the numbers of border crossers surged. In six weeks from mid-April 2018 to the end of May, almost two thousand young migrants were separated from their families at the border.

Nobody had expected such numbers: remember, the point of the policy was to *scare families away*, not incarcerate them. And because nobody had expected such numbers, nobody had done much to prepare for them. All the problems that had not been solved in 2017 remained unsolved in 2018, only this time affecting thousands of people.

When ten children are separated from their families, it's not difficult to provide them with beds and showers, to supervise their health and safety, and to keep track of the whereabouts of their family members. But by the time the policy was suspended in June 2018, at least twenty-three hundred families had been separated—and very possibly thousands more. In February 2019, the Trump administration itself conceded that it does not know how many families were separated, how many children detained.[41]

The exact fates of the children will never be known either. The majority seem to have been released to relatives already legally or illegally present in the United States. In other cases, children were sent back to their places of origin even though their families remained in detention in the United States; or the families were deported, while the children stayed for weeks or months in a foster facility here. At least seven children died in US custody.[42]

Trump never defended the family separation policy. Instead, he has repeatedly claimed that the policy was inherited from the Obama administration—and that he was responsible for ending it. Here's the most recent version of that claim, speaking with NBC's Chuck Todd in June 2019:

TRUMP: You know, under President Obama you had separation. I was the one that ended it. Now I said one thing, when I ended it, I said, "Here's what's going to happen. More families are going to come up." And that's what's happened. But they're really coming up for the economics. But once you ended the separation. But I ended separation. I inherited separation from President Obama. President Obama built, they call them jail cells. They were built—

TODD: Let's talk about what's happening now.

TRUMP:—by the Obama—

TODD: Your administration, and—

TRUMP: I'm just telling you—

TODD:—you're not doing the recreation. You're not even schooling these kids anymore. You've gotten rid of all that stuff.

TRUMP: We're doing a fantastic job under the circumstances. The Democrats aren't even approving giving us money. Where is the money? You know what? The Democrats are holding up the humanitarian aid.[43]

This was all massively disingenuous, of course. But if "cruelty were the point," Trump would not engage in such disingenuousness.

"People nowadays do not understand what cruelty is," wrote Oscar Wilde in 1897. During his own time in prison, Wilde had witnessed with horror that quite young children were incarcerated together with adults. After his release, he wrote about the case of a warder at Reading Prison—a man named Martin—who lost his job for giving sweet biscuits to some of those imprisoned children. Wilde wanted his readers to understand that the cruelty done in English prisons was not inflicted by sadists. The cruelty he had witnessed, he wrote,

> is simply stupidity. It comes from the entire want of imagination. It is the result in our days of stereotyped systems, of hard-and-fast rules, of centralization, of officialism, and of irresponsible authority.[44]

Trump's cruelties were inflicted because Trump recognized that he had lost control of the situation and did not know what to do to retake control. He was cruel because he was inadequate to the job, and rather than look inadequate, he preferred to try brutality. When that failed, Trump tried to shift blame—again an act of inadequacy.

Trump never mastered the presidency. The only part of the job he ever really understood was how to use the presidency for plunder and corruption. And even here, how successful was he really?

The opportunities exist for a dishonest president to gain wealth on a post-Soviet scale. *Vanity Fair* reported in October 2019 on a pattern of "Trump chaos trades": huge options contracts bought or sold only hours before Trump did something to roil financial markets.[45] Some question whether these transactions revealed insider trading or whether they were an optical illusion, like the mind concocting a "horse" or "duck" out of the clouds in the sky. Yet even if somebody were trading on advance knowledge of Trump's actions, who would believe that the trader was Trump himself or his family, rather than some ruthless operator who found a way to access Trump's unsecured telephone yakking? Trump cheats suppliers and workers, lies to his bankers and to tax authorities. But a criminal scheme as delicate as "chaos trading" seems utterly beyond his ken. It requires the involvement of high-grade brokers backed by advanced computers. Trump hires Michael Cohens and Rudy Giulianis and is puzzled by the iPhone X. Instead of pocketing billions by sophisticated financial crime, Trump preferred low-grade graft.

Net-net, how much can Trump have pocketed from Vice President Pence's two-day stay at Trump's Irish golf course? How much from Bahrain hosting its national day celebrations at the Trump hotel in Washington, DC? How much from the Secret Service renting golf carts at Trump golf courses? How much from air force officers being billeted at the Turnberry in Scotland? How much by doubling the admission fees at Mar-a-Lago after the Electoral College installed him in the presidency?[46] How valuable were Ivanka Trump's Chinese trademarks, really?

No question, Trump extracted dishonest millions from the presidency. Between Trump's inauguration and April 2019, at least $4.7 million of Republican Party funds flowed to his clubs, hotels, and resorts.[47] Millions more came from lobbyists and foreign governments eager to ingratiate themselves with a sleazy administration. Yet Trump's grifts were always those of the small-scale hustler. He convicted himself in the eyes of the public as the most corrupt president in American history, all probably for less money than Michelle Obama earned from her book and speaking fees.

Trump was both con artist and mark: his own first victim. His incompetence burned through a half-billion-dollar inherited fortune. He tried to replace that fortune by scams and swindles that continued after he won the presidency. He could not stop, because he could not afford to stop: he owed too much money. All the most ambitious crooked dealings of his presidency involved not plans to make money but frantic expedients to avoid losses caused by his own ineptitude and that of his equally feckless son-in-law. Jared Kushner pressured Chinese and Persian Gulf investors for a bailout for his top-of-the-market bad bet on an Eisenhower-era office building on Fifth Avenue. Trump misused the presidency in hope of driving business to the money-losing golf courses he had bought with cash from unknown sources. He wanted to stage the 2020 G-7 Summit at his Doral resort near Miami less to earn a buck, more to cover costs by occupying rooms otherwise disastrously empty. As his reelection chances dwindled, he put his Pennsylvania Avenue hotel on the market in a frantic bid to cash out before a 2020 defeat destroyed the hotel's rent-for-access business model.

Trump was lofted to the presidency by delusions of grandeur and fantasies of revenge. He exploited those emotions in others to his own advantage. Yet he himself was as blinded by delusions and fantasies as any of his followers.

He lost chances to expand his voting coalition because he could not stifle expressions of his rage and hate. He discredited himself with soft supporters because he could not govern his behavior. A more cold-blooded Trump might have been a more successful villain. Instead, Trump believed the legend that his own actions sabotaged. He could never see realities as they were. The ultimate dupe of the Don was Donald himself. Which is how he, the most flagrant lawbreaker ever to hold high office in the United States, could lead chants of "lock her up" about his political opponents. He demanded lynch law for others, impunity for himself. The construction of that impunity would be one of the few successful building projects of the Trump presidency. Unless Americans act now to demolish it, Trump's construction of impunity will shadow the American landscape for years to come.

CHAPTER TWO

The Wall of Impunity

The man tasked to breach Trump's wall of impunity was Special Counsel Robert Mueller. Mueller was assigned to delve to the bottom of the Trump-Russia connection. He never reached it because he did not allow himself to try. Mueller had always done things by the book. But "the book" contained no chapter describing anything like a Trump presidency. The upright and conservative Mueller discovered himself unequal to the unforeseen emergency. This was not a purely personal failure. It was shared across a range of elite Washington institutions. On the eve of the 2016 election, a Pulitzer prize–winning columnist opined in the *Washington Post*:

> If Trump wins, he'll be held more or less in check by the House and Senate, because that's the way our system of government is set up. Not even Republicans are eager to follow Trump's lead.[1]

I cite that column—published under the headline "Whoever Wins, We'll Be Fine"—not to single it out, but precisely because it was so *un*-singular. The keepers of the institutions could imagine Donald Trump testing the system. They could not imagine the system failing the test.

Yet the system did fail. No failure was as spectacular or as consequential as Robert Mueller's. Mueller's failure would ultimately tempt Donald Trump to try again to pervert an election with foreign help, this time by extorting Ukraine. Trump's attempted extortion led to his impeachment in Congress, ending with the United States Senate as one more institution that failed its task of holding to account a lawless president.

Mueller made five crucial decisions that guaranteed his work would deliver no useful result.

First, Mueller decided that he would look only for prosecutable crimes: conspiracy to violate election law, that sort of thing. Questions like "Do Trump businesses owe money to Russian entities?" were none of his business, because it's not illegal to owe money to Russian entities.

Second, even if he did find prosecutable crimes, he would not prosecute them if he deemed the criminal too ignorant to know the law—which is how Donald Trump Jr. escaped prosecution for soliciting campaign help from a Russian national at the famous June 2016 Trump Tower meeting.

Third, Mueller decided he would look only at the period of the 2015–2016 election cycle. Questions like "Did Russian money save Trump from ruin in 2008?" were again none of his business, because that all happened (if it happened) too long ago.

Fourth, the only crimes that Mueller would look at were crimes committed by persons near Trump, not Trump himself—since Mueller accepted the Department of Justice guidance that a serving president cannot be indicted.

Fifth, Mueller would not even report *evidence* that Trump had committed crimes, on the following theory.

1. Since the president could not be charged, he, therefore, could not stand trial.
2. Since the president could not stand trial, he would not have an opportunity to defend himself at trial.

3. Since the president would not have the opportunity to present his defense, it was therefore unfair to the president even to publish *information* that the president could not rebut in court. (Never mind that the president had ample other ways to present his side of the story.)

None of this added up to the "exoneration" that Trump claimed from the Mueller report. Mueller's assessment of the facts was certainly damning. The Trump campaign, Mueller reported, "expected it would benefit electorally from information stolen and released through Russian efforts." The Trump campaign, Mueller continued, "welcomed" this Russian help. But Mueller decided there was nothing much he could do about any of this—and little more that he should say about any of it. Nor would Mueller even challenge Trump's frequent stonewalls. Evidence was missing, perhaps destroyed. Witnesses were evasive or—like President Trump himself—unavailable. Mueller acknowledged that his investigation had found itself "not able to corroborate witness statements through comparison to contemporaneous communications or fully question witnesses about statements that appeared inconsistent with other known facts."[2] As a result, central issues in the investigation went unexplored. Oh well, what can you do?

If curiosity killed the cat, then any cat owned by Robert Mueller can look forward to a long, full life. The special counsel showed himself remarkably devoid of the cat-killing quality of curiosity even when he unearthed the most suspicious behavior. Mueller confirmed that Trump's campaign manager, Paul Manafort, had shared proprietary campaign information with a Russian businessman with close ties to the Russian government. Some questions that might pop into your head if you had discovered that fact:

What use, if any, had the Russian authorities made of the polling information delivered to them by Paul Manafort?

Did Manafort's information shape the illegal Russian social media advertising campaign in support of Trump?

How much did Manafort know about that illegal advertising when he shared the campaign's proprietary polling?

The Mueller team's answer: Beats us, we couldn't find out.
Again, once Mueller reached his conclusion that the Putin government wanted Trump to win, you might wonder:

Why?

Why did Russia's Putin so badly want Trump to win?

What connections bound Trump to Putin?

Did Putin have some kind of hold over Trump—financial or otherwise?

The Mueller team's answer: Not our department. We can only tell you that he and his team lied persistently and flagrantly about the Trump Tower Moscow project.

But was Trump Tower Moscow the only Trump-Russia connection? Or were there others?

If others, what? When did they start? How important were they to Trump's business?

In particular, did Russian sources provide the otherwise inexplicable $400 million for the all-cash acquisition spree that Trump began in 2008 after nearly going bankrupt for a third time?

The Mueller team's answer: We did not think those questions relevant to our work.

It was evident from the start that Trump's Russia connections were (a) substantial, (b) compromising, (c) undisclosed, and (d) probably not illegal at the time private citizen Donald Trump entered into them. I published that assessment in the *Atlantic* in May 2017,[3] before the special counsel investigation even began—and repeated it on television dozens of times over the following two years. What mattered was not prosecuting crimes but discovering the nature of Putin's grip upon Trump. Yet after all the work done by Robert Mueller, we still cannot answer the central question of the Trump presidency: What does the president owe—and to whom does he owe it?

That question cast its shadow deep into the Ukraine scandal too.

In May 2019, Trump fired a career ambassador to Ukraine because she had got herself disliked by corrupt officials in that country and in Russia—an early sighting of the Ukraine scandal that would lead the House to open an impeachment inquiry in September. The chairman of the House Foreign Affairs Committee accused the administration in writing: "It's clear that this decision was politically motivated, as allies of President Trump had joined foreign actors in lobbying for the Ambassador's dismissal."[4]

Who were those foreign actors?

How did they exert such sway over US foreign policy?

Not our department, replied the Mueller team. All those reports that Trump relied on Russian funds for his post-2006 golf-course-buying spree? The Mueller team either did not look into them or did not report on them.

Not that any information would have made a difference to Trump's hardest core following. In the fall of 2019, a nonpartisan research organization studied the distinctive attitudes of Republicans who watched

Fox News as their primary source of information. Among that group, 55 percent said there was virtually nothing President Trump could do that would change their minds about supporting him.[5]

Trump's followers live in an isolated knowledge community that has developed its own situational ethics. They wanted to lock up Hillary Clinton for sending and receiving emails on a personal server, not caring even slightly when Ivanka Trump did the exact same thing or when Trump outright blabbed to the Russian foreign minister secrets much more vital than anything Clinton could possibly have risked. They plunged into the QAnon fantasy of a wise and good Trump poised to crush a global ring of child molesters—in order to avoid the reality of a malignant Trump who by his own admission had preyed upon teenage beauty pageant contestants.[6]

Have you ever known anyone swindled by a scam? It's remarkable how determined they remain, and for how long, to defend the swindler—and to shift blame to those who tried to warn them of the swindle. The pain of being seen as a fool hurts more than the loss of money; it's more important to protect the ego against indignity than to visit justice upon the perpetrator. We human beings so often prefer a lie that affirms us to a truth that challenges us.

Any Trump supporters who allowed themselves to recognize Trump's swindle would immediately confront other, even more hurtful, doubts. If Trump was lying, did that imply that their trusted friends on radio and television had deceived them too: Sean and Rush and the *Fox & Friends* gang? Fox News and the Facebook feed have become for many Americans friends more intimate and more trusted than family or neighbors. The validation of their prejudices by television and Facebook is a validation of themselves. And so, for the sake of flag and faith, millions of decent conservative Americans countenanced scandals, wrongs, disloyalty, and crime.

It's illegal for federal employees to overspend on travel to benefit themselves or their colleagues. In 2012, a senior executive at the General Services Administration was sentenced to three months in prison, three months under house arrest, and three years of parole for taking personal side jaunts and overspending on lavish retreats for his staff.[7]

Yet when Vice President Pence visited Ireland in 2019, he wasted hundreds of thousands of taxpayer dollars by staying not in Dublin, the site of his meetings, but at Trump's golf course 180 miles away, on literally the opposite coast of the island. Pence tried to make things right by paying for his room personally, but that only added a direct personal payoff to Trump to the many other ethical breaches of the trip. Any other federal employee who wasted travel expenses to direct money to his supervisor's profit would find himself in serious trouble: facing at least a firing, possibly prison time if the behavior was egregious enough. Not Pence. Not the Trump staffers who meet every Tuesday evening with lobbyists at the Trump hotel in Washington, DC.[8] In the George W. Bush White House, you showed you belonged by wearing cowboy boots; in the Trump White House, by repaying some of your salary into the boss's pockets.

It is illegal for government employees to use their positions to engage in certain political activities. They are especially forbidden to engage directly in election campaigns while on the government payroll. Presidential counselor Kellyanne Conway violated this law— the Hatch Act—so persistently and flagrantly that she triggered an internal investigation. In June 2019, the investigation reported that Conway had broken the law repeatedly and intentionally.

If Conway had been a career government employee, she would have been dismissed from her position immediately. By ancient courtesy, however, the enforcement of the Hatch Act upon political appointees is left to the president directly. The investigation therefore concluded with a recommendation to the president that Conway be subject to "appropriate disciplinary action": in other words, that she be fired.[9]

Trump disregarded the recommendation. Conway mocked the finding to reporters. As one read the recommendation to her, she replied: "Blah, blah, blah. If you're trying to silence me through the Hatch Act, it's not going to work. Let me know when the jail sentence starts."[10]

Sometime in campaign 2020, some federal worker will get excited about the election and post something intemperate on Facebook or do something else to infringe the 1942 law. She will be disciplined—fired if the offense is egregious or visible enough—and she will know that this law that applies to her was ignored in the much worse case of Kellyanne Conway. Or perhaps in 2020, the law will be extra-scrupulously obeyed by federal workers—because they will already know that there is one law for Trump cronies and a different law for everybody else.

No other major democracy operates so political a system of law enforcement as the United States. The ninety-three US attorneys are all political appointees. They report to an assistant attorney general for the Criminal Division, also a political appointee. The assistant attorney general reports to a deputy attorney general and finally the attorney general—ditto all political. Ideally, while people are appointed to those posts for political reasons, they do not do their jobs in a political way. Americans can be proud that this ideal is so often voluntarily met. But when not voluntarily met, the ideal is difficult to enforce—as has been seen.

In other democracies, the equivalents of the assistant attorney general for the Criminal Division are career civil servants. The British attorney general has no role in the operation of the Crown Prosecution Service. Germany's general federal prosecutor is even more insulated from politics. Thus it is through almost all the developed world. Problems arise in these systems, too, of course. The Justin Trudeau government in Canada was rocked by the prime minister's attempt to lean on prosecutors in that country to go easy on a corporation that had been generous in its campaign contributions to his party. But in those other countries, the brute political pressure that Trump applied via Bill Barr on the Department of Justice is much less likely to have an effect.

The Trump years demonstrated the very great extent to which presidential cooperation with the law is voluntary, especially if he or she retains a sufficient blocking vote in Congress. At one point in 2019, Trump simultaneously refused all cooperation with twenty distinct congressional investigations—testing whether there was much Congress could do about it. There proved surprisingly little. Congress's contempt powers lag far behind those of courts. As the Congressional Research Service warned in 2017:

> A number of obstacles face Congress in any attempt to enforce a subpoena issued against an executive branch official. Although the courts have reaffirmed Congress' constitutional authority to issue and enforce subpoenas, efforts to punish an executive branch official for non-compliance . . . will likely prove unavailing in many, if not most, circumstances.[11]

Even outright lying to Congress can prove exceptionally difficult to punish. "Almost no one is prosecuted for lying to Congress," concludes the leading law review article on the subject. "In fact, only six people have been convicted of perjury or related charges in relation to Congress in the last sixty years."[12] Those words were published in 2006, but a report by *Roll Call* in 2018 found they still held true. The pitcher Roger Clemens was indicted for lying to Congress about steroids in 2009. He was acquitted on all charges in 2012.[13] If you're a Trump executive-branch official, you must like your chances of getting away with lying—and worse.

Some wonder: Why doesn't Congress act? But there is no "Congress" anymore; there are only the two parties in Congress. The members of the two cannot even agree on methods of evidence or standards of behavior. Florida Republican congressmember Ted Yoho spoke for troublingly many members of his caucus when he said that he "works for the president, he answers to the president."[14] Yoho's district around Gainesville, Florida, voted 41 percent against President Trump in 2016. Those voters are also Yoho's constituents, but he does not answer to any of *them*. In his mind, he is a party man first and only.

Congress as an institution cannot function on this kind of partisan mentality. There can be no meaningful oversight of the executive if the only standard is "yay team!" and "boo team!" The party of the president should be just as keen as the other party to enforce subpoenas and punish contempt—because both parties in Congress should feel the same concern for the powers of Congress. But of course, that's not how things work.

Almost all Republicans in the House of Representatives, and the great majority of Republicans in the Senate, will act to defend a president they despise against charges they know to be true. The worst of them will hare after crazy conspiracy theories. Most, though, will voice their concern and then find ways to avoid their duty. The system that protects all of us has failed because the protectors of that system have failed to protect it for us.

Democracy does not fly on autopilot. If the people responsible for the institutions of democracy will not do the job, the job will not be done. While the job goes undone, the United States and the world careen toward conflict and crisis.

CHAPTER THREE

World War Trump

American presidents have more power over foreign affairs than domestic policy. Much more than at home, it is abroad that a president can define the United States according to his own ideas. Those ideas—Jimmy Carter's commitment to human rights; Ronald Reagan's anticommunism—shape the world and the future. Donald Trump, too, had a vision, and we all will be coping with those consequences for many years to come.

For Donald Trump, life is a struggle for dominance. In every encounter, one party must win, the other must lose. The tough will prevail. The weak will be victimized—and they will deserve it. He explained his philosophy in a 2007 speech.

> It's called "Get Even." Get even. This isn't your typical business speech. Get even. What this is, is a real business speech. You know in all fairness to Wharton, I love 'em, but they teach you some stuff that's a lot of bullshit. When you're in business, you get even with people that screw you. And you screw them 15 times harder. And the reason is, the reason is, the reason is, not only, not only, because of the person that you're after, but other people watch what's happening. Other people see you, and they see how you react.[1]

He added later:

> If you're afraid to fight back people will think of you as a loser,
> a "schmuck"! They will know they can get away with insulting
> you, disrespecting you, and taking advantage of you. Don't let
> it happen! Always fight back and get even.[2]

Trump imagined the relationship between nations in the same way. You were either predator or prey. Ukraine was prey to Trump when he extorted it to help his reelection. The United Kingdom was prey when Trump dangled promises of a US-UK trade deal to entice Britain out of the European Union. Canada was prey when Trump abused national security exceptions to impose tariffs on a national security partner. The weaker the victim, the more aggressively Trump bullied it.

Axios reported in November 2018 on a Trump meeting with Iraq's then–prime minister, Haider al-Abadi:

> "It was a very run-of-the-mill, low-key, meeting in general,"
> a source who was in the room told Axios. "And then right at
> the end, Trump says something to the effect of, he gets a little
> smirk on his face and he says, 'So what are we going to do about
> the oil?'" . . .
> [T]he Iraqi prime minister replied, "What do you mean?"
> according to the source in the room.
> "And Trump's like, 'Well, we did a lot, we did a lot over there,
> we spent trillions over there, and a lot of people have been
> talking about the oil.'"
> Al-Abadi "had clearly prepared," the source added, "and he
> said something like, 'Well, you know Mr. President, we work
> very closely with a lot of American companies and American
> energy companies have interests in our country,'" the source
> added. "He was smirking. And the president just kind of tapped
> his hand on the table as if to say 'I had to ask.'"[3]

Trump has also been fascinated by plans to seize Afghanistan's putative mineral wealth, the *New York Times* reported in July 2017: "Mr. Trump, who is deeply skeptical about sending more American troops to Afghanistan, has suggested that this could be one justification for the United States to stay engaged in the country."[4]

Past presidents saw their job as building a world system that worked for all liberal democratic nations. President Dwight Eisenhower urged this truth in his First Inaugural Address back in 1953. "We are persuaded by necessity and by belief that the strength of all free peoples lies in unity; their danger, in discord."[5] Past presidents believed that the United States was empowered by cooperation with allies. "We recognize we will benefit more from a strong and equal partner than from a weak one," said Bill Clinton in January 1994.[6]

Trump discarded this commitment to cooperation. The Trans-Pacific Partnership had been negotiated under two previous presidencies to balance Chinese power. Trump called TPP "a rape of our country"[7] and withdrew three days after becoming president. Trump quit the Paris climate accords and abandoned the Transatlantic Trade and Investment Partnership before it could get started. Trump upended trade agreements like the North American Free Trade Agreement and the South Korean agreement. He raged against the World Trade Organization. He reneged on a refugee domiciling agreement with Australia, insulted heads of government in Canada and Germany, urged the United Kingdom to exit the European Union, and then hit the British with trade penalties once they were isolated and weakened. "Trade wars are good, and easy to win," he promised Americans as he imposed tariffs on steel, aluminum, appliances, and other goods.[8] Trump tweeted on June 1, 2019:

When you are the "Piggy Bank" Nation that foreign countries have been robbing and deceiving for years, the word TARIFF is a beautiful word indeed! Others must treat the United States fairly and with respect—We are no longer the "fools" of the past![9]

Trump is haunted by a fear that people might ridicule *him* as weak. In January 2016, the *Washington Post* counted more than one hundred times that Trump claimed he had heard people "laughing at us"[10] before he even entered politics. As president, Trump has imagined the whole American nation as an extension of his ego. The mockery he fears for himself, he then projects onto the world. The *Washington Post* counted more than a dozen instances in Trump's first six months in office when he complained that "the whole world" is "laughing at us"—because "they think we're stupid."[11]

International cooperation, free trade, collective security—illusions, sick jokes. Strong nations compelled their dependents to pay for protection. They imposed tariffs, seized oil. If they did not, they were suckers. As Trump complained in his 2017 inaugural address:

> We've made other countries rich while the wealth, strength, and confidence of our country has disappeared over the horizon . . . The wealth of our middle class has been ripped from their homes and then redistributed across the entire world.

Instead of subsidizing other nations, the United States should collect tribute from them.

> America shouldn't be doing the fighting for every nation on Earth, not being reimbursed in many cases at all.
> If they want us to do the fighting, they also have to pay a price and sometimes that's also a monetary price. So we're not the suckers of the world. We're no longer the suckers, folks. And people aren't looking at us as suckers.[12]

In Ukraine, Trump demanded that the payment be directed to him personally. He leaned on the British government to close wind turbines that, in his opinion, marred the seaside view from his golf courses. That plan failed, but he did secure Scottish planning permission to develop housing sites on his golf course land. He sought to hold the 2020 G-7 summit at his Doral resort near Miami. The Trump Organization has acknowledged payments of at least $1 million from foreign governments in 2018, mostly for stays and events at the Trump hotel in downtown Washington. (This figure has not been independently verified, and the underlying paperwork has not been disclosed as of the end of 2019. The true figure could therefore well prove higher.[13])

But even when he was acting in a supposedly public-spirited way—for the United States, not for himself—Trump still brought to his foreign policy the spirit of a mafia racket. Over his decades of talking to the media, Trump has espoused both pro-life and pro-choice views on abortion. He supported the wars in Afghanistan, Iraq, and Libya and then opposed those wars. He has denounced racial prejudice and appealed to racial prejudice. Yet there is one belief on which Trump has never deviated from perfect consistency: his disdain for America's post-1945 alliances in Asia and Europe. None of them paid. Every one of them made a sucker of the United States.

In 1987, Trump bought full-page ads in the *New York Times*, *Washington Post*, and *Boston Globe* for an open letter from himself to the American people. He headlined the letter, "There's Nothing Wrong with America's Foreign Defense Policy That a Little Backbone Can't Cure." Over his signature, appeared these words:

> Let's help our farmers, our sick, our homeless by taking from some of the greatest profit machines ever created—machines created and nurtured by us. *Tax* these wealthy nations, not America. End our huge deficits, reduce our taxes, and let America's economy grow unencumbered by the cost of defending those who can easily afford to pay us for the defense of their freedom. *Let's not let our great country be laughed at anymore.* (Italics added)[14]

Trump challenged David Sanger of the *New York Times* in March 2016: "Why are we always the ones that fund everybody disproportionately, you know? So everything is like that. There's nothing that's not like that."[15]

Trump preferred authoritarian client-states like Saudi Arabia to democratic rule-of-law allies. At least from authoritarian states, it was possible to extract benefits: loans for his son-in-law, trademarks for his daughter, income for himself. "I like the strong ones," Trump reportedly told friends—meaning not strong *allies* like Germany but strongman *leaders* like Vladimir Putin. With the strong leaders, Trump could strike deals for mutual advantage, quietly and with no fuss from parliaments and press. Except for Israel and the Philippines, there was not a democratic country on earth where the relationship with the US did not deteriorate between 2017 and 2020. Sixty-six percent of Australians have zero confidence in Trump to do the right thing in world affairs. Seventy percent of Britons have zero confidence in him. Seventy-five percent of Canadians have zero confidence. Ninety percent of French and Germans have no confidence in him.[16] More alarming still: almost half of Germans have come to regard China as a more reliable partner than Trump's America.[17]

Trump has scrambled the never-easy-to-manage relationship between South Korea and Japan. In October 2018, the South Korean Supreme Court ruled that former South Korean slave laborers could bring actions against Japanese companies whose corporate ancestors had been active in Korea during the Japanese occupation of 1910 to 1945. Japan responded by imposing new restrictions on technology transfer to South Korea. South Korea retaliated in kind. In August 2019, China offered to mediate. This was a disingenuous troll, of course, a way for China to score points off Japan and win friends among South Korean nationalists. Precisely for that reason, the United States should have wanted to head it off at the pass—but of course Trump was AWOL, since he saw all sides as adversaries trying to rip off the United States. When North Korea resumed testing missiles in spring 2019, Trump shrugged. "North Korea fired off some small weapons, which disturbed some of my people, and others, but not me," he tweeted.[18] Those weapons could only reach South

Korea and Japan, so who cared? The security of those allies did not concern him—and those allies noticed.

American interests suffered from Trump's disregard for friends and partners. While an illiberal, authoritarian regime like China can successfully act alone, the United States benefits from the support of wealthy and powerful democratic allies. When the United States sought to infiltrate the Iranian nuclear program, it used information gained from German contractors. To counteract Chinese influence in the Philippines, Japan has committed eleven times as much development aid as the United States. French troops fight the battle against Islamic paramilitaries in West Africa. Almost all the cost of reconstructing the former Warsaw Pact countries of Central and Eastern Europe—including Ukraine—has been borne by the European Union, not the United States. The United States has not fought a war by itself since Panama in 1990. Canadian troops spearheaded the US ground campaign against ISIS in Iraq in 2016 and 2017. Germany has provided the second-largest NATO force in Afghanistan. The first agency to discover the Russian hack of the Democratic National Committee's emails was not the US National Security Agency or Central Intelligence Agency but the Dutch intelligence agency AIVD—although that's one form of allied help that Donald Trump surely did not welcome.[19]

Trump weakened all these habits of cooperation. Under Trump, the United States looked unpredictable and untrustworthy. Despite a strong domestic economy—and a big cut in the corporate income tax at the end of 2017—direct foreign investment in the United States dropped significantly in the second year of Trump's presidency, from $277 billion to $252 billion. Only Brexit-wobbled Britain dropped more. Over that same period, almost every other economy reported major increases in foreign investment, not only such always attractive countries as Australia and Canada, but also statist France and tariff-slammed China.[20]

During the 2016 campaign, Trump intermittently positioned himself as an "antiwar" candidate. "Unlike other candidates for the presidency, war and aggression will not be my first instinct," Trump said in April 2016, his campaign's only attempt at a major foreign policy address.[21] "You're going to end up in World War Three over Syria if we listen to Hillary Clinton," he told Reuters in October 2016.[22]

But Trump was not a conflict resolver in the mold of Jimmy Carter or Herbert Hoover, presidents who abhorred violence and cherished the peaceful resolution of differences. Trump excitedly celebrated violence. "I'm good at war. I've had a lot of wars of my own. I'm really good at war. I love war in a certain way," Trump boasted at a November 2015 rally in Iowa.[23] "I would bring back waterboarding," he said in the February 2016 Republican candidates' debate in New Hampshire. "And I would bring back a hell of a lot worse than waterboarding."[24] "I'm the most militaristic person there is," he said in an August 2015 Fox-sponsored candidates' debate.[25] "I would bomb the shit out of them!" he vowed on November 13, 2015. The belligerent talk continued after Trump's election. He threatened to incinerate North Korea: "Fire and fury like the world has never seen."[26] He growled nuclear menace at Iran too: "If Iran wants to fight, that will be the official end of Iran."[27] He threatened to close the border with Mexico. "If Mexico doesn't immediately stop ALL illegal immigration coming into the United States through our Southern Border, I will be CLOSING . . . the Border, or large sections of the Border, next week."[28] He vowed to stop all foreign assistance to El Salvador, Guatemala, and Honduras.[29] He warned he might reimpose a "full and complete embargo" on Cuba.[30]

The candidate whom New York Times columnist Maureen Dowd hailed as "Donald the Dove" back in 2016[31] in 2019 ordered the assassination of Iran's terror commander, General Qassem Soleimani. By then, Trump was supporting a widening proxy war in Yemen and was ordering thousands of additional troops to Iraq—the latest steps toward direct conflict with the most populous and, after Israel, the most militarily capable state in the greater Middle East.

Trump did not renounce war against other nations. He renounced cooperation with other nations.

"We reject the ideology of globalism!" President Trump told the United Nations in September 2018.[32]

"Our mission is to reassert our sovereignty," Secretary of State Michael Pompeo declared in a speech in Brussels in December of that year.[33]

What those words have meant in practice has been a narrow, selfish definition of US interest backed by power, never by fairness or reason. Trump expected that brute self-assertion would bring foreign capitulation and easy profit.

That expectation was soon disappointed. Trump never even seemed to know what it would mean to "win" a trade war. But even worse than the material cost of Trump's me-first vision of US leadership has been the moral effect.

In the throes of World War II, the great free-trading Secretary of State Cordell Hull reviewed the misery that America First nationalism had wrought on his world.

> After the last war, too many nations, including our own, tolerated, or participated in, attempts to advance their own interests at the expense of any system of collective security and of opportunity for all. Too many of us were blind to the evils which, thus loosed, created growing cancers within and among nations; political suspicions and hatreds; the race of armaments, first stealthy and then the subject of flagrant boasts; economic nationalism and its train of depression and misery; and finally, the emergence from their dark places of the looters and thugs who found their opportunity in disorder and disaster.[34]

Chastened by that memory, the Americans of the postwar era committed themselves to a new kind of world. It's not a defect of the system that Germany no longer fields a giant Wehrmacht, that Japanese merchant shipping is guarded by American warships and aircraft rather than Japan's own. It's not a rip-off that South Korea pays for beef and fruit by selling electronic goods, or that the United States pays for electronic goods by selling beef and fruit. That was the plan all along. Trump talks of "great deals," but he can feel certain that he has scored a great deal for himself only if he has imposed misery and ruin on his counterparty.

The emotions that animate Trump are dark and violent. "Maybe hate is what we need if we're gonna get something done," he said in a 1989 television interview.[35]

Trump intensely admires those who deploy violence to preserve their power and wealth. As Trump gushed over Kim Jong-un on the flight home from the Trump-Kim summit in Singapore, Fox News's Bret Baier reminded the president: "He's clearly executing people."

"He's a tough guy," replied Trump admiringly. "Hey, when you take over a country—tough country, with tough people—and you take it over from your father . . . I don't care who you are, what you are, how much of an advantage you have—if you can do that at twenty-seven years old, that's one in ten thousand that can do that. So he's a very smart guy. He's a great negotiator. But I think we understand each other."[36]

"He's a strong person, he has very good control," Trump said of the murderous Saudi crown prince, Mohammad bin Salman. "He's seen as a person who can keep things under check. I mean that in a positive way."[37]

Should the United States champion human rights against authoritarians like Turkey's Erdoğan? Candidate Trump said no. "When the world looks at how bad the United States is, and then we go and talk about civil liberties, I don't think we're a very good messenger."[38]

Isn't Vladimir Putin a killer? "I think in terms of leadership he is getting an A and the president is not doing so well," Trump said in a September 2015 TV interview.[39] Newly elected President Trump shrugged off Putin's crimes. "There are a lot of killers. We have a lot of killers. Well, you think our country is so innocent?"[40]

Should North Korea's human rights abuses matter to US foreign policy? "A lot of other people have done some really bad things. I could go through a lot of nations where a lot of bad things were done."[41]

Trump had fond words even for dictators deposed and deceased. Of Saddam Hussein, he said on the 2016 campaign trail, "He was a bad guy—really bad guy. But you know what he did well? He killed terrorists. He did that so good. They didn't read them the rights. They didn't talk. They were terrorists. Over."[42]

Interviewed in 1990 by *Playboy* magazine, Trump condemned Mikhail Gorbachev as insufficiently brutal, unlike the rulers of communist China.

Q: What were your other impressions of the Soviet Union?

TRUMP: I was very unimpressed. Their system is a disaster. What you will see there soon is a revolution; the signs are all there with the demonstrations and picketing. Russia is out of control and the leadership knows it. That's my problem with Gorbachev. Not a firm enough hand.

Q: You mean firm hand as in China?

TRUMP: When the students poured into Tiananmen Square, the Chinese government almost blew it. Then they were vicious, they were horrible, but they put it down with strength. That shows you the power of strength. Our country is right now perceived as weak . . . as being spit on by the rest of the world—[43]

"America First" does not exert strength. It invites everybody else in the world system to bend rules and test limits in their own perceived short-term self-interest, while delegitimizing instrumentalities of power that defend US interests and uphold American values. On those rare occasions when Trump did speak about values, he spoke not of human rights and liberty—but of white ethnic identity.

We write symphonies. We pursue innovation. We celebrate our ancient heroes, embrace our timeless traditions and customs, and always seek to explore and discover brand-new frontiers. We reward brilliance. We strive for excellence and cherish inspiring works of art that honor God. We treasure the rule of law and protect the right to free speech and free expression. . . .

What we have, what we inherited from our—and you know this better than anybody, and you see it today with this incredible group of people—what we've inherited from our ancestors has never existed to this extent before. And if we fail to preserve it, it will never, ever exist again.[44]

These words—taken from President Trump's speech in Warsaw in July 2017—open by defining the "we" as those who participate in the most particularly European of all cultural forms: symphony writing. It defines freedom not as an ideal sought by all, but as the patrimony available to descendants of certain ancestors. If "we" fail to preserve it, it will never exist again, because nobody but "us" can attain the pinnacles of human achievement. Ironically, this paean to European superiority was delivered as Trump stood on a platform alongside a president and prime minister whose government were that very week fighting a fierce political battle to destroy the independence of Poland's judiciary—and who had already corrupted and politicized Poland's broadcast media.

Trump assumes, "I get poor when you get rich." He asserts, "I command, you defer." This blighted view of life and politics can lead only to conflict and failure. America has done best for itself when most generous to others; it has most enhanced its security by sharing that security with friends, partners, and allies. The golden age of America to which Trump frequently wishes to return was an age of American generosity. Trump instead incites selfish nationalism, rising protectionism, and accumulating conflict. The little Trumps of Europe, Asia, and Latin America think to empower themselves by emulating the example of the big Trump of the United States.

How does the United States warn Vietnamese and Korean people against the Chinese state's rising threat to their neighborhood while an American president habitually insults his own neighbors?

How to warn against the geopolitical implications of corruption and dirty money under a president who pockets payments from foreign governments and owes his own election in considerable part to a Russian espionage intervention?

How to stand for any liberal, democratic, or humane principle or value under a president who so noisily repudiates them all? In his own life, Donald Trump has cheated anyone foolish enough to trust him: contractors, creditors, wives. That a great nation should cherish its reputation for good faith—that is an alien idea to him.

Flat-out incomprehensible to him is the idea that a superpower might use its strength, not to dominate and exploit, but to institute rules that benefit all nations, including itself. In one of the last speeches of his presidency Ronald Reagan urged Americans always to trade in freedom. "In war, for one side to win, the other must lose. But commerce is not warfare. Trade is an economic alliance that benefits both countries. There are no losers, only winners."[45] Under Trump, Reagan's party has left behind Reagan's wisdom, making losers of us all.

Trump leaves behind a country less admired, less trusted, and therefore less strong and less secure. He has made American power a cause of worry to other free nations, not a source of reassurance. He has emboldened crooks and bullies, done damage to the world trading system, and accelerated the American decline he promised to reverse. Most deadly of all, Donald Trump has whistled up a violent global insurgency against liberal democracy inside the countries of the West: fought by men who kill to express their hatreds of Muslims, of Jews, of nonwhite immigrants—and who look to Donald Trump as their inspiration, if not their leader.

CHAPTER FOUR

White Terror

After the murderous attack on the Pulse nightclub in Orlando, candidate Donald Trump suggested that President Obama was somehow implicated in the mass killing. The shooter, an American-born Muslim, had sworn allegiance to ISIS and cited ISIS ideology as his motive for a crime that killed forty-nine people and wounded fifty-three. The next morning, Monday, June 13, 2016, Trump telephoned in to Fox News's morning program.

> Look, we're led by a man that either is not tough, not smart, or he's got something else in mind. And the something else in mind—you know, people can't believe it. People cannot, they cannot believe that President Obama is acting the way he acts and can't even mention the words "radical Islamic terrorism." There's something going on. It's inconceivable. There's something going on.

Trump then called for Obama to resign because of that "something going on."

> He doesn't get it or he gets it better than anybody understands—it's one or the other, and either one is unacceptable.[1]

In case Trump had not made himself sufficiently clear, he repeated his insinuation later that same morning in a call to NBC's *Today* program:

> Well there are a lot of people that think maybe he doesn't want to get it. A lot of people think maybe he doesn't want to know about it. I happen to think that he just doesn't know what he's doing, but there are many people that think maybe he doesn't want to get it. He doesn't want to see what's really happening. And that could be.[2]

This slander that Obama secretly sympathized with Islamic terrorists was only too typical of the grotesque behavior of candidate Trump. Perversely, however, Trump's determination to argue Pulse = Muslim = Obama led Trump to one of the few relatively humane statements of his 2016 campaign. In his acceptance speech at the Republican convention in Cleveland a month after the Pulse shooting, Trump vowed,

> Only weeks ago, in Orlando, Florida, forty-nine wonderful Americans were savagely murdered by an Islamic terrorist. This time, the terrorist targeted our LGBT community. As your president, I will do everything in my power to protect our LGBT citizens from the violence and oppression of a hateful foreign ideology.

Detractors correctly observed that Trump cared for the safety of gay Americans only in order to accuse Muslims. Yet the commitment had been put on the record, and that was something. Something else had been put on the record, too—and that would prove even more important to the Trump presidency.

Pulse shooter Omar Mateen does not seem to have received any direction or support from ISIS or any other international terrorist organization. ISIS inspired Mateen, but Mateen did not report to ISIS, even to the extent that there was any ISIS to report to. Mateen exemplified a new kind of international terrorist movement: a virtual movement that shared ideas and rhetoric rather than money and weapons. Just such a movement of international terror would kill hundreds of people worldwide in the Trump years, a movement of white racial resentment that often looked to Donald Trump as its inspiration and voice.

The year 2019 suffered a peak in mass shootings in the United States, forty-nine shootings in total according to computations by the Associated Press, *USA Today*, and criminologists at Northeastern University. (The researchers defined a "mass killing" as taking four or more lives apart from the perpetrator's.) The majority of those killed died at the hands of a stranger—typically a white male loner impelled by grievances against society.[3] The deadliest mass shooting in US history (as of the end of 2019) occurred in October 2017. Stephen Paddock, a sixty-four-year-old white man, opened fire at a music festival in Las Vegas from a thirty-second-floor hotel room. Paddock killed 58 people and wounded 413. More than 400 other people were injured in the rush to escape the attack. After firing thousands of rounds in only ten minutes, Paddock killed himself by a gunshot in his mouth.

Paddock had professed support for Donald Trump to friends in the weeks before his crime, but police found no evidence of a specifically ideological or political motive for Paddock's attack. Other mass shooters, however, did express stronger pro-Trump feelings in their explanations of their crimes.

In the manifesto he posted before his attack on a New Zealand mosque in March 2019, Brenton Tarrant wrote that he shared a "common purpose" with Trump. Tarrant's attack left fifty-one people dead, dozens more wounded. Tarrant explained his views in a series of questions and answers.

Q: Were/are you a supporter of Donald Trump?

A: As a symbol of renewed white identity and common purpose? Sure. As a policymaker and leader? Dear god no.

In August 2019, Patrick Crusius opened fire upon a predominantly Hispanic crowd in El Paso, Texas. Crusius killed twenty-two and wounded many more. His manifesto cited the New Zealand shooting, half a world away, as his inspiration. "This attack is a response to the Hispanic invasion of Texas," he wrote. He blamed politicians "of both parties" for enabling mass immigration and insisted, "My opinions on automation, immigration, and the rest predate Trump and his campaign for president." Yet among Crusius's complaints about Hispanic immigration into Texas was that it could shift the state's politics from Republican to Democrat—not a complaint you'd expect to hear from a person wholly alienated from the political system and equally hostile to both parties.

Robert Bowers, who killed eleven and wounded six in a Pittsburgh synagogue in October 2018, stated on his social media account that he had not voted for Trump. "Trump is a globalist, not a nationalist. There is no #MAGA as long as there is a kike infestation."[4] But even as Bowers condemned Trump, he acknowledged that many of Bowers's fellow racists *did* like Trump. Bowers reposted two social media images in which Trump is photographed apparently listening attentively to a man in kippah and Jewish Orthodox garb. In both, the Jewish man was supposedly instructing Trump:

"Your character will appear to the public as a white racist. It's how we control Whites."

"Yes sir," balloons a word bubble beside the Trump image.

"The character we've chosen for you," continues the Jewish overlord in Bowers's reposted fantasy

is of a good, strong white leader who is acting in the interests of his country. We must keep whites asleep for a few more years so they are totally outnumbered by our non-white minions and can never regain their country. Do this and we'll keep your family safe & wealthy, and we won't tell anyone about your trips to Lolita Island.[5]

Bowers's message to his fellow racists was that Trump's (authentic and laudable) racism against nonwhites could not succeed unless joined to an attack on the Jews masterminding the plot against the white race.

Santino William Legan attacked the Gilroy Garlic Festival, a family-oriented food fair held about thirty miles southeast of San Jose, California, in July 2019. He killed three, wounded seventeen. His manifesto said nothing specifically about President Trump. His social media account promoted the nineteenth-century racist and misogynist tract "Might Is Right." Legan explained his action as an attack on the "hordes of mestizos and Silicon Valley twats" attracted to the festival.

In 2017, domestic political extremists murdered thirty-seven people in the United States, according to figures compiled by the Anti-Defamation League. (The ADL did not count the Las Vegas shooter as a political extremist.) Domestic political extremists killed fifty people in 2018. These figures were slightly lower than the figures for 2015 and 2016: seventy and seventy-two, respectively. But unlike 2015 and 2016, in the Trump era, political murders

> were overwhelmingly linked to right-wing extremists. Every one of the perpetrators had ties to at least one right-wing extremist movement, although one had recently switched to supporting Islamist extremism.[6]

The figure for 2018 would have been even higher if the pro-Trump pipe bomber Cesar Altieri Sayoc had been more successful with the fourteen devices he sent to twelve targets of Trump attack tweets, including former director of national intelligence James Clapper and Democratic presidential candidate Kamala Harris.

Trump—or anyway, whoever was managing Trump's Twitter that day—did issue a clear condemnation of right-wing extremist violence on the one-year anniversary of the Charlottesville demonstrations.

"I condemn all types of racism and acts of violence. Peace to ALL Americans!"[7] At other times, however, Trump's expressed more equivocal views about political violence. On September 29, 2019, Trump tweeted a threat that removing him from office by impeachment would lead to "a Civil War like fracture in this Nation from which our Country will never heal."[8] Pro-Trump militia groups seized on Trump's words with glee. "We ARE on the verge of a HOT civil war. Like in 1859. That's where we are."[9]

Interviewed by Breitbart.com in March 2019, President Trump boasted of his supporters' propensity to violence.

> It's so terrible what's happening. You know, the left plays a tougher game, it's very funny. I actually think that the people on the right are tougher, but they don't play it tougher. Okay? I can tell you, I have the support of the police, the support of the military, the support of the Bikers for Trump—I have the tough people, but they don't play it tough until they go to a certain point, and then it would be very bad, very bad. But the left plays it cuter and tougher.[10]

Trump has fantasized about political violence since he declared for president in 2015. He encouraged his supporters to punch and beat protesters and offered to pay the legal bills of anybody who got arrested during a beating. But recently, Trump has changed the way he has spoken about violence: not as an individual action—but as his last best hope for retaining power. Here he is in September 2018:

> They're so lucky that we're peaceful. Law enforcement, military, construction workers, Bikers for Trump—how about Bikers for Trump? They travel all over the country. They got Trump all over the place, and they're great. They've been great. But these are tough people. These are great people. But they're peaceful people, and Antifa and all—they'd better hope they stay that way. I hope they stay that way. I hope they stay that way.[11]

Similarly, the National Rifle Association began posting videos in the fall of 2017 that approached the verge of direct incitement, fantasizing about violence against political opponents while pitying themselves as somehow the true victims of aggression by others. Here's host Dana Loesch in a video released on October 20, 2017:

> We are witnesses to the most ruthless attack on a president, and the people who voted for him, and the free system that allowed it to happen in American history. From the highest levels of government, to their media, universities and billionaires, their hateful defiance of his legitimacy is an insult to each of us. But the ultimate insult is that they think we're so stupid that we'll let them get away with it. These saboteurs, slashing away with their leaks and sneers, their phony accusations and gagging sanctimony, drive their daggers through the heart of our future, poisoning our belief that honest custody of our institutions will ever again be possible. So they can then build their utopia from the ashes of what they burned down. No, their fate will be failure and they will perish in the political flames of their own fires.[12]

The radio-talk-show host and NBC contributor Hugh Hewitt blurbed a series of fantasy novels in which heroic Red State Americans perpetrate commando attacks on Blue State targets. In 2018, the *American Conservative* marked the September 11 anniversary by posting an article that predicted that the Mueller Report would compel Trump supporters to resort to violence.[13]

In May 2019, the former Breitbart columnist and enthusiastic Trump supporter Milo Yiannopoulos urged his fans to ready themselves for domestic insurgency.

> I abhor political violence. Let me be clear about that. But when someone takes away your freedom, your speech and your ability to protect yourself and your family, there aren't many options left. At least, that's how citizens quickly come to feel.

It is getting close to the time when, per America's founding documents, citizens will start forming into well-regulated militias in preparation for the lawful defense of the Constitution. And maybe I'm the right person to sketch out how that should work.

You know, maximum cell size. Encrypted comms. Like I said, I abhor violence. But civil war is coming, and, if it does, well-meaning but poorly informed and relentlessly de-platformed conservatives are going to need a handbook.[14]

Weird right-wing street gangs have formed in the Trump years, Proud Boys and Patriot Prayer, that seek out confrontations with black-masked anarchist groups, often dubbed Antifa, for "antifascist." ("Antifa" is antifascist in the same sense that the Democratic People's Republic of Korea is a democratic people's republic.)

Like Islamic extremism, the new extremist politics spans a spectrum of behaviors. Some inspire violence, some condone it, some commit it. The new extremist movement resembles ISIS in particular in that—unlike say the IRA and PLO terrorists of the 1970s and 1980s—its ideologists and its gunmen are not personally known to one another. There is no central command. The movement's ideologists place content on TV or on the Internet; the gunmen find it and are actuated by it.

Unlike networked Islamic movements, however, the new politics of white extremism are marked by a large element of irony, spoof, and grift. Did Milo Yiannopoulos "mean it" when he offered himself as an expert on urban terrorism? Or was he just emitting empty words in pursuit of a dishonest dollar? The novels endorsed by Hewitt that fantasize about a Red State war on Blue America may have borrowed a lot from William Pierce's *Turner Diaries*. But their author is not a neo-Nazi on the margins of society. He's a well-compensated lawyer in Los Angeles, a frequent guest on cable TV, who is attempting to bust into the entertainment industry. The confrontations staged by the Proud Boys are less 1930s-style mob violence intended to "win the streets," more performances choreographed to create viral videos for YouTube. The performers in NRA video spots growled, "We're coming for you, *New York Times*" and "consider this the shot across your proverbial bow" and "we're going to laser-focus on your so-called honest pursuit of truth."[15] They would then express shock and dismay that anybody would hear a *threat* in words they insisted were intended purely metaphorically.

The pipe-bomber Sayoc himself had confessed that he had selected his targets based on Trump's tweets. Trump accepted no responsibility, however. He instead accused news media who reported on the pro-Trump motive for Sayoc's bombs of attempting to "score political points against me and the Republican Party."[16] The Pittsburgh synagogue killer fantasized that a global Jewish conspiracy headed by George Soros was masterminding illegal immigration to the United States and Europe. Even *after* the synagogue shooting, Trump still repeated on November 1, 2018, that "he wouldn't be surprised" and "a lot of people are saying" that George Soros paid for the caravans.[17] Yet Trump and his supporters reserved the right to be affronted and offended if anyone noted the similarity between Trump's rhetoric and the Pittsburgh shooter's.

Almost any set of ideas, when taken to extremes, can justify authoritarianism and violence. The antiwar movement of the 1960s mutated into the bombings and robberies of the Weather Underground. The civil rights movement produced the Black Panthers. Advocates of animal welfare committed eleven hundred violent acts against persons and property between 1976 and 2004, according to the FBI.[18] The authors of those acts are responsible for their own crimes. The moral test comes in the way that law-abiding advocates of a set of ideas react to lawless people who share some of their ideas. Are they unambiguous in their condemnation? Do they recalibrate anything in their message that might act as incitement? Do they cooperate with law enforcement to punish wrongdoers and prevent future wrongdoing? This is what was asked by American conservatives of American Muslims in response to Islamic terrorism. The targets of the new extremist violence can now pose the same demand to President Trump and his supporters.

Trump's left-wing critics sometimes argue: *Racism and authoritarianism were always present within American conservatism. Trump only "says the quiet part out loud," making explicit what was always implicit. In a way, Trump is an improvement, at least now everybody can see what the issues are.*

But the move from unspoken to spoken is a big move. It's one thing to hold an unconscious, unexamined bias. It's a different thing to articulate that previous bias as a conscious and willing belief. The winning conservatism of Richard Nixon, Ronald Reagan, and the two Bush presidents may sometimes have drawn power from deep and dark energies in the American soul. That conservatism also contained those energies. Hate crimes against Muslims spiked in the immediate aftermath of September 11. Thanks in great part to leadership by President George W. Bush, including a mosque visit within a week of the attacks, the spike after September 2001 was quickly curbed in 2002.[19]

Trump conjured the dark energies that his predecessors had sought to contain. Did he fully control them? Did he even understand them? He imagined support for him as a "Trump" movement, which is why he imagined he personally could get away with anything even shooting a man on Fifth Avenue—and why he deluded himself that he could bequeath that movement to his underachieving children as a family property.

But Trump belonged to his movement as much as or more than his movement belonged to him. It's bigger than him, it's more dangerous than him, and it will have to be reckoned with even after Trump himself departs this scene.

How to describe this movement? What to call it?

Its supporters like to call it "nationalist"—but it is anything but "nationalist." The new movement's version of "nationalism" attaches them not to the multiracial American nation with its capital in Washington, DC, but to a multinational white race with a capital in Moscow. The most fundamental concept in the politics of the new movement is the divide between friend and enemy, but for the new movement, the divide cuts *through* nations, not between them. Fellow citizens can be enemies; faraway co-racialists can be friends.

This replacement of nation by race may explain why so many Trump supporters felt untroubled by Russian help for the Trump candidacy—or the flow of foreign money to Trump personally. The Trump movement linked itself to similar movements around the world. It cared as much or more about Britain quitting the EU and Muslim migration to Europe as about anything happening in this country. The pro-Trump Breitbart.com has run almost as many stories about the UK Brexiteer Nigel Farage as about US vice president Mike Pence; more about the British immigration provocateur Tommy Robinson than about Tom Cotton, the leading immigration restrictionist in the US Senate. One of Trump's favorite TV hosts, Fox News's Tucker Carlson, lent credence on his program to Russian claims that NATO membership for the Adriatic nation of Montenegro would somehow trigger World War III.[20] Montenegro's armed forces number twenty-four hundred people. It has no tanks, no combat aircraft, and two antique frigates. It had friendly relations with all its neighbors and is situated twenty-two hundred kilometers distance from the nearest Russian border. How could Montenegro possibly start a war with anybody? But what Montenegro does have is the one formerly non-NATO port on the Adriatic. For both strategic and ego reasons, it irked Putin to lose access to it. In October 2016, Russian secret services backed an election day assassination attempt and coup against Montenegro's pro-Western government. Nobody gets worked up about the danger *from* Montenegro to Russia (as opposed to the other way around) unless they are consuming some truly high-octane Russian propaganda. "I think we should probably take the side of Russia, if we have to choose between Russia and Ukraine," Carlson said on his program December 2, 2019— his second endorsement of Russian aggression against Ukraine in a week. After the first endorsement, he later said he had been "only joking," but there was no apology for the straight-faced second endorsement.[21]

Like Carlson, adherents of the new movement—whether Italian, Hungarian, British, or American—look to Russia's Vladimir Putin even more than to Donald Trump for inspiration, support, and leadership. Vladimir Putin said the evangelist Franklin Graham, on a 2015 visit to Russia, "is protecting traditional Christianity"[22] at a time when democratic leaders espouse secularism and liberalism. In a lecture at Hillsdale College in 2017, the journalist Christopher Caldwell compared Putin in the 2010s to Fidel Castro in the 1960s. Both Putin and Castro, said Caldwell, became "a symbol of national self-determination" to an international rebellion against capitalist democracy.[23]

Its detractors called the movement "white nationalist," but again, this is not quite right. The Trump movement is crammed with people of wholly or partially non-European origins, people who would not conventionally be regarded as white. The pro-Trump *Human Events* is edited by a British-born "anti-globalist" of Ismaili Muslim origins. Bombay-born Dinesh D'Souza produces books and documentaries reviling Barack Obama as an African outsider and hailing Trump's glorious leadership. David Clarke, the African American former sheriff of Milwaukee County, served as a leading spokesman for Trump's America First Action SuperPAC until 2019. Even bigger are Diamond and Silk, two sisters whose singsong YouTube videos in praise of Donald Trump delight 1.5 million followers on Facebook. The pro-Trump advocacy group Turning Point USA is cochaired by Candace Owens, a charismatic young black woman with unusual views like this: "If Hitler just wanted to make Germany great and have things run well—OK, fine. The problem is that he wanted, he had dreams outside of Germany. He wanted to globalize. He wanted everybody to be German."[24] The Gilroy Garlic Festival shooter was of part-Iranian origins.

In Western Europe, parties of the far right now welcome gays and feminists as allies against Muslim minorities. President Jair Bolsonaro won a plurality of the votes of Brazilians who define themselves as "mixed race," despite (or because of) his promise to police urban slums by machine-gunning darker-skinned gangsters.[25]

Nuremberg-law whiteness is not necessarily required by the new white supremacist movement. You don't have to *be* "white" to join up. You just have to agree that "white" is best. The *New York Times* reported in April 2019:

> At least four white extremist killers [to that date had] made statements online praising Elliot Rodger, a racist and misogynist who targeted women in a 2014 spree, before carrying out their own attacks.[26]

Rodger attributed the rage that impelled him to his mixed-race origins. "I am half White, half Asian, and this made me different from the normal fully-white kids that I was trying to fit in with . . . My first act was to ask my parents to allow me to bleach my hair blonde. I always envied and admired blonde-haired people, they always seemed so much more beautiful."

Hitler was not blond; Stalin was not Russian; Napoleon spoke heavily accented French. We are all familiar with the case of the alienated outsider who identifies himself as the ultra-insider, even committing murder to prove his point.

So how to define and describe the new movement? It is, first, radically masculinist and misogynist.

In every advanced country, the twenty-first century has proved a bewildering time for men. Job opportunities and pay have diminished for less-educated men. Management and the professions have been thrown open to women, who have enforced new norms of behavior in the workplace upon better-educated men. The ancient domestic division of labor has been upended. Men and women are more likely than ever to live apart, their sexualities no longer uniting them in marriage but antagonizing them against each other in sequences of mutually disappointing relationships.

These resentments provided an indispensable political resource to Donald Trump. In 2015, he retweeted the insult: "If Hillary Clinton can't satisfy her husband what makes her think she can satisfy America?"[27] Although he soon deleted it, the brutal message that Clinton was not sexy enough to lead reverberated through Trump world. Yet at the same time, she was also too womanly: faint, weak, ill. Under the "SickHillary" and "HillarysHealth" hashtags, Trump dirty tricksters like Roger Stone spread false rumors of a mysterious Clinton illness—rumors that I heard repeated by sophisticated Wall Street donors as well as online trolls. In prepared speeches in August 2016, Trump spoke the accusation in his own voice. "She lacks the mental and physical stamina to take on ISIS," Trump said in Youngstown, Ohio, on August 15, 2016. "To defeat crime and radical Islamic terrorism in our country, to win trade in our country, you need tremendous physical and mental strength and stamina. Hillary Clinton doesn't have that strength and stamina," he repeated in West Bend, Wisconsin, the next day.[28] To many Trump supporters, including many I personally heard from in 2016, Hillary Clinton had no name. She was simply "The Cunt."

Men who seethe with sexual anger easily shift to racial hatred against other men who are supposedly getting much *more* sex than they are cosmically entitled to. Those supposedly oversexed men are often imagined as belonging to a different religion, ethnicity, or race. Alien men are the enemy to be battled; women are the prize to be appropriated and controlled.

The new movement, second, is implacably hostile to science, reason, and objective truth. The leaders of Italy's Five Star movement are anti-vaxxers.[29] Poland's Law and Justice Party is animated by the belief that the plane crash that killed a former president in 2010 was a plot by Poland's then government, rather than the accident all independent experts agree it was. The Alternative for Germany dismisses the science of climate change as an elitist hoax.[30] The brainpan of Donald Trump, of course, bubbles with false information of all kinds.

President Trump campaigned against independent media as "enemies of the people," installed cronies and representatives of vested interests to head science agencies,[31] and eliminated scientific advisory panels that deliver unwelcome expertise on issues like climate policy.[32] Hungary's Viktor Orbán has driven his nation's only independent university out of the country. Both Hungary and Poland have crassly politicized their broadcast media.

Instead, the new movement subordinates reality to power. "The struggle of man against power is the struggle of memory against forgetting," wrote the Czech novelist Milan Kundera.[33] He was thinking of the persistent falsification of history by Soviet communism. His words also applied to President Trump's aggressive disinformation.

"What you're reading and what you're seeing is not what's happening," President Trump told a veterans' group in July 2018.[34] In June 2019, Trump erroneously claimed that Russia had withdrawn "most of their people" from Venezuela. That claim was immediately contradicted by an official Kremlin statement, which insisted that Russian specialists would continue to assist the Venezuelan government to maintain its military hardware. Asked about the contradiction, Trump told journalists:

Well, let's just see who's right. You know what you're gonna do? You're gonna see in the end who's right. You just watch it. Okay? And we'll see who is right.

Another journalist then posed another question. Trump interrupted to add: "Ultimately I'm always right."[35] (Russian specialists continued to travel to and from Venezuela to assist that country through the fall of 2019.[36])

Third, the new movement's concept of power is personal, not institutional. When Colonel Alexander Vindman testified to the House Intelligence Committee about Trump's extortion of Ukraine, Vindman was accused of disloyalty—not to the Constitution, to which he swore loyalty, but to Trump, to whom he did not.[37] Loyalty is due to persons, according to the new movement, not to impersonal institutions. "I need loyalty, I expect loyalty," Trump told FBI director James Comey at their fateful dinner. Trump associate Roger Stone explained how Trump understood "loyalty": "Support Donald Trump in anything he says and does."[38]

Trump collapses all politics into one question: for him or against him, regardless of what he does, regardless of anything the supporter might previously have believed. Formerly normal Republicans are zombified. Trump's third press secretary, Stephanie Grisham, became a source of robotic statements of North Korean obsequiousness. Asked on *Fox & Friends* in October 2019 whether the president regretted describing career civil servants and internal Republican critics as "human scum," she replied:

> No, no, he shouldn't. The people who are against him, and who have been against him, and have been working against him since the day they took office are just that. It is horrible that people are working against a president who's delivering results for this country and has been since day one. And the fact that people continue to try to negate anything he is doing and take away from the good work he is doing on behalf of the American people, they deserve strong language like that.[39]

Should we call this new movement fascist? We can see parallels, especially the fascination with violence, an essential element to fascism old and new. This is most especially true in the United States, with its cult of the gun and dress-up paramilitaries. Yet in Europe, too, we see a resurgence of street hooliganism, attacks on welfare facilities that house migrants, and even political assassinations.[40]

But there are differences as well, and they are important.

Fascism fetishized youth and energy. These new illiberal movements are movements shaped by the nostalgia of the elderly. They look backward to a supposedly better time, not forward to a utopia of national redemption through conquest and war.

The fascists of old imposed repression when they took power. For all Trump's bluster and threats, he has signally failed to do that—and even in Hungary, Viktor Orbán must settle for harassment and economic reprisal. Modern rule-of-law regimes are much more robust than those of ninety years ago.

Fascism promised to protect order and property against communist revolutions. Hard as Fox News works to frighten its viewers with the menace of Antifa and the New Black Panthers, modern property owners do not feel the fear on which classic fascism battened.

While these new movements are sustained by many of the same human impulses as animated fascism, they have evolved into something distinct and new. The would-be fascists of the 2010s face stronger and better organized democracies in a world trending toward more prosperity, not less, as in the 1930s. When scientists examine a species that resembles another, but only incompletely or imperfectly, they add the suffix *oid*. A chemical compound that's not quite an alkaline is an *alkaloid*; an orbiting space rock not quite a planet is a *planetoid*. In the same way, Trump and his ilk are *fascoid*—near it, but not quite the same, a failure even as fascists.

This time, the forces of freedom represent the stronger side. With will and savvy, the fascoids can be beaten—faster, more decisively, and less painfully than their predecessors.

To beat them, though, it's necessary to reckon with the sources of their appeal.

In an April 1938 Fireside Chat, President Franklin Delano Roosevelt explained how democracy could be lost if it failed to address pressing social problems.

Democracy has disappeared in several other great nations—disappeared not because the people of those nations disliked democracy, but because they had grown tired of unemployment and insecurity, of seeing their children hungry while they sat helpless in the face of government confusion, government weakness—weakness through lack of leadership in government. Finally, in desperation, they chose to sacrifice liberty in the hope of getting something to eat. We in America know that our own democratic institutions can be preserved and made to work. But in order to preserve them we need to act together, to meet the problems of the Nation boldly, and to prove that the practical operation of democratic government is equal to the task of protecting the security of the people.[41]

The challenge issued by Franklin Roosevelt in 1938 has returned to face us today. Trump may fall to ill health, mental breakdown, or the hazards of politics. Whatever his personal fate, he has remade the Republican Party in his image. He has taught even opponents to emulate behaviors they once would have regarded as utterly unacceptable. He has excited imitators across the world. As the communists of the 1930s cooperated across borders in the Third International, so today's illiberal authoritarians form a new . . . Trump International.

The new movement, like Trump himself, manages both to combine deadly dangerousness with clownish absurdity. The real Nazis seized a state; these bozos lurk on Gab. Yet they can kill. They are losers, but losers with guns. They cannot be eliminated, but they can be rendered harmless. Neutering them, though, will require more than one successful election. To contain and reverse the global movement to illiberal authoritarianism, it will be necessary to do more—much more—than eject that movement's mouthpiece president from the Oval Office.

Yet even that first step may prove challenging enough. If votes alone determined the outcomes of American elections, Trump would never have become president in the first place. Over the first years since the 2016 election, what comes out of the American ballot box has only drifted further away from what goes into it.

CHAPTER FIVE

"Real" versus "Unreal" Americans

Americans used to tell their national story as one of progress toward personal equality and political democracy. That story is inscribed into the evolving text of the US Constitution. The Thirteenth Amendment to the Constitution abolished slavery. The Fourteenth secured civil rights regardless of race. The Fifteenth guaranteed the right to vote regardless of race. The Sixteenth allowed the federal government to tax Americans as individuals on an equal basis. The Seventeenth instituted direct election of US senators. The Nineteenth extended the vote to women. The Twenty-Third amendment enfranchised residents of the District of Columbia. The Twenty-Fourth forbade poll taxes. The Twenty-Sixth reduced the voting age to eighteen. Along the way, the Voting Rights Act of 1965 policed state and local attempts at disenfranchisement.

The US political system remained anti-majoritarian in many important ways, of course: the two senators per state rule, judicial review by the Supreme Court. Yet these anti-majoritarian features were legitimated as wise restraints upon an otherwise representative system. They balanced an apparatus otherwise powered by the principle, "Here the people rule."

The president in particular was seen as embodying the will of the people. While it remained theoretically possible that a candidate could lose the popular vote and win the Electoral College, that had last happened in 1888. For twenty-seven consecutive presidential elections, 1892 through 1996, the person who won the most votes in total also won the most Electoral Votes. In twenty of those twenty-seven elections, the winner outdistanced the loser by at least five percentage points of the votes cast. In ten of the twenty-seven, the winner won more than 55 percent of the popular vote. The rickety eighteenth-century constitutional architecture consistently yielded a robustly democratically legitimate result in the twentieth century.

Then, in the twenty-first century, the old architecture abruptly stopped working. In the election of 2000, 547,000 Americans had preferred former vice president Al Gore over Texas governor George W. Bush. The Supreme Court pronounced Bush the winner, with a final Electoral result of 271–266.

Back in 1888, nobody had worried that much about a divergence between the popular vote and the Electoral College. In those days, violence and intimidation in the South and fraud and corruption in the North rendered popular vote totals only very approximate anyway.[1] But at the beginning of the twenty-first century, President-elect Bush recognized it as a serious problem that he lacked a popular mandate. He strove to gain after the election the broad national support that had eluded him on voting day. In his first speech after the *Bush v. Gore* decision, Bush promised:

> I was not elected to serve one party, but to serve one nation. The president of the United States is the president of every single American, of every race and every background. Whether you voted for me or not, I will do my best to serve your interests, and I will work to earn your respect.

At the time, the 2000 election was generally regarded as a freakish anomaly, a once-in-a-century fluke, a coin toss that had landed on the edge. The surge of unity after the September 11 attacks shoved the memory of *Bush v. Gore* to the back of the national attic, to gather dust and be forgotten. The election of 2004 seemed to return to majority rule as usual. This election was close, too, but Bush's 286–251 Electoral College victory aligned appropriately with his 50.73 percent popular vote majority.

But since 2010, anti-majoritarian outcomes have been recurring more and more often, at every level of the system. They are recurring not only because of antique legacies like the Electoral College, but in consequence of the newest rules. They are produced not by undesired glitches in the original constitutional scheme, but by present-day abuses by self-interested politicians.

In the election of 2016, Donald Trump won 46.09 percent of the popular vote: less than Mitt Romney lost with in 2012. In fact, of the ten nominees for president by the two major parties beginning in the year 2000, only *one*—John McCain in 2008—won a smaller share of the popular vote than Donald Trump in 2016.

But as in 2000, in 2016 the Electoral College again favored the Republican. Only this time, Americans confronted the uncomfortable possibility: maybe this was no anomaly. Trump misrepresented the 2016 election as an epic achievement won by his own political savvy and personal charisma. On the first Sunday after the vote, he declared that the Democrats in 2016 "suffered one of the greatest defeats in the history of politics in this country" and took credit for "a massive landslide victory."[2] This first round of boasting ignited more derision than even Trump could withstand. So, three weeks after 2016, Trump revised his claim.

> In addition to winning the Electoral College in a landslide, I won the popular vote if you deduct the millions of people who voted illegally.[3]

Taken literally, this second claim implied truly historic levels of voter fraud in favor of Hillary Clinton—a claim credible to nobody not on the payroll of either Fox News or the Trump White House and believed by precious few people even at those institutions. But many people were ready to believe that if all those extra votes for Hillary Clinton were not technically *illegal*, they were surely undesirable and improper, cast by people whose votes deservedly counted for less.

From the moment Trump entered office, he and his party faced a choice: try to do what George W. Bush did and govern to build a new voting majority behind the Trump presidency—or else accept minority status and try to find a way to hold on to power despite it.

During the impeachment debate of December 2019, Representative Clay Higgins of Louisiana delivered his remarks standing before a map of all the Red-tinted counties Trump had won in 2016.

> We face this horror because of this map; this is what the Democrats fear. They fear the true will of we the people. They are deep established D.C. They fear, they call this Republican map flyover country. They call us deplorables. They fear our faith, they fear our strength, they fear our unity, they fear our vote, and they fear our president.

How do you construe "the will of the people" from a map drawn to magnify unpeopled terrain? But that is the wrong question. The point of the Red-county map is not to elevate rocks and buffalo over people, but to elevate some people over others.

Republican member of Congress Dan Crenshaw posted a video on Twitter in August 2019 to argue that Republican states deserve more say than Democratic states even if they cast fewer votes. Republicans, he argued, are "more representative of the entirety of the country . . . Smaller, more rural states have their voice both in the Congress and when electing our president . . . 51 percent of the population could tell the other 49 percent what to do, even if that 51 percent were concentrated in the most populous states."[4] Instead, it is fairer for the 49 percent to tell the 51 percent what to do.

How can this be justified in a supposedly democratic society?

Like Tony Perkins—whom we met in the introduction predicting in 2014 that evangelical Christians would soon be packed off in boxcars to concentration camps—conservatives have convinced themselves that the country stands at five minutes to midnight, forever.

"America is drawing perilously close to a tipping point that has the potential to curtail free enterprise, transform our government, and weaken our national identity in ways that may not be reversible," Paul Ryan told the American Enterprise Institute in 2011.[5] "We are locked into an existential battle for the future of western civilization," Rush Limbaugh told his radio audience in 2018. "The other side is playing for keeps, and will stop at nothing to win."[6]

If Trump loses the 2020 election, one of Trump's most imaginative TV defenders argued, "The nation will cease to be a constitutional, democratic republic."[7] Broadcaster Glenn Beck concurred. He told Sean Hannity on the latter's Fox program:

> If the Republicans don't win in this next election, I think we are officially at the end of the country as we know it. We may not survive even if we win, but we definitely don't if the Republicans lose with Donald Trump.[8]

Trump is the last chance, the only barrier against the loss of all that real Americans hold dear. How would it be justified to throw away almost two and a third centuries of Americanism just because misguided Californians and New Yorkers voted in a herd for socialism and abortion? From a pro-Trump point of view, such a scenario is terrifyingly plausible.

If Californians vote in 2020 at the same rate as in 2008, instead of the lower rates of 2012 and 2016, then Democrats will pull a net total of half a million more popular votes just out of that one state. Posit a similar turnout surge in New York, New Jersey, Michigan, and other states with high minority populations, and it is very easy to imagine Trump losing the national popular vote in even a tight 2020 election by more than 4 million instead of 2016's 2.87 million.

Yet at the same time, Trump's majorities among rural voters and white voters could actually rise. Trump's 2020 campaign plan, as often publicly discussed by his managers and strategists, is to flip just two smaller states with non-Hispanic white populations of over 85 percent—Minnesota and New Hampshire—while adding two more of Maine's four split Electoral Votes to the single EV Trump won in Maine in 2016. The Electoral College arithmetic just barely works, even if Trump loses any one of these vulnerable 2020 states: Indiana, Iowa, Michigan, Georgia, North Carolina, or Wisconsin.

So what does America look like if Trump *twice* wins the Electoral College while losing the popular vote? If three out of the four Republican presidential terms of the twenty-first century were won without a popular mandate? "He got elected by an overwhelming majority of 63 million Americans who came out and supported him and wanted to see his policies enacted," said press secretary Sarah Huckabee Sanders of Trump in October 2018.[9] It sounded unconvincing then. It will sound even more ridiculous should the next election prove even more lopsided. At some point, Republicans may be driven to argue explicitly: with the country composed of the wrong kind of majorities demographically, it cannot be governed by majority rule electorally.

Trumpists believe both:

This country needs to be governed in the name of the great majority of its everyday plain people, not self-satisfied elites;

and

Voting is a privilege not a right, the United States is a republic not a democracy, and we should not choose our leaders just by counting who got the most votes.

You might think it would provoke a headache to hold on to both those seemingly contradictory beliefs. Trumpism is not even aware of them as contradictory. Embedded in Trumpism is the distinction between "people" and "the people." Not all people belong to "the people." More and more people emphatically do *not* belong—which is why Trump's absurd claims about illegal voting resonated so powerfully. The Trump supporters who hear that claim may not have believed that literally millions of illegal aliens voted. But they could easily believe that millions of people voted who should never have been accepted as voters in the first place. One of President Trump's few supporters in the technology world, venture capitalist Peter Thiel, wrote in 2009: "I no longer believe that freedom and democracy are compatible." Thiel explained,

> Since 1920, the vast increase in welfare beneficiaries and the extension of the franchise to women—two constituencies that are notoriously tough for libertarians—have rendered the notion of "capitalist democracy" into an oxymoron.[10]

Thiel—a graduate of Stanford and Harvard Law School who now heads a hedge fund—would seem the epitome of all that a Trump voter might resent. But his ideas about who should not participate in the political system might strike many a MAGA hat wearer as very congenial.

Yet even if all Americans remain formally entitled to vote, the weighting of votes becomes ever more unequal as the political system lags behind shifts in population. As the veteran political observer Norman Ornstein often points out: by 2040, 70 percent of the American population will live in fifteen states. Thirty percent of the population will live in thirty-five states. Think about what this means. That widely distributed 30 percent will be disproportionately white, disproportionately nonurban, disproportionately older than fifty years of age. They will control seventy seats in the US Senate, enough to override a presidential veto. If they all support the same candidate for president, that candidate will begin every election with a 40-vote head start in the 538-vote Electoral College. The 30 percent who live in thirty-five states are only three states short of the number necessary to amend the US Constitution.

Both parties have always tried to game the American political system. But since 2010, the system has been gamed in a way unlike anything since before the civil rights era. You see the erosion of democratic self-rule most strikingly at the state level.

In the elections of 2018, Republicans won 47 percent of all votes cast for the Michigan state legislature. They won 53 percent of the seats.

Republicans won 48 percent of votes cast for the North Carolina state legislature—and 54 percent of the seats.

In Ohio, Republicans won an authentic majority, 51 percent of votes cast. That slim margin of votes translated into a crushing majority of 62 percent of the seats in the statehouse.

Most extreme of all: in Wisconsin, 45 percent of the vote yielded 64 percent of the seats in the state assembly.[11]

In June 2019, former Wisconsin governor Scott Walker responded on Twitter to complaints about the gerrymandering of his state, of which he was a considerable author. Walker reproduced a map of Wisconsin's seventy-two counties, the great majority of them tinted Republican Red. He wrote atop the map:

> This map says it all. Democrats win by big margins in places like Madison (which counts the same as any other vote in statewide races) but that doesn't mean they should have a larger share of the seats just because they win by big margins in some districts.[12]

Walker is suggesting that each state needs to be organized like the whole country: with some areas systematically overweighted, and others systematically underweighted. But in Wisconsin, the overweighting is even more aggressive than it is nationally.

Four Democratic-leaning counties due south of the city of La Crosse are crammed into two legislative districts, while heavily Republican Waukesha County west of Milwaukee gets ten legislative seats all to itself.

In every other democracy that draws geographical constituencies, the job of drawing boundaries is assigned to some kind of independent agency. As the saying goes: "In other countries, the voters choose the politicians; in the United States, the politicians choose the voters."

The practice of party-drawn districting has always been a gross political evil. But the state and federal redistricting after the 2010 Census occurred at an especially bleak moment. The slow recovery from the 2008–2009 financial crisis had elected Republicans across many states—and those post-2010 Republicans were feeling panicky and desperate about their future under President Obama.

Faced with such a threat to all they held dear, Republicans saw no place for compromise. They wrote maps to guarantee they would win even if they lost.

Not only are votes unequally weighted, they are not always allowed to be cast in the first place. The state of Georgia purges from voter rolls any name that does not exactly match its identity in the state's driving records. Suppose the Department of Motor Vehicles records a Gloria Hernandez-Miranda (with a hyphen) living at 123 Maple Street. If that person at that address registers to vote without a hyphen, she risks being expunged by Georgia law. Georgia law does allow for an appeals process, whereby people improperly excluded can ask for reinstatement. That process does not move fast. As of voting day 2018, fifty-three thousand such appeals were pending. In that year's gubernatorial election, the Republican margin of victory was fifty-five thousand. The winner, Brian Kemp, was the secretary of state who oversaw the voter purge. Of the fifty-three thousand people whose appeals were unresolved by voting day, 70 percent were black.[13]

How do they get away with it?

Back in the civil rights era, the Supreme Court struck down state districting maps that favored rural over urban areas on the principle "one man, one vote." But more conservative courts have backed away from such scrutiny. Unless someone is fool enough to put in writing an explicit racial animus—as happened in North Carolina in the redistricting after the 2010 Census—federal courts have effectively resigned from voting oversight. As late as 2018, the US Supreme Court suggested that it was at least theoretically possible for a state gerrymander to go too far disadvantaging one party at the expense of the other. The confirmation of Justice Brett Kavanaugh in October 2018 finished off that possibility. In a pair of cases in June 2019—one involving the Wisconsin gerrymander, another a tidied-up North Carolina gerrymander minus the more blatant racism of a previous version—the US Supreme Court ruled that partisan gerrymandering was no business of the federal courts. Disenfranchised persons remained free to try their luck in state courts under state law. Thoughts and prayers!

Of course, as the Republican Party has morphed under Trump into a party of white ethnic chauvinism, partisan gerrymandering necessarily implies racial gerrymandering. When "belly of the beast" congressman Clay Higgins lauded the bright-Red map of the interior of the country, he was worshipping his own handiwork. In Higgins's state of Louisiana, about 1.46 million votes were cast for Louisiana's six congressional seats in the election of 2018. Republican candidates won about 57 percent of those votes. Yet they took five of six seats. The single seat they lost was artfully drawn to include *both* the state's biggest cities, New Orleans and Baton Rouge, *both* of them majority African American. In a state that is one-third African American, the congressional delegation is only one-sixth black. You see similar patterns across the Republican states. Mississippi is only 58 percent non-Hispanic white. In 2019, white Republicans held three of its four congressional seats. Alabama is 67 percent non-Hispanic white. In 2019, white Republicans held six of its seven seats.

The gerrymanders in Wisconsin and North Carolina, the registration purges in Georgia and Florida, voter ID laws everywhere—

all exert obviously disproportionate racial effect. This behavior was supposedly outlawed by the Voting Rights Act of 1965.

In 2006, President George W. Bush signed a twenty-five-year reauthorization of the act. "The right of ordinary men and women to determine their own political future lies at the heart of the American experiment," he said at the signing ceremony. The act had "broken the segregationist lock on the ballot box. . . . My administration will vigorously enforce the provisions of this law, and we will defend it in court."[14]

But the courts decreed otherwise. The Supreme Court vitiated a crucial enforcement section of the Voting Rights Act in 2013. The Trump Justice Department has shown little interest in the remaining sections of the act. The Civil Rights Division of the Justice Department lacked any confirmed head until October 2018. The eventual choice, John Gore, had previously worked as an employer-side lawyer at a big Washington, DC, law firm. Under Trump, the division initiated 50 percent fewer actions than it had done under President George W. Bush[15]—and many of those energies have focused on defending religious groups who feel oppressed by ordinances requiring them to accommodate gays and lesbians.[16]

As the Republican Party becomes ill adapted for political competition on equal terms, it has redefined its political goals. Instead of thinking how to compete in cities, how to reach the religiously unaffiliated, how to appeal to nonwhites, it invests its energies in the brutal project of preventing those groups from voting.

A telling indicator:

Republicans got crushed up and down the ballot in the state of Virginia in November 2019. Democrats won control of both houses of the state legislature for the first time since the mid-1990s. Democrats already held both the state's seats in the US Senate, as well as all the statewide elected offices of governor, lieutenant governor, and attorney general, atop their victory in the state in the presidential race of 2016. The chair of the Republican Party of Arizona reacted to the debacle by tweeting a county-by-county map of Virginia that showed much of southern and western Virginia still Red, under the caption: "Should we look toward an #ElectoralCollege type system at the state level?"[17]

The conservative political theorist Harvey C. Mansfield observed in the *Wall Street Journal* in 2016: "Trump makes it clear that, for him, winning dishonorably is better than losing honorably."[18] Mansfield did not mean that observation as a compliment, exactly, but many of his readers surely interpreted it that way.

Conservatives have long taken for granted that they represented America's great "silent majority," a phrase coined for Richard Nixon in 1970. But as they have glumly accepted that this is not true, that they have lost their former majority, conservatives have made their peace with rougher and rougher methods to hold power.

In March 2017, the *Washington Post* sent a reporter to the town of Wilmington, Ohio, seventy miles southwest of Columbus, a "town of rolling farmland and main streets shaded by grain elevators." The surrounding county had voted 75 percent for Donald Trump five months before. The *Post* reported that Wilmington remained Trump Country still.

> "The Russia thing doesn't fit too well here," Harold Rowland said in between bites of his breakfast at McDonald's. "Nobody really cares."[19]

Voters also did not care about Trump scandals in Monticello, Iowa;[20] Evansville, Indiana;[21] Little Hocking, Ohio;[22] Mesa, Arizona;[23] Laurel, Mississippi;[24] and Luzerne County, Pennsylvania,[25] among innumerable other dispatches from the heart of Trump country. (Luzerne is mentioned twenty-four times just in Salena Zito's and Brad Todd's often-cited book about the 2016 election, *The Great Revolt*.)

The town of Wilmington, Ohio, numbered slightly under thirteen thousand people in 2017, about the same as the Westwood neighborhood of Los Angeles around UCLA. Luzerne is a bigger place—317,000—but it still numbers fewer than Manhattan south of Washington Square Park. The entire state of South Dakota is home to fewer people than Maryland's Prince George's County.

The American political system does not treat the people of Prince George's County as the civic equals of the people of South Dakota. Indeed, people in South Dakota would regard it as a hideous injustice if they ever *were* treated as equals to the people of Prince George's County. The people of the American interior are the "real Americans," who deserve unceasing flattery and extra consideration. "We grow good people in our small towns, with honesty and sincerity and dignity," said Sarah Palin in her vice presidential acceptance address at the Republican convention in 2008. (She was quoting without attribution from Westbrook Pegler, a conservative columnist of the 1940s who ended as a supporter of the John Birch Society.) Can you imagine for a second the hell that would erupt if anyone spoke in similar terms at a political convention about America's big cities or great univerities? *We grow good people on the Upper West Side of Manhattan. . . .* It is unimaginable.

Yet maybe it is time to begin to imagine the unimaginable, for the people of New York City and Houston, of Las Vegas and Chicago, of the bay areas around Tampa and San Francisco to repeat after Glenn Beck in 2009—only this time, accurately:

> While the voices you hear in the distance may sound intimidating, as if they surround us from all sides—the reality is very different. Once you pull the curtain away you realize that there are only a few people pressing the buttons, and their voices are weak. The truth is that they don't surround us at all.
> We surround them.[26]

The compliment paid to the old "silent majority"—that they are the people who do the work and pay the taxes only to see their hard-earned money siphoned away for the benefit of people entrapped in dependency hundreds of miles away—that hardworking and tax-paying silent majority now lives on America's coasts and in America's cities.

On the campaign trail in 2008, Palin praised small towns as the most patriotic and pro-American parts of the country. That is ceasing to be true as well.

In a July 2018 poll conducted for Yahoo, 40 percent of self-identified Republicans professed unconcern if Russia again helped them win an election. Of that 40 percent, 29 percent agreed it would be "inappropriate, but not a big deal" if Russia helped Republicans keep control of Congress in that year's elections; 11 percent went further and said it would be fully "appropriate."[27] This seems a freakish result. Yet when Quinnipiac asked in September 2019 if it should be impeachable to ask "a foreign leader for help in defeating an opponent in an upcoming election," 68 percent of Republicans replied, "No."[28]

The stability of a democratic system depends on the willingness of players to play by agreed fair rules. The voters care about outcomes, not processes, as confirmed by an ominous study carried out by Matthew Graham and Milan Svolik of Yale University.

Graham and Svolik presented a sample of voters with a choice of candidates: one to their liking, one not. They then added the information that one of the candidates had said or done something that attacked the basics of democracy: endorsed a very unfair redistricting plan, supported a plan to reduce access to voting machines in strongholds of the other party, even backed a project to enable a governor of their party to rule by decree in defiance of a legislature controlled by the other party. Graham and Svolik found that only about 15 percent of voters would punish a co-partisan for such egregious behaviors. The strongest partisans, no surprise, were the least willing to punish. Voters instead relied on the deep human propensity for double standards to blind themselves to co-partisan abuse. Fifteen percent is not nothing. In a competitive political system, it's a lot. But in 2016, of the 435 seats in the House of Representatives . . .

177 favored one party or the other by fifteen points or more. In 2016, only seventy-two seats in the House were considered "competitive" by the veteran political observer Charlie Cook. And the problem of noncompetition is getting worse: Between 1997 and 2016, the number of competitive House seats fell by more than half.

It's political professionals and public-spirited elites who police the system. During Watergate, it was a fellow Republican, Senator Howard Baker of Tennessee, who posed the famous question of President Nixon: "What did the president know, and when did he know it?" The most memorable condemnation of Bill Clinton's immoral behavior during the impeachment crisis of 1998–1999 was delivered by a fellow Democrat, Senator Joe Lieberman of Connecticut.

Trump has defied accountability on a scale and with a consistency unequaled in modern presidential history. He refused to deliver subpoenaed documents, directed executive branch appointees not to testify, and asserted executive privilege even over people who no longer worked in the executive, like former White House counsel Don McGahn. He got away with it, for as long as he did get away with it, because of the protection of Republicans in the House and Senate.

Unaccountability is an infectious disease. The unelected Supreme Court has allowed state legislatures to become ever less representative. Distorted state legislatures gerrymander the House of Representatives. The gerrymandered House and the never-very-representative Senate in turn have protected a lawless presidency. Reforms that were written to enhance people power—the primary process to choose presidential nominees, for example—have spectacularly backfired. Instead of cleansing the process from the corrupt influences of party bosses, the primaries have empowered the most ideologically extreme factions of each party, and especially the Republican Party. Bosses wanted unifying candidates who could help the ticket everywhere in the country, so that the bosses could gain and dispense more patronage. Few liked that system while it existed, but in retrospect it seems a huge improvement over a system where the most radical on-air and online voices look for the politician who can most brutally manipulate the emotions of their listeners so as to keep angry old people watching and catheter advertisers buying time and clicks.

The antique certitude that the US Constitution artfully balanced majority rule against minority rights looks ever less credible. The old hope that America must slowly but surely trend toward democratic self-government—that hope looks sadly tarnished.

The coagulation of political power supports the concentration of economic power, as we shall see in the next chapter. As the American economy becomes less competitive, American workers and their wages lose ground. As workers lose, voters become more vulnerable to demagogues and extremists—who in their turn coagulate political power more. It's a dangerous cycle of despair and disempowerment. Yet it can be broken.

"History isn't kind to the man who holds Mussolini's jacket," Senator Ted Cruz told friends in New York in 2016.[29] Then Cruz went to work in Mussolini's cloakroom.

If American democracy is to recover, Cruz's party must be redeemed from those who bent that democracy to gain power they could not fairly win. The American economy must be redirected to serve better the people who do its work.

CHAPTER SIX

The Deep State Lie

It seems ungrateful for Trump to hate the FBI so much, considering all the FBI did to make him president. Through the 2016 campaign, the FBI's New York office leaked anti-Clinton tidbits to former New York City mayor Rudy Giuliani.[1] FBI director James Comey's formal notice to Congress on October 28, 2016, that he was reopening the investigation into Hillary Clinton's emails "in connection with an unrelated case" apparently validated Trump's campaign claims that some huge scandal was secreted within the Clinton email server. Hillary Clinton credited that notice as a crucial factor in her narrow defeat eleven days later.[2]

Trump assumed law enforcement agencies and the military would support his reactionary, chauvinist politics. It must have jolted him to discover post-election that his campaign, too, had come under investigation on counterintelligence grounds. Pre-presidential Trump had a long, complex, and mysterious relationship with the FBI and law enforcement agencies. Trump acted as an FBI informant in the 1980s, as the *Washington Post* reported during the campaign.[3] His usefulness to other FBI investigations may explain how a New York real estate figure who shared a lawyer with John Gotti and Tony Salerno escaped investigation himself.

From his earlier experiences with the FBI, Trump seems to have absorbed a transactional approach to law enforcement—the approach he deployed on James Comey at their famous dinner in January 2017. *You do me a favor, I do you a favor.* Only this time, the exchange of favors did not happen. Trump fired Comey. Jared Kushner reportedly assured Trump that Democrats would welcome the firing, ending Trump's Russia exposure once and for all. As so often happened, Kushner's advice proved less than astute. Trump for the first time in his long life of corrupt dealings found himself face-to-face with a criminal investigation he could not transact his way out of.

Trump would gradually attach the term *deep state* to every element of government that resisted his whim of the moment. According to Bob Woodward's reporting, President Trump ordered Secretary James Mattis to plan an operation intended to assassinate Syrian dictator Bashar al-Assad—an unlawful order, since assassination is prohibited by US law. Mattis reportedly listened politely, then told his staff, "We're not going to do any of that."[4] When Central American asylum seekers sought to rush the US border, Trump reportedly demanded they shoot the migrants in the legs. That unlawful command was likewise ignored.[5] Trump sought to blackmail Ukraine into fabricating dirt against likely presidential rival Joe Biden. His National Security staff mutinied and thwarted him. But it all started with Comey and the FBI, and that first encounter with cops he could not buy.

The phrase *deep state* originates in the byzantine world of Turkish politics. Kemal Atatürk, the founder of the Turkish republic, bequeathed a military and security establishment committed to secularism. For decades, Turkish politicians who wished to push their country in more Islamic directions would be balked—or even sometimes overthrown—by Kemal's heirs in the armed forces. Western political scientists adopted the term *deep state* to describe the power of the Kemalists after Kemal. Over time, the term was extended to describe other Third World societies with overmighty military and intelligence establishments, especially Pakistan. Steve Bannon absorbed the term somewhere and introduced it to Trump. Trump then diffused it through the conservative media, and especially to his pal Sean Hannity at Fox News.

In Turkey and Pakistan, the term *deep state* described how those with secret power used clandestine means to thwart the regular government. Bannon, Trump, and Hannity used the term to mean the direct opposite: how the regular government used lawful means to thwart Trump officials who abused their power.

Consider the actions at issue in Trump's impeachment trial. Congress voted military aid to Ukraine. Trump could have vetoed that aid. He could have withdrawn US recognition of the Zelensky government as the lawful government of Ukraine. He could have nominated Gordon Sondland as ambassador to Ukraine and instructed him to support the business schemes of Igor Fruman and Lev Parnas as in the national interest of the United States. He could even (probably) have directed his attorney general to open a criminal investigation of the Burisma gas company and any US person involved with it, including Hunter Biden.

These actions might have exacted a political cost, but they were all within Trump's legal authority. Trump did not do any of them. Instead, Trump used all the immense legal powers of his office to advance one policy in Ukraine. He then deployed secret nonlegal methods to advance a contradictory policy.

Or consider Trump's Russia policy. Trump could have pivoted US foreign policy to Russia. He could have appointed a secretary of state, secretary of defense, and national security advisers who shared his pro-Putin views. He could have waived US sanctions on Russia and accredited a US ambassador to Bashar al-Assad. He could have ended US naval operations in the Black Sea and withdrawn US forces from Poland and Romania. He could have invited Vladimir Putin to Camp David for talks, given a speech to Congress or to the country arguing for an alliance with Russia.

Again, Trump did not do any of that. He signed all the instruments and findings to continue preexisting Russia policy. Then he sabotaged his own policy in private, working around his own administration—treating even his note-takers and translators as spies and enemies.

Presidents hold enormous power over foreign policy. Trump did not use those powers. Trump was conspicuously uninterested in all those regular operations of the executive branch. He talked on unsecured phones, relied on Fox News rather than intelligence briefings, and disparaged his own officials as "Never Trumpers." Those disparaged officials did not defy Trump's policy. They *complied* with Trump's policy, as that policy was codified in formal orders. What they defied was the policy that Trump whispered to his cronies, the policy that Trump and his spokespeople indignantly denied they were following.

Trump disliked all formally constituted government. As Trump's former personal lawyer Michael Cohen testified, Trump talks in code. He wanted underlings who would spare him the distasteful necessity to articulate his intentions out loud. He expected them to anticipate his wishes, while preserving his deniability.

Government works by paper. Presidents issue orders by signed decision memo, creating a record of clarity and accountability. Trump hated paperwork. He erupted in rage when his first White House counsel, Don McGahn, took notes at meetings. He used insecure devices, risking surveillance by enemy spy services, rather than use methods where his own government could record him.

Trump was not a victim of the deep state: a rogue government-within-a-government that sabotaged lawful authority. It was *Trump* who was his own deep state, sabotaging on the sly the policy that he himself had ordered in writing.

Trump instinctively mistrusted all the law enforcement functions of government. He assumed, however, that the military would salute and obey any order, no matter how illegal. It must have stunned him to discover that the armed forces declined to act as his toy army.

Senior military leadership resisted Trump's wish for a big parade down Pennsylvania Avenue. Donald Trump had returned enthralled from a 2017 Bastille Day visit to Paris. He had stood in a place of honor in a reviewing stand as troops, weapons, and military bands passed before him. He was seen to mouth "So good" to his wife, Melania.[6] Trump returned home from Paris determined that he must have a parade in Washington for Veterans' Day 2017.

The Pentagon found reasons why it could not be done. Heavy military vehicles would chew up the streets of Washington, DC. The symbolism was inappropriate while US troops were still engaged in combat against ISIS and the Taliban. Anyway, it would all cost too much. Defense planners estimated that the parade Trump wanted would cost the federal government and the District of Columbia a total of $92 million, rather than the White House figure of $12 million—an estimate the Pentagon leaked to journalists, just in case.[7] The more fundamental cause of reluctance was not financial or symbolic, but human: the military has a lot of real work to do, and it did not want to impose useless extra tasks on its personnel for no better reason than to amuse an infantile president.

Yet Trump kept ordering the parade. A compromise was reached in time for the Fourth of July 2019. Trump got a flypast by each of the armed services, including the Coast Guard, but no marching troops, no rolling vehicles.

We were promised an armored division motoring along Constitution Avenue. We got Trump standing behind two parked tanks.

Notably, the service chiefs declined to attend Trump's salute to himself in the guise of a salute to the military. Whatever excuse they offered, it was hard to mistake the very real reservations senior officers felt about Trump's leadership. A poll by the *Military Times* in 2017 found notably low approval of Trump among the officer corps: about 30 percent favorable, about 53 percent unfavorable.[8] Insiders suggested that the higher the rank, the worse the opinion of Trump—an assessment confirmed when, in an unprecedented rebuke to a serving president, all four service chiefs took public stances after Trump's "good people on both sides" comments after the Charlottesville neo-Nazi march in August 2017.

At 1:42 p.m. on Saturday, August 12, a man intentionally drove a car into a group of counterprotestors at Charlottesville, killing one of them, a thirty-two-year-old woman named Heather Heyer. Over the next few days, Trump's reaction to the incident would provoke angry reaction from Congress, corporate America, even his own senior staff. Chief White House economic adviser Gary Cohn told friends he wanted to resign; so many CEOs did resign from White House advisory panels that the administration chose to close all of the panels down.

But before any corporate leaders spoke, one of the very first protests was voiced by the most senior of America's naval officers, Chief of Naval Operations John Richardson. At 8:31 on the evening of Heyer's death, Richardson tweeted:

Events in Charlottesville unacceptable & musnt be tolerated @USNavy forever stands against intolerance & hatred.[9]

As Trump doubled down, his service chiefs delivered unmistakable rebukes. At 6:51 p.m. on Tuesday, August 15, Marine Corps commandant Robert Neller tweeted:

No place for racial hatred or extremism in @USMC. Our core values of Honor, Courage, and Commitment frame the way Marines live and act.[10]

Army chief of staff Mark Milley tweeted at 4:50 (Eastern Time) on the morning of August 16.

The Army doesn't tolerate racism, extremism, or hatred in our ranks. It's against our Values and everything we've stood for since 1775.[11]

At 10:01 a.m. Eastern on the morning of August 16, air force chief of staff Dave Goldfein recycled Hillary Clinton's 2016 campaign slogan.

I stand with my fellow service chiefs in saying we're always stronger together—it's who we are as #Airmen[12]

Goldfein was capped at 11:27 a.m. Eastern that same day by the top general in the National Guard, Joseph Lengyel.

I stand with my fellow Joint Chiefs in condemning racism, extremism & hatred. Our diversity is our strength. #NationalGuard[13]

Maybe the most eloquent statement of them all came from Secretary of Defense James Mattis. Visiting Jordan August 21, 2017, Mattis stopped to talk with US personnel. Somebody captured his words on video: "Our country right now—it's got some problems. You know it, and I know it. It's got problems that we don't have in the military. You just hold the line, my fine young soldiers, sailors, airmen, and Marines. You just hold the line until our country gets back to understanding and respecting each other, and showing it, and being friendly to one another—all that Americans owe to one another."[14]

These comments never mentioned Trump. They did not need to. Everybody heard them, including Trump. Mattis slowly lost his hold on the president and resigned at the end of 2018.

Early in the Trump years, some feared that Trump might try to politicize the military in his direction. It soon became clear, however, that Trump lacked the knowledge and focus to sway military promotions policy. Trump's standing within the military deteriorated through 2018 and 2019, not only among officers but enlistees too. The December 2019 *Military Times* poll found that a plurality of troops of all ranks now disapproved of Trump's presidency, and 45.8 percent "strongly disapproved."[15]

Most of the time, Trump kept out of the military's way. Despite his dislike of NATO, Trump did not block military plans first to deploy troops to Poland and Romania, then to build permanent bases east of the former NATO–Warsaw Pact boundary. He did not withdraw troops from the Korean peninsula (although he never relented in his zeal to send South Korea a giant bill for its defense[16]). In summer 2019, he heeded the uniformed military's warnings about launching a shooting war versus Iran. He heeded advice to end the escalation with Iran in January 2020.

But every once in a while, Trump burst loose. He would do something wild, send the military scrambling to work around him—or to contain him. The supreme example: the betrayal of America's Syrian Kurdish allies in October 2019. Trump took military officials utterly by surprise when he greenlit the Turkish invasion of Kurdish-held areas of Syria, so much so that US forces actually came under fire from the Turkish advance. To avoid US casualties, US forces actually withdrew from their positions, surely the first time one NATO ally has retreated from an attack by another.[17] General Joseph Votel, former head of Central Command and leader of the fight against ISIS until 2019, condemned Trump's abrupt move in the *Atlantic* as a breach of trust. He observed, "The decision was made without consulting U.S. allies or senior U.S. military leadership. . . ."[18] Dozens of Kurdish civilians and soldiers were killed by Turkish forces; tens of thousands of people were displaced. Trump did not care about any of those human consequences. The military scrabbled to find something he did care about and succeeded: Syria's puny oil reserves. The *Washington Post*, October 25, 2019:

> President Trump was persuaded to leave at least several hundred troops behind in Syria only when he was told that his decision to pull them out would risk control of oil fields in the country's east, according to U.S. officials.
>
> Trump had rejected arguments that withdrawing U.S. forces would benefit American adversaries, while endangering civilians and Kurdish allies, but he tweeted Thursday that "we will NEVER let a reconstituted ISIS have those fields."
>
> Defense Secretary Mark T. Esper confirmed on Friday that troops would remain in eastern Syria to prevent the oil fields from being retaken by the Islamic State.[19]

The *New York Times* reported on October 30, 2019, the net result of Trump's bold decision in Syria:

> Every day in northeastern Syria, waves of American troops are pulling out under President Trump's order this month that paved the way for a Turkish offensive that included assaults on the Pentagon's allies, the Syrian Kurds.
>
> And at the same time, a separate wave of American troops from the opposite direction is pouring back in.
>
> In fact, once the comings and goings are done, the total number of United States forces in Syria is expected to be about 900—close to the 1,000 troops on the ground when Mr. Trump ordered the withdrawal of American forces from the country.[20]

Trump would express frustration later that he received less credit for the killing of ISIS leader Abu Bakr al-Baghdadi than he felt due. At a November 1, rally in Tupelo, Mississippi, Trump complained that the military dog that cornered al-Baghdadi got better publicity from the raid than he did. (Trump insisted that he was happy about this, in that familiar way where he would cite grievances and then add in a long-suffering tone, "but that's okay," about things that plainly he found radically *not* okay.) Trump wanted Americans to equate the Baghdadi mission to the 2011 raid that killed Osama bin Laden in Abbottabad, Pakistan. The two operations differed, however, in four ways detrimental to Trump's reputation.

1. President Obama intensely involved himself in operational details of the bin Laden mission, including the fateful decision whether to use one stealth Black Hawk helicopter (a choice that offered greater hope of penetrating Pakistani airspace undetected) or two (a choice that offered a greater margin of safety should anything go wrong). Obama opted for two, a decision vindicated when one of the Black Hawks crashed. Trump, by contrast, was kept largely in the dark

about the Baghdadi mission by a military that did not trust him not to blurt operational details—as he in fact did in his boastful announcement speech the day after the attack.[21]

2. The killing of bin Laden capped a decade-long effort to destroy al-Qaeda as a striking force. The Baghdadi mission killed an inhumanly brutal terrorist, an individual if possible even more psychopathically cruel than bin Laden. But it occurred as Trump was wrecking US security architecture in the region. When the smoke lifted over Baghdadi's compound, it was Russia, Turkey, and Iran that had achieved their strategic objectives in Syria. Trump, by contrast, had betrayed the Syrian Kurds who had provided the information for the raid and enabled its success. The bin Laden raid proved the United States could strike anywhere. The Baghdadi raid was followed by Trump's attempted destruction of America's striking power.

3. Obama did not seek personal credit for the raid. His brief and dignified statement afterward spoke only of "the United States" and praised the special operators who conducted the very dangerous mission. Trump not only preened, boasted, and bragged for an excruciating three-quarters of an hour—but he pressed military commanders to take time from their work to sit in full uniform for a staged photo with him at the center, to the visible discomfort of the military participants.

4. Trump's account of what happened was crammed with bizarre lies, including his claim to have heard Baghdadi "whimpering, screaming, and crying." No other person viewing the raid heard any such sounds. It was not possible to hear them, because US forces remained at a bomb-range distance from Baghdadi and his hostages in the moments

before he killed himself. "I don't have those details," said Secretary of Defense Mark Esper. "I'm not able to confirm anything else about his last seconds. I'm just not able to confirm that one way or another," said Frank McKenzie, head of Central Command.[22] Trump's voracious ego pushed him to falsify the story—which predictably caused Trump's own falsifications to *become* the story.

Trump's national security team persistently treated *him* as a national security threat, or at least, a national security problem. They marginalized him, ignored him, or willfully misinterpreted his instructions. For example:

In March 2018, Russian agents attempted a dual assassination on British soil of a defected ex-agent and his daughter. The Russians used a toxin developed in the former Soviet Union. They smuggled the toxin into the United Kingdom, a recklessly dangerous act that violated treaties and international law. The intended targets survived, but a British woman with no connection to the targets was accidentally fatally poisoned. Trump at first refused to blame Russia for the murder. When that position became untenable, Trump insisted on only the most limited possible sanctions. When European allies decided they would expel Russian officials from their countries, Trump grudgingly agreed. "We'll match their numbers," the *Washington Post* reported Trump saying. "We're not taking the lead. We're matching." US officials chose to interpret this to mean that the United States would match the total number of EU expulsions, about sixty. When Trump learned that the individual EU member states had expelled fewer—about four each from France and Germany—he erupted in rage.

The president . . . was furious that his administration was being portrayed in the media as taking by far the toughest stance on Russia.

His briefers tried to reassure him that the sum total of European expulsions was roughly the same as the U.S. number.

"I don't care about the total!" the administration official recalled Trump screaming. The official, like others, spoke on the condition of anonymity to discuss internal deliberations.

Growing angrier, Trump insisted that his aides had misled him about the magnitude of the expulsions. "There were curse words," the official said, "a lot of curse words."[23]

As Trump became more familiar with the job, he became wilier about eluding his officials to advance his personal agenda. Defenders of Trump demand, *And what exactly is so wrong with this? Trump was the president; was he not entitled to conduct foreign policy as he wished? Who elected those officials who circumvented him, by what right did they thwart him again and again and again?*

The short answer was given at the Constitutional Convention of 1787 by Gouverneur Morris, who would later head the drafting committee for the final text. Morris explained that he had at first opposed an impeachment provision. His generation of Americans well remembered how impeachment powers had been abused by British Parliaments to punish officials without fair trials. Morris reminded the convention that Charles II, king of England from 1660 to 1685, had been bribed by Louis XIV, king of France. The president of the United States might be even more susceptible to such temptations:

He may be bribed by a greater interest to betray his trust; and no one would say that we ought to expose ourselves to the danger of seeing the first Magistrate in foreign pay without being able to guard agst [sic] it by displacing him.

The people who wrote Article II of the Constitution did not imagine that it conferred on the president the right to auction US foreign policy to the highest bidder, in the manner of Charles II. The president's constitutional powers are a "trust," to be discharged in the public interest, not his own. How to *tell* when a president is acting selfishly, rather than for the public purpose? One sure sign is when the president tries to bypass the executive branch that exists to serve him.

During World War II and the Cold War, the FBI often carried out surveillance missions against suspected spies and foreign agents. The FBI's powers were constrained by law after Watergate. Until the mid-1970s, however, the agency surveilled more or less anybody it regarded as a counterintelligence risk—most notoriously, Martin Luther King. Yet even the FBI obeyed some limits. One of those limits: it stayed out of party politics. So when Richard Nixon decided he wanted to bug the headquarters of the Democratic National Committee, he had to constitute his own private intelligence organization, the so-called Plumbers. When Nixon's burglars were arrested, the president tried to avert an FBI investigation of the crime by mobilizing the CIA to claim the burglary as a foreign-intelligence matter. This was the plan recorded by the "smoking gun" tape that forced Nixon's resignation in August 1974.

Nixon might have imagined that "when the president does it, that means that it is not illegal," as he said to David Frost in their famous 1977 interview. But if Watergate stands for anything, it is the principle that presidential action—even presidential action supposedly in the name of national security—*can* be illegal. Trump knew this, which is why he tried to build his own private government to circumvent the regular government. Presidential actions can be illegal even if they fail, as Nixon's blame-the-CIA scheme failed and as Trump's extort-Ukraine scheme failed.

Presidential actions can be illegal because presidents, too, are bound by law. One of the president's most absolute powers under Article II is his or her power to pardon. Presidents can pardon anyone for any federal offense. As Donald Trump has demonstrated, they can pardon for almost any reason: to reward someone who wrote flattering articles about them, to win racist votes in Arizona, to impress a Kardashian. But even this almost absolute power has limits. If a president outright sold pardons for bribes, he or she would be impeached. A president's power over foreign policy is more limited than his or her pardon power. When Congress votes aid to a partner like Ukraine, the president must release it—that's not optional. If the president tries to leverage that aid for his own purposes, he violates numerous federal statutes that forbid using official powers to extract personal benefits. The US government does not neatly silo presidential power from congressional or judicial power. Each power interacts with the others. Even unsuccessful wrongs can be punished. Like Trump's Ukraine extortion scheme, Nixon's "smoking-gun tape" discussed an idea that was not ultimately put into effect.

What Trump meant by "the deep state" was nothing other than the rule of law. Trump wanted a government that he could deploy at his whim, for his own personal purposes. He wanted an attorney general who would serve him as the gangsterish Roy Cohn had served him in his early business career. He recruited as his immediate entourage people who thought in that same autocratic way. But the executive branch was just too big—and Trump's attention span too brief—for him to change all of it in time.

A comic example of the interplay:

At the annual Al Smith fundraising dinner in New York in October 2019, former secretary of defense Jim Mattis joked about his experience in the Trump administration.

> I'm not just an overrated general. I am the greatest, the world's most overrated . . . I would just tell you too that I'm honored to be considered that by Donald Trump because he also called Meryl Streep an overrated actress. So I guess I'm the Meryl Streep of generals . . . And frankly that sounds pretty good to me. And you do have to admit that between me and Meryl, at least we've had some victories . . . I earned my spurs on the battlefield . . . and Donald Trump earned his spurs in a letter from a doctor . . . I think the only person in the military that Mr. Trump doesn't think is overrated is . . . Colonel Sanders.[24]

One of Trump's most assertive defenders, Sebastian Gorka, denounced Mattis on his radio program.

> What on Earth do you mean, Mattis? Secretary General Mattis? At least we've had some victories? What are you referring to? Are you referring to the man who was elected by 63 million Americans, who is your commander in chief to this very day? . . . Act like a bloody marine, why don't you, instead of taking the piss out of your commander in chief? . . . Not only is it un-American, it's not the values of the Corps.[25]

Marines swear loyalty to the Constitution, not a commander in chief. Yet neither Trump nor avid supporters like Gorka could wrap their minds around the concept of impersonal authority, of institutions and laws binding upon everyone, including the president.

They think, if the president is boss, the president is entitled to do what he pleases. The nation's laws are not instructions directing him but nuisances impeding him. Trump has communicated that anticonstitutional mode of thinking to two-fifths of the nation.

Yet even as Trump defied the "deep state" of the rule of law, his administration empowered the "deep state" of economic monopoly and privileged favor-seeking. In almost every way that can be measured, the US economy has become more concentrated in the twenty-first century.[26] Growth has slowed, wages have stagnated, but profits have soared as powerful interests extract higher returns for themselves. Health care offers the worst example, higher education a nasty runner-up, but the effects are felt throughout the economy. In the 1990s, Americans paid less than Europeans for Internet connections and mobile telephone services; in the 2010s, Americans paid substantially more.

Political power converts into economic benefit. That problem has only worsened in the Trump years, with the Trump tax cut and the Trump tariffs the leading culprits. In December 2019, the Federal

Reserve released the first close study of the impact of Trump's economic policies on consumer welfare. The language of the study was delicate, but the conclusions were damning. "We find that tariff increases enacted in 2018 are associated with relative reductions in manufacturing employment and relative increases in producer prices." And while some might argue that hurting consumers is an acceptable price to pay to revive US manufacturing, "our results suggest that the tariffs have not boosted manufacturing employment or output, even as they increased producer prices."[27]

The Trump tax cuts were justified in great part as a means to entice US corporations to book their profits where the US government could tax them. The *New York Times* reported in December 2019 that this purpose had been stealthily defeated by deft lobbying of the Trump Treasury department.

> Through a series of obscure regulations, the Treasury carved out exceptions to the law that mean many leading American and foreign companies will owe little or nothing in new taxes on offshore profits, according to a review of the Treasury's rules, government lobbying records, and interviews with federal policymakers and tax experts. Companies were effectively let off the hook for tens if not hundreds of billions of taxes that they would have been required to pay.[28]

The defeat of the attempt to tax offshore profits partially explains why the Trump tax cut expanded the federal budget deficit so much more than projected back in 2017. As recently as January 2019, the Trump Office of Management and Budget promised that the Trump tax cut would not push the budget deficit beyond $1 trillion until fiscal year 2022. By August 2019, OMB had to concede that the deficit would exceed $1 trillion in the fiscal year that would begin October 1, 2019.

Deficits are taxes postponed. They will eventually be repaid one way or another. Repaid how? And by whom? The interoperation of an increasingly dysfunctional democracy with an increasingly plutocratic economy implies that taxes avoided in the present by those best able to pay will be repaid in the future by the least able.

It's a grim formula and one that should badly cost this administration at the polls. But every election asks the inescapable question: Compared to what?

CHAPTER SEVEN

How to Lose to Trump

Heading into the election of 1980, Republicans faced a dangerous dilemma. Ronald Reagan championed a bold platform of conservative ideology. Reagan's principal party rival, George H. W. Bush, offered a whispered message of caution: remember how the extremist Barry Goldwater led this party to disaster. Memory of the debacle of 1964 had guided Republicans for a political generation. Republicans had rejected Reagan for the presidency in 1968 in favor of the more ideologically moderate Richard Nixon. They rejected Reagan again in 1976 in favor of renominating the incumbent president, Gerald Ford. Bush hoped to shut out Reagan a third time by touching the familiar pain point.

This time, though, the Republican rank and file had other ideas. They sensed that President Carter was desperately vulnerable. Seven million Democrats would vote against Carter in party primaries in 1980. Republicans glimpsed the opportunity of a lifetime. They could afford the exciting choice. They nominated Reagan.

Nominating Reagan represented a hazardous gamble, at least according to the hitherto understood rules of American politics. This time, the gamble paid off. Liberal Democrats split from Carter to vote for the independent candidacy of John Anderson. Reagan won 489 electoral votes with only 50.7 percent of the popular vote—and proceeded to launch the most ambitious redirection of the US government since 1932.

Fast forward to 2020. Many Democrats glimpse an opportunity in Trump akin to that offered by Carter in 1980. Isn't this their chance to seize the moment, to stake everything on the exciting choice, not the safe choice?

Big liberal moments do not arrive that often in America. Progressives endured a parched half century from 1965 to 2009. After the loss of the House to Tea Party Republicans in 2010, who knew how long progressives must wait for their next opportunity? Now, thanks to the unpopularity of Donald Trump, liberal dreams again beckon on the horizon: Medicare for All, student loan forgiveness, taxes on wealth, amnesty for the undocumented, confiscation of AR-15 assault rifles. The Democratic Party has veered sharply to the left over the past fifteen years. Try to imagine any national Democrat repeating on a Democratic platform the words below written by a would-be nominee for president back in 2006:

> When I see Mexican flags waved at proimmigration demonstrations, I sometimes feel a flush of patriotic resentment. When I'm forced to use a translator to communicate with the guy fixing my car, I feel a certain frustration.[1]

Those un-Woke words were published by then-senator Barack Obama, in the vanished world of 2006.

"As president, I will not support driver's licenses for undocumented people . . ." That pledge was spoken by then-senator Hillary Clinton in November 2007.[2]

Fast forward a dozen years.

At the second of the two Democratic debates in Miami in June 2019, co-moderator Savannah Guthrie challenged the candidates on stage: "This is a show of hands question and hold them up so people can see. Raise your hand if your government plan would provide [health-care] coverage for undocumented immigrants."

Michael Bennet, Joe Biden, Pete Buttigieg, Kirsten Gillibrand, Kamala Harris, John Hickenlooper, Bernie Sanders, Eric Swalwell, Marianne Williamson, and Andrew Yang all signaled "yes."[3]

In twelve years, the Democrats—including supposedly the most moderate of them, Vice President Joe Biden—had shifted from "no to driver's licenses" for illegal aliens to "yes to government health coverage" for illegal aliens. Could they not anticipate the obvious Trump counterattack? It arrived within minutes via Twitter:

> All Democrats just raised their hands for giving millions of illegal aliens unlimited healthcare. How about taking care of American Citizens first!?[4]

An NPR/Marist poll at the end of July 2019 found that not only did 93 percent of Republicans oppose government health care for illegal immigrants, but so did 40 percent of Democrats. Altogether, two-thirds of Americans rejected the idea endorsed by all the Democratic presidential candidates.[5]

Democrats must know that math. They cannot act on it. The years since 2014 have been aptly nicknamed the "Great Awakening." Former liberals and progressives have veered sharply leftward, especially on issues of race, gender, and immigration. White liberals express more liberal views on immigration than Hispanic Americans. White liberals are readier to attribute negative outcomes to racism than are black Americans. They are committed to views on gender and gender identity radically rejected by other Americans.

Zach Goldberg at Georgia State University has tried to quantify the speed and intensity of this swing.

> The first half of this decade [the 2010s] appears to have been a watershed for white liberal racial consciousness. The picture that emerges from the various points of data is one in which white liberals and social media created a kind of outrage feedback loop. White liberals started spending ever increasing shares

of their time in a medium—social media and internet news sites—at the same moment that, for multiple reasons, that medium produced a higher volume of race-related moral outrage stories relative to other forms of journalism. Exposure to the stories on those sites, in turn, generated moral outrage among white liberal readers who then fed that emotional response back into the sites, which catered to their appetites as consumers, thus powering the feedback loop.[6]

This feedback loop drives Democratic politicians to unsustainable positions. Senator Elizabeth Warren tweeted on August 29, 2019: "As president, I'll reverse the Trump administration's cruel 'Remain in Mexico' policy and ensure that asylum seekers will be welcomed at ports of entry."[7] In the first half of 2019, the United States received one hundred thousand asylum seekers *per month*. More than half of those admitted as asylum seekers never bother to file a formal application. Most asylum petitions that are filed are rejected—but only after a process that spans years. Rejected asylum seekers then drop out of the system and remain as illegal immigrants. Vanishingly few rejected asylum seekers ever leave the United States. As I write, the largest source of African asylum seeking is the Democratic Republic of the Congo. To reach the United States, Congolese will typically exit their own country, transit neighboring Angola, fly from Angola to Ecuador, and then travel by bus from Ecuador through five more countries—Colombia, Panama, Nicaragua, Honduras, and Guatemala—to enter Mexico and thence reach the US border. That's a long way to travel if you are supposedly fleeing for your life. In fact, the asylum system is obviously being gamed. The intensely policy-minded Warren had to appreciate the recklessness of what she was saying. Her approach would do at the US border what Germany inadvertently did in August 2015: invite a surge of entry from all over the world, overwhelming the US immigration system and radicalizing US politics. Yet she could not say no.

The great Democratic challenge entering 2020 is that the tone and style of much of progressive politics offends large numbers of Americans who have had their fill of President Trump.

No question, Trump is in big trouble, especially with women.

Trump's numbers among women, bad at the start, have shriveled into the miserable. Through the first half of 2019, polls consistently showed that more than 60 percent of American women disapproved of Trump's handling of the office.[8] More than 70 percent of women believed Trump respects women less than men.[9]

Trump polled worse among nonwhite women than among white women, but north of 55 percent of white women disapproved of him even before the economic news began to turn bad in the summer of 2019. White women with college degrees disapproved of him by a margin of around 58 percent, again across multiple polls. Women voted as they felt. In 2018, women voted for Democratic candidates for Congress over Republican by a margin of nineteen points, according to CNN exit polls.[10]

Women do not like the ideas of Trump's party much better than they like its leader. A 58 percent majority of women prefer a more activist government that provides more services rather than a less-expensive government that provides fewer.[11] Seventy-two percent of women want assault weapons banned.[12] Only 30 percent of American women believed Trump Supreme Court nominee Brett Kavanaugh told the truth at his confirmation hearing; 45 percent believed his accuser, Christine Blasey Ford.[13]

The Trump campaign frets about these numbers, but there is not much they can to do to overcome them. The trouble starts with the candidate. In 1992, businessman Donald Trump told *New York* magazine about women: "You have to treat 'em like shit."[14] He has lived that philosophy all his adult life: barging into the dressing rooms of teen pageant contestants to leer at them, groping and grabbing at least two dozen women, deploying the *National Enquirer* to defame women who rebuffed or offended him, disparaging the appearances of women who accused him of rape or assault. There's no rebound for Trump from this history. But American politics is always a binary choice, and while Trump cannot recover, his opponents can sink themselves.

A University of Virginia poll in the summer of 2018 found that 62 percent of Americans of all races strongly or somewhat agreed that "political correctness threatens our liberty as Americans to speak our minds."[15] Obviously, different people understand different things by the vague term *political correctness*. But at a minimum, the term reveals unease with the cultural norms that dominate Democratic politics. And while progressives may scoff that the term merely ratifies the concerns of conservative white men, the dislike of political correctness reaches much further. Latinos—and especially Latino men—are actually more likely than whites to complain of political correctness as a leading problem facing the country.[16] In a poll for the Marist Institute, 54 percent of white women without a college degree agreed "political correctness has gone too far."[17]

Nor is it a trivial matter that whites and men do so strongly feel themselves beleaguered by cultural change. In January 2019, South Carolina's Winthrop poll conducted a fascinating experiment. Winthrop polled people of all races across eleven Southern states. One question was phrased in two slightly different ways. Half of the people surveyed were asked whether they agreed that "whites have privileges that non-whites do not have." The other half were asked whether they agreed that "non-whites face barriers that whites do not face." Logically, of course the two questions mean exactly the same thing. But they yielded very different answers. When asked whether they enjoyed special "privilege," only 50 percent of whites agreed. Among the most conservative whites, only 36 percent agreed. But when asked whether nonwhites faced extra "barriers," 70 percent of all whites *and a majority even of the most conservative whites* agreed.[18]

People do not like being negatively judged. When they feel negatively judged, they hunker down. On the other hand, people do have a sense of fairness. When that is appealed to, they respond more generously.

The parlor games that permit people in public forums to speak of whites and men in terms they would never use to speak of other groups exact an important real-world price from American society. They provoke a truculent reaction that otherwise would have lain quiet.

Progressive politicians may feel that provoking this reaction is worthwhile if it can mobilize a progressive populist surge. This vision of politics bumps into some inhospitable realities. Of those Americans who did not vote in 2016, the majority—52 percent— were white. Among those who did not vote despite being registered (and those are the nonvoters most likely to show up in 2020) the white majority was even bigger. Nate Cohn of the *New York Times* estimates that in the industrial Midwest, the population that was registered to vote in 2016 but that did not cast a ballot was 68 percent noncollege white.[19] In other words, the most accessible pool of nonvoters in the most decisive region of the country are precisely the group *least* likely to respond to "Woke" messaging on immigration, race, and gender.

Yet the Woke messaging keeps flying. Speaking in New York's Washington Square on September 18, 2019, Senator Warren let fire this zinger. "We're not here today because of famous arches or famous men. In fact, we're not here because of men at all."[20] But if Warren ever arrives in the White House, it will be because of men—not all of them, obviously, but sufficient numbers of them. And the lesson of the Trump presidency is that insulting voters loses their votes.

Those who aspire to conjure up a counter-Trump movement of militant progressive forces imagine that American demographics have tilted to the point that a politics of (in their view) righteous grievance can outvote the (in their view) wrongful grievance that Trump has summoned up. They are kidding themselves about their math, but even if they were correct, what kind of answer would that be?

Trump is president not only because many of your fellow citizens are racists, or sexists, or bigots of some other description, although surely some are. Trump is president also because many of your fellow citizens feel that accusations of bigotry are deployed casually and carelessly, even opportunistically. Anti-racism can easily devolve from a call to equal justice for all into a demand for power and privilege. *We speak, you listen. We demand, you comply. We win, you lose.*

Trump campaigned in 2016 as a "different kind of Republican." He was not Paul Ryan, scheming to deprive you of your Medicare and Social Security. He was not George W. Bush or Dick Cheney, plunging into far-off wars. He was not Mitt Romney, offering a big tax cut to rich people like himself. Trump promised to *raise* taxes on rich people and to use the money to build roads and bridges. He denounced foreign wars and promised a foreign policy of nonintervention. He excoriated the trade deals you blamed for taking away your jobs. Maybe above all . . . he talked like you and like people you knew.

Now, Trump's greatest vulnerability heading into 2020 is that on economic issues, he has accumulated a record as a very conventional Republican. Trump did cut taxes for the rich, after saying he would raise them. He did take away the health coverage of millions of people—and tried and failed to take away the coverage of millions more. The roads and bridges never got built. NAFTA's still there in all but name, but a new washing machine costs almost $100 more at Walmart because of Trump's tariffs on imports from China, South Korea, and other trading partners.[21] Other prices are rising, too, especially food.[22]

Precisely because Trump got maneuvered away from a relatively popular set of messages in 2016 onto a relatively unpopular set of policies in 2020, he will face little choice but to amplify the rancor of his identity politics before the presidential election. Trump will run a campaign in 2020 compared to which even his 2016 campaign will look mild and restrained. "Send her back!" will replace "Lock her up!" Air Force One will carry rage, resentment, and racism across the land. Facebook ads will grope for every dark and fearful impulse; micro-targeting will try to activate every primordial prejudice.

Trump's political malpractice has opened the door to a new era of activist, reformist government. Yet an open door is only an invitation. That invitation can still be refused if it is phrased the wrong way—or if it leads in the wrong direction. Americans are ready for reform, but they are left alienated and frightened by the Great Awokening that has seized activist progressives. Donald Trump cannot win reelection in 2020 by his own efforts. But the election can be thrown away by people who will not meet voters where they are.

Trump and his supporters appreciate the potentially destructive power of the ultra-progressive Left better than anyone. When Steve Bannon praises Bernie Sanders and when *Fox & Friends* promotes Tulsi Gabbard, they are not expressing sincere admiration. They are grasping the life vest that can save them from the shipwreck. One credible poll has found that 12 percent of those who supported Sanders against Clinton in 2016 switched to Trump in the general election.[23] If the ultra-progressives are thwarted from foisting an unelectable candidate upon the Democratic Party from the inside, perhaps they can be coaxed and manipulated to boost a Trump-rescuing third-party candidacy from the outside. It's become evident over the Trump years that there exists a militant progressive constituency who regard Trump as a much lesser evil than Hillary Clinton or Joe Biden. This constituency may be small, but in 2016 it proved sufficient to tip a close election to Trump. Trump is hoping the trick can be repeated.

You are either helping Trump—or stopping Trump.

Part II

A NEW AGE OF REFORM

CHAPTER EIGHT

Unrigging the System

Sometimes in the Trump years, it seemed like the country was regressing into a dark past. Yet away from the antics in Washington, the American conscience remained alive—and active. In October 2017, the actress Alyssa Milano tweeted: "If you've been sexually harassed or assaulted write 'me too' as a reply to this tweet."[1] Milano may not have originated the phrase—people dispute that—but no question she sent it viral. Over the next two years, the #MeToo movement would upend the careers of prominent men in business and media: Louis C.K., Placido Domingo, Mark Halperin, Garrison Keillor, John Lasseter, Matt Lauer, Paul Marciano, Les Moonves, Charlie Rose, Eric Schneiderman, and Harvey Weinstein, the man at the center of it all.

In 2018, Congress reversed a twenty-two-year-ban and allowed federal funding for gun-safety research, one of a string of victories for the gun-safety movement in the Trump years, including a November 2018 ballot initiative in Washington State that raised minimum age of purchase and imposed new storage requirements and "red flag" laws in Delaware, Florida, Hawaii, Illinois, Maryland, Massachusetts, and Rhode Island.

The National Lynching Memorial opened in Montgomery, Alabama, in April 2017. In September 2019, the state of Maryland erected a marker to the forty black men known to have been lynched in that state between 1854 and 1933. That same month, Harris County, Texas, announced a program to memorialize the four men known to have been lynched in that jurisdiction.

Six states passed new restrictions on plastic waste in 2019: Connecticut, Delaware, Maine, New York, Oregon, and Vermont, following the earlier lead of California, Hawaii, and the District of Columbia. Dozens of local governments adopted plastic-restricting ordinances too. The number of electric cars on the road in the United States more than doubled between 2016 and 2018. Coal's share of the market for US electricity generation was cut in half over the decade after 2008, from about one-half to about one-quarter—and is still falling. Smaller coal plants have been closing for a decade. Now mega-plants are closing too. Arizona's Navajo Generating Station emitted as much greenhouse gas per year as half a million passenger cars. It closed in 2019, as did Pennsylvania's Bruce Mansfield plant.

Tolerance is rising in all kinds of measurable ways. In the half decade from 2014 to 2019, support for same-sex marriage would rise from 52 percent to 62 percent.[2] Trump's misogyny, bigotry, corruption, and general cruelty have powered a revulsion against misogyny, bigotry, corruption, and cruelty. Just as Watergate was followed by a surge of reforms in federal and state governments in 1974–1978, so the Trump period seems likely to be followed by a new era of political reform.

But reform of what kind? The next Democratic president and the next Democratic congressional majority will owe their power to millions of conservative-leaning people who want a more ethical and effective government after the squalor of the Trump years. Many Democrats themselves recognize the urgency of moderation. A *New York Times* poll of Iowa Democrats in October 2019 found that they preferred a "more moderate" to a "more liberal" candidate by ten points. They preferred "finding common ground" to "fighting for bold progressive change" by twelve points. They preferred "improving the existing healthcare system" to "Medicare for All" by fourteen points.[3]

Democracy is tested by its ability to deliver security, prosperity, and justice. Relatively modest reforms to the US system could improve all those outcomes. This is not to negate the value of bigger ideas: changes to the voting system, changes to the campaign-finance system. But those things are hard to do. They raise constitutional issues. Even if the courts approve them, they are beset by unintended consequences. So much of the present dysfunction of the federal campaign finance system can be traced to the unexpected decision of the US Supreme Court back in 1974 that *donation* limits were constitutional but *spending* limits were not constitutional. Without limits on spending, every player in the system had powerful incentives to work around the donation limits, making mockeries of them too. Further rounds of reforms have failed, and often backfired.

The first laws requiring disclosure of federal campaign donations were adopted in 1910 and 1911, then toughened in 1925. But until 1971, it was legal for campaigns to accept cash. Not until 1972—and especially after 1974—does election finance step into the sunlight. Now the fog is rolling in. Very probably the majority of all the money spent to determine the elections of 2020 will be spent by nobody-knows-who on not-easy-to-say-what. It is not easy to know how to restore transparency without making a dozen other problems worse.

Any big idea will require a big consensus in favor of reform, and such consensus is unlikely. More challenging still, any big idea will require permission from a more-conservative-than-ever federal judiciary—and such permission is even more unlikely. Yet there are very feasible *small* reforms to protect American democracy from any repeat of the authoritarian minority rule and flagrant criminality of the Trump administration.

PUBLISH TAX RETURNS

Post-Trump, it is no longer acceptable that presidents decide for themselves whether or not to release their tax returns. If tax publication had been compulsory, Trump would never have run for president in the first place. He would never have dared; he had too much to hide.

The question is: Where to draw the line? Even politicians have rights to privacy—and so do their spouses.

The tightest rule is that several years of returns—three?—be published on the date that a person accepts a major-party nomination for president; and that annual publication by a president be compulsory. Financial disclosure rules also need to be revised for modern times. The present rules were drafted in a less plutocratic era, to cast light on the finances of affluent professionals and successful business executives. They are utterly defeated by the network of trusts and closely held corporations in which the modern rich stash their assets—and, maybe even more important when those rich enter politics, their debts.

At the same time—and this disclosure may prove even more important in the long run to the integrity of the US economy—America's experience with the Trump Organization demonstrates why more needs to be done to ensure that the government always knows who owns which assets, not only financial assets but real estate assets too.

The federal government has begun imposing "know your customer" regulations on Realtors in cities with high rates of secret real property ownership, especially New York and Miami. Candidates for president and presidents should disclose not only the assets they own but also those they control through corporations or benefit from through trusts.

NUKE THE FILIBUSTER

If Democrats win the Senate in 2020, they should promptly abolish the legislative filibuster: the ability of a minority of as few as forty-one senators to delay indefinitely the enactment of legislation. Don't study or debate it. Just do it. There will be a lot of yelling, but in the immediate shock of a decisive election, the measure can be shoved through fast. Former Democratic majority leader Harry Reid eliminated the filibuster of judicial nominations in 2013. Republicans benefited from that rule in the Trump era, leading some conservatives to taunt Democrats that they should blame Reid for the rightward turn of the judiciary. But if a party holds the presidency and fifty-plus seats in the Senate, why should it not be able to confirm judges? If the nominations are extreme—if the Senate is unrepresentative—that party will soon enough bring political trouble upon itself, as the Trump-McConnell Republicans have done. But it would be reckless to learn from the 2013 precedent that a minority of a minority should be able to veto legislation of all kinds forever.

Republicans enjoy a built-in advantage in the Senate. Since they will more often be in the Senate majority, the abolition of the filibuster will advantage them in important ways. But without that abolition, the metropolitan majority of the US population will never be able to govern itself at all—because while Democrats may sometimes win more than fifty Senate seats, they will almost never be able to win more than the sixty necessary to overcome a filibuster.

The filibuster is not in the Constitution. It's not in the law. It's just a Senate rule, one that has been reshaped and reformed often before—and one that has almost invariably been used to protect privileged interests that are already abundantly protected in other ways too. The arguments in its favor are laughably self-serving. In an August 2019 op-ed in defense of the legislative filibuster, Senate Majority Leader Mitch McConnell invoked the authority of Thomas Jefferson: "great innovations should not be forced on slender majorities."[4] But as is, even *great* majorities are prevented from pursuing even *small* innovations. As of 2018, the fifty states and the District of Columbia were home together to 327 million people. A law passed by senators representing 290.4 million of them can effectively be vetoed by senators representing 36.6 million of them, or 11 percent. This coalition of the ultra-smallest is admittedly unlikely. It includes deep-Blue Hawaii and Vermont as well as ultra-Red Mississippi and Wyoming. But a coalition of the twenty-one smallest states that elected at least one Republican senator sometime between 2010 and 2018 still numbers only 53.5 million, or 16.1 percent.

The filibuster is advertised as a protection for the interest of smaller states. It does not serve that purpose very well. The most damaging thing done to small states in the past five years was President Trump's decision to sacrifice farm exports to pursue his trade war. The filibuster did not protect farmers from that misguided mistake.

Indeed, most often, the real effect of the filibuster is to enable big donors in big cities to buy influence with veto-wielding senators in tiny states for much less than the cost of persuading their own senators. Once the filibuster is gone, not only will nobody except the crassest interest groups miss it. Nobody except the crassest interest groups will ever understand how or why it could have existed in the first place.

STATEHOOD FOR THE DISTRICT OF COLUMBIA

Then, bring the Senate a little closer into line with the American population by conferring statehood upon the residential areas of the District of Columbia. Many people wrongly imagine that such a change would require a super-majority or even a constitutional amendment. But once the filibuster is ended, Congress could admit "New Columbia" to statehood by majority vote of two houses, plus a presidential signature.

The new state would have a population greater than Wyoming or Vermont. At its present rate of growth, New Columbia will overtake Alaska and North Dakota before 2030. New Columbia would be less dependent on federal assistance than twenty-one other states, including not only poor states like Mississippi and Louisiana but relatively prosperous ones like Texas and Georgia.[5]

DC statehood would also deprive conservative congressional Republicans of their favorite test kitchen for serving unpalatable culture war dishes to an unwilling population. The new state could write its *own* rules on guns, abortion, and other emotive subjects rather than have those rules written for it by out-of-touch, out-of-district legislators who answer to other voters rather than its own.

Under present demographic conditions, DC statehood would promptly add two Democratic senators, with a high likelihood that one or both would be African American. This would help to redress both the partisan and racial unrepresentativeness of the Senate.

There would be some tough complexities to work out, especially since many valuable blocks of the city would have to be carved out for a new shrunken federal zone under the Congress, the monuments, the White House, and the blocks in between. The money discussions could be rancorous.

But in the end, there would be a Senate that looked a little more like the actual country than it does today.

ADOPT A MODERN VOTING RIGHTS ACT

The United States needs a new Voting Rights Act to fill the void left by the Supreme Court in 2013. The Voting Rights Act of 1965 committed the federal government to upholding the voting rights of racial minorities. Those rights were originally guaranteed by the Fifteenth Amendment of 1870. The Southern states quickly made a nullity of the amendment. By the 1890s, black Americans had been disenfranchised across the former Confederacy. The 1965 Act restored those long-lost rights by requiring suspect states and municipalities to obtain federal approval for changes to their voting rules.

The court's 2013 voting-rights decision made one valid point: The Voting Rights Act of 1965 was premised on the supposition that voting rights abuses were uniquely likely to recur in the future in areas where they had occurred in the past.

The section struck down in 2013 applied only to Alabama, Alaska, Georgia, Louisiana, Mississippi, South Carolina, and Virginia, as well as to parts of North Carolina, Arizona, Idaho, and Hawaii. That did seem out of date. Hawaii has evolved into a very good actor on voting rights. Meanwhile, states that were not subject to federal scrutiny in 1965 have regressed into very bad actors, Wisconsin maybe the worst of them all.

A new federal voting rights law is needed, but one that addresses the abuses of the present, not the memories of the past. It could test the sincerity of Republican concerns about voter ID by providing a federal tamper-proof form of identification to all citizens at no cost to them. Republicans would likely object, which would at least put that issue to bed once and for all. A new Voting Rights Act would need to look at new issues: not only the location of voting installations but equal access to reliable voting technology and equal waiting periods in richer and poorer neighborhoods. A two-hour queue deters voters as surely as the old methods of threat and intimidation. A new Voting Rights Act would be founded on the real-world observation that under present circumstances, partisan gerrymandering functions indistinguishably from racial gerrymandering.

DETER GERRYMANDERING

Most ideas to counter gerrymandering founder on one of two fearful difficulties: the difficulty of persuading the Supreme Court to reverse a very recent precedent, or the difficulty of gaining two-party buy-in for a reform that will at any given moment benefit one party more than the other—or both.

The new Census in 2020 offers a new opportunity for a unilateral gerrymander fix.

The Democratic National Committee could hire a commission of experts—political scientists, retired judges, demographers—to draw best-practice maps for every state and federal district in the country. The goal would be to draw maps that maximize the chance that seat balances, state and federal, will align with votes cast—while also respecting other imperatives: town boundaries, racial balance, and so on.

Then issue an invitation to Republican states: if you guys will adopt fair maps that honestly reflect our strength in the states you happen to hold in 2021–2022, then we'll adopt maps that honestly reflect your strength in the states we hold. You can see all the maps right here; you're not buying a pig in a poke. And if you have good faith revisions to offer, hey, we're all ears.

And if not . . . well then after our wins in 2020, we will do unto you as you did unto us after your wins in 2010. Politicians may not wish to *talk* that way. But they can *think* that way.

The longer-term goal should be of course to get redistricting out of the hands of politicians altogether. But until that institutional reform can be agreed upon, deterrence will have to substitute for fairness.

There's something else that badly needs doing, but that will take more time and national thought.

DEPOLITICIZE LAW ENFORCEMENT

President Trump abused the Department of Justice in a way unimagined since Nixon's attorney general John Mitchell perjured himself and obstructed justice to cover up the Watergate scandal. Yet Trump arguably did worse than Nixon. Nixon abused the Department of Justice mostly defensively, to protect himself from law enforcement. Trump deployed the Department of Justice as a weapon against his perceived enemies. The Trump Department of Justice sought to bring a criminal case against former acting FBI director Andrew McCabe on grounds so flimsy that a federal grand jury refused to indict—a highly unusual rebuff. Trump's attorney general Bill Barr flew about the planet pressuring US allies to endorse Trump's false claims that the Democratic National Committee hacked itself, that Russia was innocent, and that Trump was the victim of an Australian-led plot to concoct a Russian hoax. Decisions by Trump's Department of Justice helped run the Mueller investigation into ineffectuality. The Department of Justice litigated to help Trump postpone release of tax returns and business records from committees of Congress entitled to see them.

Did President Trump's request for a dirt-on-Biden "favor" from Ukrainian president Volodymyr Zelensky amount to a violation of federal campaign law? The *Washington Post* reported on September 26, 2019, that the decision "no" was made personally by Trump's assistant attorney general for the Criminal Division, Brian Benczkowski.[6] Benczkowski had been confirmed by the Senate in July 2018 by a vote of only 51–48.[7] Opponents of the nomination objected that Benczkowski lacked significant criminal-justice experience. Even more worrying, he had represented Russia's Alfa Bank—a bank at least allegedly implicated in Trump's Russia dealings—but declined to recuse himself from Trump-Russia matters.[8] Benczkowski's decision of no-violation may have been supportable, but it did not command confidence as either independent or impartial.

The federal criminal justice system seems a legacy of the nineteenth century, when American parties intertwined themselves into the workings of government. It seems merely antiquated that jobs like the director of the National Oceanographic and Atmospheric Administration or the Centers for Medicare and Medicaid Services remain patronage jobs that change when administrations do. Trump has underscored how profoundly hazardous to democracy it can be for criminal justice to be administered in such a way.

It would require a big overhaul of the US government to create a fully nonpolitical criminal justice system at the federal level. The US attorneys are not sufficiently remunerated to secure long-term commitment by highly capable lawyers. People want those jobs precisely because they expect to convert a four-year service into another opportunity in politics or the private sector. That would have to change—and changing it would ramify all through the system of federal job classification and pay. But at least we can identify the problem and the goal: converting the assistant attorney general for the Criminal Division from a political to a career job analogous to other top prosecutors in other advanced democracies.

After the Watergate scandal, Americans embarked on a major cleanup of their federal and state governments. Between 1973 and

1978, Congress passed major new laws on campaign finance and ethics in government. It adopted new rules on lobbying, created the House and Senate Intelligence Committees, and generally tried to clean up—not only Watergate, but many abuses of power that had accreted through two world wars, a Great Depression, and a Cold War.

At the same time, Congress also deregulated important areas of the US economy. In 1972, the federal government regulated the interest rate on checking accounts; routes and fares for passenger aviation, trucking, shipping, and rail freight; the price of oil and natural gas; stockbrokers' commissions—all while enforcing a private monopoly on telephone services. By the end of 1982, all those rules had been swept away.

Most of these reforms have met the test of time, or at least seemed to do so until Donald Trump arrived in Washington to smash up the joint. Yet it is also paradoxically true that, to the extent we can measure, Americans seemed more satisfied with their dirty pre-Watergate government than their cleaner post-Watergate government. "The people are better. The results are worse." Tip O'Neill delivered that verdict on his thirty-five years in Congress shortly after his retirement in 1987. The Congress of 1952 held more alcoholics, more racists, more expense-account chiselers, more philanderers, and more sexual harassers than the Congress of 1987. Yet those same alcoholic, racist, chiseling, philandering, and harassing members built the interstate highways, launched the space program, balanced budgets, and generally got the business of the nation done in a way that dumbfounds us all these decades later.

Trump arose because Americans felt their government was not delivering for them. Those feelings will not vanish when and if Trump does—especially not if the next president takes office amid a Trump-bequeathed recession, Trump-bequeathed trade wars, Trump-bequeathed debt and climate crises, a Trump-bequeathed crack-up of US alliances, and Trump-bequeathed confrontations with China and Iran. To stabilize democracy, democratic government must be seen to succeed on the things that matter most.

CHAPTER NINE

Uniting "Us" and "Them"

On the eve of the 2018 election, Gallup asked Democrats and Republicans to choose their top voting concerns from a pre-set list. Among Democrats, 87 percent selected health care as their top concern, tied equally with "the way women are treated in American society." Among Republicans, 84 percent selected immigration, second only to "the economy" at 85 percent.[1]

That disparity seems another proof of a society that cannot even agree on the questions, let alone agree on the answers.

How can things look so different to different people? Don't Republicans get cancer? Don't Democrats care about national identity? Must everything be subordinated to clashing cultural identities?

As recently as 2006, then-governor Mitt Romney believed he could win the Republican nomination and the US presidency by championing universal health insurance in his then-state of Massachusetts. As recently as 2007, future Democratic presidential candidate Senator Bernie Sanders opposed the Kennedy-McCain immigration reform as too likely to undercut American workers' wages.

The parties hardened their positions on these core issues only after 2008, a sign of the post-recession era's ultra-polarization. The consequence has been the frustration of both parties' highest hopes.

The Democrats did enact the Affordable Care Act in 2010, but they have not been able to protect it from Republican sabotage at the federal and state level. Nor have they themselves clutched the program to their hearts. Through 2019, insurgent Democrats like Bernie Sanders and Elizabeth Warren criticized the Affordable Care Act almost as savagely as any Republican. They promised to replace the ACA with a wholly new approach to health care, a universal federally managed "Medicare for All." A decade after the enactment of Social Security in 1935 and Medicare in 1965, those two programs might as well have been written into the Constitution, they were so secure. A decade after enactment of the ACA, however, it remains contested and uncertain. Post-ACA, only slightly more than one-third of Americans agree that the US health-care system is something to be proud of.[2]

Republicans in their turn have been frustrated on their highest priority issue, immigration. The Trump administration tightened some aspects of immigration enforcement by executive action. Trump has, however, failed to amend immigration law in any enduring way. Nor has Trump built any consensus in favor of restricting immigration. To the contrary, Trump's actions are reviled by Democrats as appalling moral outrages—"Kids in cages"—and will be reversed as soon as Trump leaves power.

Ultra-polarization prevents *either* party from consolidating its most sought-after reforms. Ultra-polarization raises the political stakes, as each party pursues maximal goals without regard to the objections of the other. At the same time, ultra-polarization perversely renders politics ineffectual, by precluding enduring achievements. In the 1990s, the Bush administration enacted the Americans with Disabilities Act and the treaty effectively ending the environmental harm of "acid rain." The Clinton administration raised the Earned Income Tax Credit and created the SCHIP program to insure children under eighteen whose families earned too much to qualify for Medicaid. Those acts all ceased to be controversial as soon as they were legislated. That kind of legitimation-by-existence ceased to happen in the ultra-polarized Obama-Trump years.

If the opposition party cannot and will not be reconciled to political facts, then the incentives of politics shift. When Hillary Clinton spearheaded health-care reform for her husband's administration in 1993–1994, Daniel Patrick Moynihan urged her to moderate her plans, conciliate her opponents. The venerable scholar-senator cautioned the impatient young First Lady: *Important measures pass the Senate 70–30 or they do not pass at all.*

That advice bespoke a vanished political world. In the Obama-Trump years, it seemed the only way to achieve big things was by cramming them down opponents' throats.

Could we reverse the grammar of politics—and gain an exit from polarization? It's natural to absorb cynicism and hopelessness from the experience of the post–Great Recession years. The ultra-polarization of politics is shaped by the structure of society. It seems futile to imagine that the process could work the other way around.

But here's another piece of advice from Daniel Patrick Moynihan to consider.

> The central conservative truth is that it is culture, not politics, that determines the success of a society. The central liberal truth is that politics can change a culture and save it from itself.

Could Moynihan's insight still hold true? Could political action begin the process of social healing? What if things can be done together that could never be done separately? What if doing them together is the only way they can be done at all? What if—by doing things together—we might change our habits of politics? What if we could end our political culture war by delivering each side its most hoped-for victory?

The crushing cost of health care and its inefficient provision degrade American life and impair American prosperity. Over three years—2016, 2017, 2018—life expectancy has dropped in the United States. Overdoses, obesity, accidents, and suicide are held to blame.

Yet think how incredible this grim trend is. US life expectancy rose even as almost half a million young Americans died in World War II. US life expectancy rose during the Great Depression, when Americans had better reason for despair than they do in the 2010s. Not since the influenza epidemic of 1918–1919—the worst global plague since the seventeenth century—have Americans lived less long on average at the end of one year than they did at the end of the year before. By 2040, on present trajectory, life expectancy in the United States will have tumbled to sixty-fourth place among the nations. By that time, *Americans will be the only people in the developed world with an average life span of less than eighty years*.[3] On present trajectory, life expectancies in China will overtake those in the United States by 2027. Already, a baby born in China can look forward to more years of *healthy* life than his or her American counterpart.[4]

It's not for lack of resources. Americans spend vastly more than anybody on health care, and those costs continue to rise. In 2019, the average cost of coverage for a family of four exceeded $20,000.[5]

Health-care costs are crowding out the money for wage increases. They frighten Americans away from quitting their jobs to start new companies. (Americans are the least likely to be self-employed of any people in the developed world, and only about one-third as likely as people in the European Union, according to data compiled by the Organization for Economic Cooperation and Development.[6])

Health costs are also the nonobvious culprit for the crushing burden of student debt. Tuition costs are up at State U. in large part because State U. is receiving less money from the state government. In fact, over the thirty years from 1987 to 2017, state spending per university student *declined* by 25 percent, after inflation. Where did the money go? Short answer: to fund the skyrocketing costs of Medicaid.[7] Over those same years, the real per-capita cost of higher education nearly doubled. Some of that increase was driven by the self-seeking behavior of universities. Within the University of California system, the number of deans and administrators swelled by 60 percent in the decade 2005–2015, while the number of faculty barely rose at all.[8] Without exonerating the academic practice of overspending on self-management, even here health care is a culprit. Maybe the UC system should not employ so many administrators, but that's not the cost that is breaking the system. The cost that is breaking the UC system is its $12 billion unfunded liability for retirement costs of past and present employees. Almost all the surge in that liability beyond the amount funded by employee contributions is traceable to the huge health-care cost inflation of the past four decades.

Yet even after spending these vast sums, when Americans fall ill, they can discover that their coverage is punctured by gaps and limits that plunge them into ruin despite all those years of payments. They face co-pays and deductibles that can exhaust whatever they have saved from wages shriveled by their health insurance. When the Pentagon pays $10,000 for an airplane toilet seat, at least it gets a seat that fits the toilet of an airplane. When Americans pay $500, $600, or $700 a month for health insurance for their families, they often find they have bought nothing at all.

Americans see doctors and go to the hospital *less* often than people in other developed nations. But when they do see doctors or go to the hospital, the services they consume cost vastly more. The typical American heart bypass operation costs more than six times as much as the same operation costs in the Netherlands, just for one example.

Every dollar of spending in the health-care system is somebody's dollar of income. American hospital corporations, American pharmaceutical companies, American diagnostic service firms are the best in the world at collecting income. That's not to blame them. Everybody wants more for himself or herself; that is human nature. But in other countries, equally powerful economic actors can negotiate effectively on behalf of patients and taxpayers.

The US government spends more per American to cover the people enrolled in Medicare, Medicaid, and other government health programs than the Canadian government spends per Canadian to cover everybody. The best of American health care is certainly the best in the world. But it's not only the best that costs more. Everything costs more. The anxiety that haunts so many Americans at any whisper of illness is also a cost to be accounted. The health care that people do not get when they need it is a cost too.

Libertarian-minded people once hoped that private insurance companies could impose discipline on health-care providers. Instead, the insurance companies found it easier to squeeze patients, who were weak and disorganized, than providers, who were strong and well-organized. The Affordable Care Act disallowed some of the insurance companies' worst practices—but without substituting any new player to do the job the insurance companies failed to do. The job will have to be done by government, and by the federal government so that providers do not play one state off against another.

Americans like to tell themselves a story about their health-care system delivering better results than the socialist systems of other developed countries. But American health care is a creation of government, too—a government that has allowed powerful interests to seize pricing power allowed them by no other democracy in the world. That's what must change.

Slogans like "Medicare for All" distract voters and officials from the real problem: not who *finances* health-care costs, but who *negotiates* those costs. The US government is the biggest health-care purchaser on earth. It's time to start acting like it, and not just on behalf of Medicare beneficiaries, but on behalf of all Americans whose incomes and standard of living is devoured by the health providers' state-capture and rent-seeking.

Reform is obviously urgently needed. Why is it so hard to achieve?

People close to the system can witness the abuses being carried out right in front of them. Yet it is all but impossible to muster political mandates for action to squeeze the abuses out of the system. Why do Americans find it so uniquely difficult to act effectively in the public interest?

We saw an answer during the Obamacare debate of 2010. Obamacare was attacked as "socialism." Yet the people most responsive to these attacks—older voters—were themselves already enrolled (or looking forward soon to enrolling) in Medicare, a system much more socialistic than anything contemplated by the Affordable Care Act. In fact, a lot of the anger against the Affordable Care Act flowed from seniors' and soon-to-be-seniors' anxiety lest the Affordable Care Act cut into the funding for *their* socialized medicine.

In other countries, the health-care system supports social unity. In Britain, the National Health Service tops the list of things that define what it means to be British. Canadians feel as intensely about their Medicare system. But in the United States, Americans with good coverage—including the socialized coverage of American Medicare—fear tumbling down the ladder to join the people with bad coverage. The beneficiaries of the dysfunctional status quo reject change that they fear will harm them and benefit others. That fear originates in America's history of racial subordination. It is sustained by the widely shared and angry perception that open immigration redirects American health-care dollars to newcomers, legal and illegal.

Those fears are often dismissed as irrational, but they contain large elements of truth. Of those who lacked health-care insurance in 2008, more than one in four—27 percent—were foreign-born.[9] When President Obama proposed to raise taxes and crimp the future growth of Medicare to cover the uninsured, it was not crazy for fifty- and sixty-something Americans to think: *If we'd had less immigration, my taxes would be lower and my Medicare would be safer.*

When all the Democratic candidates for president pledge themselves to extending coverage in the future even to illegal aliens, as we read a few pages ago, it becomes even less irrational for more conservative Americans to link the cost of health care to thinly guarded borders.

Among the American population as a whole, fewer identified as conservative at the end of the 2010s than at the beginning of the 2000s. But the health care–dependent (and highly politically engaged) baby boom cohort has veered right as the rest of society has shifted slightly left.

As late as the year 2000, only 35 percent of people born between 1946 and 1960 described themselves as "conservative." Then came the financial crisis, the presidency of Barack Obama, and the Affordable Care Act. The proportion of baby boomers who called themselves "angry at government" surged from 15 percent before 2008 to 26 percent after the financial crisis struck. By 2011, 42 percent of baby boomers were labeling themselves "conservative."

What did these boomers mean by "conservative"? Basically: government needs to do less for others so it can do more for us.

Compared to people born in the years from 1930 through 1945, boomers were *more* likely to say that government does not do enough for the elderly. Compared with those older Americans, boomers were *less* likely to agree with statements like "It is the responsibility of the government to take care of people who can't take care of themselves."[10]

Why the difference between the 1931 to 1945 cohort and the 1946 to 1960 cohort? Unlike their elders born before 1945, the boomers would grow old in a country radically ethnically different from the country in which they were born. They looked at younger Americans and seem to have thought: "Not our country, not our problem. Let's look after ourselves."

If a society allows its sense of "one of us" to weaken, so will its willingness to provide for members of that "us." That is what is happening to the United States, not only in health care, but across the spectrum of social provision.

Back in the mid-1970s, as the great immigration was beginning, the state of California ranked seventh in the nation for per-pupil spending on "current instruction" (that is, not counting capital investment and debt financing).[11] A less-diverse state willingly taxed itself to educate its children. Forty years later, California's adult population, more than 60 percent white, supports a majority Latino school population.[12] Fewer than half of California public school students meet state standards of English-language competency. California has responded to that ethnic divergence just as Representative Steve

King predicted. California's spending on its schools has plunged to twenty-ninth in the nation. (At the trough of the Great Recession, California tumbled to thirty-ninth.)[13] In the 2014–2015 school year, California spent about $10,700 per elementary school pupil, only $200 more than Missouri, a state with radically fewer resources and significantly lower costs of living.[14] But Missouri ranks forty-first in the nation for foreign-born; California far and away ranks first.

Speaking to British doctors in 1944, that eminent conservative Winston Churchill pledged his country to a future of national health insurance.

> The discoveries of healing science must be the inheritance of all. That is clear. Disease must be attacked, whether it occurs in the poorest or the richest man or woman simply on the ground that it is the enemy; and it must be attacked just in the same way as the fire brigade will give its full assistance to the humblest cottage as readily as to the most important mansion. Our policy is to create a national health service in order to ensure that everybody in the country, irrespective of means, age, sex, or occupation, shall have equal opportunities to benefit from the best and most up-to-date medical and allied services available.[15]

Churchill, though, was speaking to and for a society whose unity had been forged in the hardships of war. The American spirit of unity is dissolving—and with it, the willingness and ability of Americans to care for one another.

This dissolution has weakened the nation but strengthened the parties. Partisanship has become a much more powerful identity in the 2010s than at any time since the aftermath of the Civil War. The revenues of the two great parties have risen into the billions, as each fundraises off dislike of the other. Yet the excesses of partisanship lead the party into self-harm too.

Two examples.

The first is the Republican debacle in Kentucky in 2019. Kentucky has evolved into one of the brightest Red states. It is one of the least urbanized states east of the Mississippi. More than 40 percent of Kentucky households own guns. Kentucky elected a loudmouthed Trump-before-Trump governor in 2015. It elected a Republican supermajority in the Kentucky House of Representatives, the first Republican victory in the Kentucky lower house since 1921. Trump won the state by thirty points. On the eve of the 2019 vote, Republicans held every statewide office, including both US Senate seats.

Yet there was a warning ahead that Republicans should have discerned. No state had benefited more from the ACA than Kentucky. Four hundred and forty thousand Kentuckians gained coverage under the ACA; Kentucky's uninsured rate tumbled from 20 percent in 2013 to 7.5 percent in 2015. In the state's poor Appalachian counties, where Republicans won most overwhelmingly, the gains had been especially striking.

Republicans heedlessly used their triumphs in Kentucky elections to attack health coverage in the state. They requested and got waivers to ACA rules that enabled Governor Matt Bevin to shrink Medicaid and SCHIP enrollment by thirty-one thousand. He wrecked his own administration on that change. By 2018, a plurality of Kentuckians, 44 percent, approved of the ACA.[16] Bevin soon found himself the most unpopular governor in the country—and a loser in November 2019.

The rollback of coverage threatens Republicans outside Kentucky too. Nationwide, Medicaid and SCHIP enrollment shrank by 1.73 million in 2017 and 2018.[17] Between 2010 and 2016, the percentage of Americans with health insurance steadily rose; in 2017 and 2018, coverage declined. In the single year 2018, the number of Americans protected by health insurance dropped by 1.1 million.

Yet the Trump era also offered warnings to Democrats about their political blind spots.

Trump closed the Republican election campaign in November 2018 with two weeks of warnings about a caravan of would-be border crossers heading to the United States from Central America. Democrats dismissed Trump's angry rhetoric as bigoted flimflam. But it worked. Democrats had a good election in 2018. But so did Republicans. In the big off-year elections of the past—1994, 2006—the losing party suffered a notable decline in support. Not so in 2018.

Republican candidates for the House in the disaster year 2018 together won *more* votes than they did in their mighty victory of 2010. Republicans failed to hold the House because Democrats showed up in even greater numbers: 9 million more in total. But what marked 2018 was the success of *both* parties in mobilizing and countermobilizing. Not since 1914 had so much of the electorate voted in a nonpresidential year: 53 percent of the voting-age population.[18] Immigration and the caravan threat helped turn out those Republican votes for an otherwise unpopular president and party. In a Monmouth poll after the election, only 22 percent of respondents agreed that they were "sure" that Trump was wrong about the caravan containing terrorists.[19]

If Democrats want to perpetuate their health-care reforms, they must do a better job of solidifying a sense of national belonging. If Republicans want to safeguard the border, they must offer a better deal to those living on that border's American side.

America's master politician, Franklin Delano Roosevelt, understood how to build institutions that last. In the summer of 1941, an outside adviser to the Roosevelt administration devised a plan to reform the then-new Social Security program. The outside adviser argued that taxing payrolls discourages hiring and penalizes work. The adviser got a meeting with President Roosevelt and urged him to get rid of the payroll tax and replace it with something more economically efficient: a retail sales tax for example. The adviser recorded for posterity FDR's reply.

We put those payroll contributions there so as to give the contributors a legal, moral, and political right to collect their pensions and their unemployment benefits. With those taxes in there, no damn politician can ever scrap my social security program. Those taxes aren't a matter of economics, they're straight politics.[20]

FDR cared most about creating a sense of "right" and "belonging." That's why your Social Security benefit comes enumerated by an account number, backed by a printed card. In real life, what you pay into Social Security is only very hazily related to what you will collect. But in the minds of tens of millions of Americans, Social Security is *earned*, and therefore it is *owned*. Like the British National Health Service, like Canada's Medicare, it is a defining aspect of what it means to belong to this particular national community.

The Affordable Care Act was written without reference to that need for belonging. Maybe that is why the ACA remains so weak, so vulnerable to attack by state governments, partisan majorities in Congress, and ideologically motivated courts. When the Democratic candidates for president unanimously endorsed extending federal health-care benefits to illegal aliens, they were discarding the wisdom of Franklin Roosevelt.

Often in politics, things that cannot be done separately can be done together. Back in the mid-1980s, conservatives wanted to cut tax rates; liberals wanted to eliminate tax breaks. The two ideas converged in the tax reform of 1986. In the mid-1990s, Newt Gingrich and Bill Clinton swapped expanded health coverage for poor children for a cut in the capital gains tax. The No Child Left Behind law of the Bush administration joined conservative enthusiasm for testing to liberal wishes to concentrate federal funds on the poorest school districts. The food stamp program (now known as SNAP and delivered via a plastic card, not stamps) is supported by a coalition of Democratic urban liberals and Republicans from farm states. Convergence is possible, and health care plus immigration is the most favorable place for such convergence.

Because of America's tortured racial history, immigration is often imagined—by proponents and opponents alike—as a subordinate theme within the larger racial narrative. Either we are encouraging immigration in order to do racial justice or we are discouraging immigration to preserve America's white identity. But even if all immigration into the United States were to cease tomorrow, the country's racial crossover points would be bumped back by only a few years. America is already majority nonwhite among the under-eighteen population. The non-Hispanic white population will begin to shrink in absolute numbers about the year 2024. By 2027, non-Hispanic whites will cease to be a majority among the under-thirty age group. By 2033, non-Hispanic whites will be in the minority among under-forties. Regardless of immigration policy, the country as a whole will cease to be majority non-Hispanic white sometime in the mid-2040s, according to 2018 Census projections.[21]

The challenge for the United States is to make a success of the future it has already chosen.

In this atomized new world, Americans need one another more—and trust one another less. As recently as 2006, the United States numbered only 300 million. Under present policies, the United States will reach 400 million by the year 2050. Immigrants and their children will drive almost all of that growth. Those newcomers earn significantly less than natives, so the natives will bear the larger share of the costs of educating and insuring the newcomers. As we have witnessed under Trump, this is a course leading only to conflict, and possibly democratic breakdown.

By enhancing mutual provision, we add meaning to national belonging; by adding meaning to national belonging, we enable mutual provision. The people who most clearly recognize the interconnectedness between belonging and provision are the people who seek to defeat both. It's not remotely a coincidence that the American social insurance system grew most during the period 1930 to 1970, when the proportion of foreign-born in the population reached its nadir. In 1970, 97 percent of the people resident in the United States held citizenship and the rights of citizenship, the historic peak. Nor is it a coincidence that the immigration surge since 1980 has coincided with a period of maximal skepticism about the ability of government to act fairly in a national interest.

> The political era between the 1930s and the 1970s marks what might be called a "great exception"—a sustained deviation, an extended detour—from some of the main contours of American political practice, economic structure, and cultural outlook. During this period, the central government used its considerable resources in a systematic, if hardly consistent, fashion on behalf of the economic interests of nonelite Americans in ways that it had not done before or since.[22]

So Jefferson Cowie wrote in his history of midcentury America, *The Great Exception*—and he was right. Low immigration was not the only cause of this exception, but it was a cause and also a symptom: a society deeply concerned for the welfare of employees will think differently about immigration than a society dominated by the preferences of employers.

The boomer generation, of which I am just barely a member (I was born in 1960), has bequeathed to America a more individualistic and expressive culture. Boomers are highly attuned to their personal rights, less attentive to collective responsibility. From sex, drugs, and rock-and-roll in their youth; through divorce, guns, and motorcycles in midlife; and now to Fox News and Medicare in their older age, the boomer motto has been, "I gotta be me."

The expressive individualism of the boomers did much good. It emancipated women and unleashed vital new creativity. But it also severed bonds of solidarity between citizens. Unions dwindled. The state retreated. Borders lowered. The market advanced. Americans find themselves less likely to live in families, less likely to adhere to a church, less likely to be enrolled in a union, less likely even to belong to a club. The well-being of the less adaptable, the less inventive, the less astute has remorselessly declined.

When immigration numbers swell too fast—if voters perceive that authorities have lost control of the borders—then citizens turn to authoritarians to impose order. The mass movement of immigrants into Germany in the summer of 2015 brought to power an illiberal, authoritarian government in Poland the next month—and reinforced Viktor Orbán in Hungary after he had nearly wrecked his power base by imposing heavy taxes on Internet use. That migration was decisive in the Brexit vote the next summer, since the United Kingdom's then-lively job market—not Germany's sluggish one—was the preferred ultimate destination of many migrants. The Central American surge to the US border in the summers of 2014 and 2016 helped elect Donald Trump in 2016. Trump hoped he could use the even bigger surge of the first half of 2019—and his militant fight to repulse that surge—as his best argument for reelection in 2020.

To defeat Trump and to prevent new Trumps, the United States (and other advanced societies, too) must control their borders and strengthen their nationality and their social-insurance systems to foster the sense of belonging that has ebbed away as our societies become more diverse, more interconnected, more plutocratic.

I get the merits of the case for covering the ten million or so illegal residents of the United States. The majority of those people have resided in the United States for more than a decade.[23] What *is* to happen when those people get sick? Even more awkwardly: What is to happen when they grow old? Are we really to contemplate a future in which millions and millions of elderly US residents will be shrugged off in illness or frailty because they entered the country illegally back when Bill Clinton was president?

Yet if we include those uninvited, unauthorized residents of the United States in the most valuable benefit offered by the national community, are we not also inviting tens of millions of more to break the law after them? It will be a hugely expensive project to cover even the population *already* illegally present. About half the illegal population of California, for example, earn incomes low enough to qualify for Medi-Cal, should it become available to them.[24] If the American health-care system is to be stabilized, not only must costs be controlled, but eligibility must be defined and enforced.

The path to citizenship that Democrats want for illegal residents must begin with demonstrated proof that large illegal immigration flows have been stopped forever. Canada is a country generally regarded as uniquely welcoming to immigration. Yet in July 2011, the second-highest Canadian federal court ruled that illegal aliens have no right to health-care coverage—and this decision remains the law to the time of writing. The Canadian policy of refusing health care to unauthorized immigrants is so uncontroversial within Canada that, so far as I can tell, nobody seems ever to have bothered to conduct a public poll about it. It just seems obvious to all concerned: you come to Canada legally, you get health care as part of the deal; if not, you don't. If a society has an ethic—"This we will do for you whether you can afford it or not, just because you are one of us"—then it must have a meaningful definition of "one of us."

Perhaps you object to yielding one inch to the illiberal, xenophobic, and reactionary message of Donald Trump. Yet when the threat of communism stalked the Western world during the Great Depression and after the devastation of World War II, wise leaders did not say: *No, not an inch.* They said: So long as we suffer mass unemployment, pervasive destitution, haunting fear—our people will be susceptible to communism's promise. To defeat communism, it must be deprived of its most powerful complaints, its most alluring arguments.

Some conservatives of those days argued that any concession to social concerns must lead to the total overthrow of capitalism and democracy. But most conservative-minded leaders were wiser than that. They understood that old-age pensions, unemployment insurance, and policies to smooth recessions were weapons *against* communism, not pathways to communism. As Theodore Roosevelt said more than a century ago: "Reform is the antidote to revolution . . . social reform is not the precursor but the preventive of socialism."[25] To save democracy from illiberal authoritarianism, democrats must deny the authoritarians their most powerful weapons, their most appealing arguments. Against communism, that means responding to social concerns. Against fascists, that means responding to national concerns.

Illegal immigration must be curtailed, not with a wall on the border, but with inspections and meaningful penalties against employers of illegal labor. Employers must be provided with some convenient and reliable means to confirm whether their workers are legally present or not. That will imply new forms of tamper-proof identification. The present system of checking worker status against Social Security numbers is designed to fail.

In the twenty-first century, borders are being tested more and more by immigrants who present themselves as asylum seekers. The laws and treaties governing asylum were written after the Second World War with the victims of Nazism and communism in mind. Those laws and treaties guarantee every asylum claimant an individual hearing—which is why a nation's asylum system comes crashing down when asylum seekers start showing up by the hundreds of thousands and then the millions, as they have done in Europe and the United States since the middle 2010s. The new mass wave of asylum seekers yearns to escape poverty, lawlessness, the loss of farms to environmental degradation. But they are seldom fleeing *individual* persecution of the kind to which the asylum system was intended as an answer. The large and growing problems of Central America and West Africa call for humane international solution, but the migration of millions of their people to other countries is not that solution—and if we are not realistic about that truth now, we will stoke reactionary movements compared to which the Trump episode will seem a pale dawn glimmer of a red and terrible day.

The legal immigration process needs to be reinvented too. The United States accepts more than a million legal immigrants a year. Why? Because that's the number that was set in 1991 to tidy up after the amnesty of 1986 legalized a great number of single young men who wished to bring their families after them from Mexico and the

Philippines. Thirty years later, the great majority of those emigrating legally to the United States remain relatives of relatives of relatives of those who gained status in 1986. How does this make any sense? The right to live in the United States is a huge prize. That prize should be bestowed in the American interest to people who have something specific to offer the United States. It's my personal view that the ceiling on legal immigration should be lower, should return to the pre-1986 figure of a little under 600,000 a year rather than the present 1.2 million. But more important than the number of immigrants should be the composition of immigration: more people who come to meet a gap in the US labor market; fewer who come because a relative got here first.

The United States runs an immigration policy as if it were a country facing a desperate labor shortage. In fact, the United States faces a desperate social cohesion shortage. Immigration done right can tighten the bonds of nationhood. Done wrong, as the United States is doing it, mass immigration only intensifies the mutual suspicions of American society—and impedes any effort to rewrite the social contract to offer a better deal to the average American.

There are extreme fringes in the immigration debate for sure, and no moderate policy will appease them. As in the 1950s, so it is today, the goal is not to convert convinced extremists, but to render them harmless by denying them followers. Voters are often attracted to wrong answers, but they are always right when they identify problems. If the voters are led astray, then the responsibility of democratic leadership is not to reprove them but to rescue them.

American conservatives take pride in their nation, but mistrust the nation's state. American liberals value the state, but feel discomfort with the concept of "nation." Yet it is the power of the state that makes of the nation something more than a phrase of speech; it is the idea of the nation that legitimates the power of the state. Democracy depends on both, because only when there is both a nation and a state can there be an electorate to choose and remove leaders by peaceful balloting after collective deliberation.

CHAPTER TEN

Greener Planet, Better Jobs

Liberal societies flourish on optimism, fail on pessimism. Hannah Arendt explained the vulnerability of her German contemporaries to radical evil: "The worst have lost their fear and the best have lost their hope."[1] Without hope, good people drift into passivity.

In our time, there are two great sources of fear disabling democracy. One was addressed in the last chapter: fear that the long-settled populations of Europe and the United States will be displaced by new immigration. The other fear haunts the younger and the environmentally minded: that humanity is destroying the environment that sustains human civilization. Congresswoman Alexandria Ocasio-Cortez, livestreaming on Instagram from her kitchen, mused in February 2019: "There's scientific consensus that the lives of children are going to be very difficult. And it does lead young people to have a legitimate question: Is it OK to still have children?"[2]

Whatever their thought processes, it's evident: young Americans are answering that question with a no—or, at least, with a "not now."

The 325 million Americans of 2017 gave birth to fewer babies than did the 160 million Americans of 1953. Behind the statistics lies a world of individual disappointment: surveys find that women across the developed world are having fewer children than they would ideally like. Lyman Stone of the American Enterprise Institute ingeniously combined data sequences to compute that American women collectively wish they had at least 20 percent more children than they actually do.[3] The shortfall is even greater in Europe.[4]

There are many practical reasons why young people hesitate to have children. Those who attend college emerge laden with debt. Those seeking work in cities face daunting housing costs. The downward trend in the wages of noncollege men reduces their eligibility as marriage partners. As women's work becomes better paid, so, too, does the cost to women of stepping out of the labor force to bear and raise children. Even a short absence for one child imposes measurable costs. The larger the family, the higher the loss to the mother's lifelong income.[5]

The US government tries to offset these burdens with direct aid to parents. Since 2017, the US tax code has provided a $2,000 tax credit for every citizen child under age seventeen. Up to $1,400 of that credit can be refunded in cash even if the parents do not pay enough tax to use the full credit. Smaller credits are paid for children over age seventeen.

Obviously, these credits are not sufficient to the job. Two thousand dollars might clinch the deal for the couple deciding whether to have a child this year or wait till next. But it will hardly overcome the large uncertainties faced by people unsure whether they can afford to have a child in the very first place. Counteracting all *those* drags would cost hundreds of billions a year. Who would contemplate spending that?

Yet the US political system does not hesitate to spend much vaster sums to provide security to those in the later part of life. Social Security, Medicare: those already cost more than a trillion and a half dollars per year, and will soon cost more. Developed societies are caught in a vicious cycle of self-consumption. As they age, their voters became ever readier to spend on the elderly, ever stingier with the young—even willing to sacrifice the future altogether to ease the present generation on its passage through and out of life. Nowhere do you see the conflict between generations presented more acutely than in the climate debate.

Climate rejectionism has become a central theme of modern conservatism. Either it's not happening, or it's not happening because of human action, or there's nothing to be done about it—or sometimes all three—have become doctrinal positions on the modern Right. Obviously, there are important economic interests at play here. But economics alone cannot explain the kind of personal offense conservatives take to the climate claims. To many, the topic feels like an aggression. To borrow a term they like to mock, it *triggers* them—and most especially when the topic is raised by younger people.

"A 16-year-old Swedish girl whose contempt for adults is breathtaking is an international hero," complained the radio host Dennis Prager of the sudden celebrity of climate activist Greta Thunberg.[6] Breitbart contributor John Nolte tweeted: "I can't tell if Greta needs a spanking or a psychological intervention . . . Probably both."[7] Radio host Erick Erickson declared Thunberg a mouthpiece for manipulative adults. "No, I am not going to be lectured to by a 16 year old just because she gets access to a prince's private yacht."[8] A contributor to the Daily Wire fumed: "The notion that policymakers ought to consider proposing policy due to the fraught and hysterical pleas of a 16-year-old is, naturally, insane."[9] The British anti-environmentalist journalist Brendan O'Neill wrote, "The green cult has pushed Ms Thunberg into the position of its global leader, its childlike saviour, the messiah of their miserabilist political creed . . . They have pumped her—and millions of other children—with the politics of fear."[10] Thunberg even earned a sarcastic Trump tweet: "She seems like a very happy young girl looking forward to a bright and wonderful future. So nice to see!"[11]

Climate change advocacy as generational impertinence: it's not a new idea. Almost a decade ago, then–Fox News star Glenn Beck played a video clip of former vice president Al Gore on Beck's Fox program. In the clip, Gore said: "There are some things about our world that you know that older people don't know." Beck erupted indignantly:

> Here he is speaking in front of 12- and 13-year-olds. *There are things that you know that older people don't know.* Excuse me?
>
> What are those things that parents don't know that their children do?
>
> Can we please ask the media and the politicians—how is it now that kids are smarter somehow than their parents?[12]

As American conservatives have felt the ebb of cultural power away from them, they have come to feel watched and judged. They do not like it. "How does it feel to be a problem?" memorably asked W. E. B. Du Bois.[13] Du Bois was writing about the African American experience. The question might now be retorted upon the petroleum-burning American way of life.

That pickup truck, powerful enough to haul a stack of lumber, that you drive from your subdivision to the office park? Problem.

The polystyrene packaging that keeps your barbecue brisket warm and moist? Problem. (As is the methane-emitting bovine source of the brisket itself.)

The bright-green lawn irrigated for your golfing pleasure? Problem.

The air-conditioning that chills your retirement condo? Problem again!

In the age of Trump, conservatism has functioned less as a body of ideas, more as a defense of a distinctive way of life: the American way as white baby boomers remember it from when they were young. They remember split-level homes on suburban lots, Santa at the mall, and leggy blondes on TV. They do not want to be guilted about drinking from a plastic straw or driving a big car. On the eve of the impeachment vote, Trump's favorite congressman, Matt Gaetz of Florida, appeared on Fox News with pro-Trump radio host Mark Levin to describe the stakes in the impending impeachment battle. Arrayed against the president, said Gaetz, are those who uphold "a worldview where you eat nothing but kale and quinoa, where those of us who cling to our Bibles and our guns and our fried foods and real America are looked down upon."[14]

It's not only annoying Swedish teenagers who are looking down. A consensus of know-it-all scientists corroborates the impudent teen. Then, when you express your disgust with the scientists as a bunch of impractical idiots working for globalist billionaires . . . your own children look at you as if *you* were the idiot. It's galling.

The Trumpist Right habitually applies the jibe *snowflake* to disparage the supposedly overtender feelings of modern youth. Yet no group of Americans complains more about microaggressions than the Trump base and Fox News audiences. No issue wounds their ego more than climate. They believe they should be on top, they should write the rules. Instead, they are told that they are ignorant, they are wrong, they are killing the planet. It's insulting, it's intolerable. That's why they love Trump. He doesn't put up with any of that crap. He shows everyone who's boss, who's *entitled* to be boss—and it's not a bunch of liberal hippie scientists who probably bicycle to work.

Possibly there was a timeline in which climate change did not have to be a partisan issue. The first world leader to raise the alarm in a public forum was Margaret Thatcher, in her 1988 speech to Britain's Royal Society and then again in 1989 in a speech at the United Nations.[15] In a September 2000 speech, presidential candidate George W. Bush promised to regulate carbon dioxide as a pollutant.[16] In the first months of the Bush administration, an internal argument erupted whether to honor that promise. History should remember the two White House staffers who led the fight to uphold it: John Bridgeland and Gary Edson.[17] But they lost; Vice President Cheney won. Soon September 11 struck, then we were enmired in Iraq, then beset by the global financial crisis. The climate issue receded. It receded, too, because the pace of global warming temporarily slowed between 1998 and 2012. "Temperatures peaked in 1998," climate skeptics could say. Yes, we had passed through a hot phase in the 1990s, but now things seemed to have stabilized. What's the panic?

But the holiday ended. The world began to warm again, and faster than ever. Two thousand sixteen overtook 1998 as the hottest year ever. Two thousand seventeen exceeded 2016. Two thousand eighteen exceeded 2017.

Through the second Obama term, world emissions of greenhouse gases had held more or less steady. Many experts hoped that perhaps they had plateaued, that reduction could begin soon. Instead, global emissions jumped 2 percent in the single year, 2017.[18] They continue to rise. The planet continues to cook. And the political passions set in motion by the warming are accelerating, too—pushing many on the Left away from democracy and liberalism as immigration has radicalized those on the Right.

The illiberal turn is strongest in Europe, where Green Party activists in many countries are urging a "climate emergency" whereby governments would impose radical state controls upon the economy. What would a "climate emergency" look like?

> It would require a high level of government intervention, backed by effective planning, policy and legislation, to drive action that is swift, resolute and impactful. The state would need to openly communicate the magnitude of the threat and consequences of inaction; and then draw on all its own resources *and* the full capacity of its citizens and market participants to drive an effective response. The economic mobilisation [*sic*] during WWII continues to be the best reference point for the scale and pace of economic and social intervention required.[19]

A permanent war economy is not compatible with a free society. And indeed, some seem attracted to the climate cause precisely as a new excuse for old visions of state-directed collectivization.

> Forget everything you think you know about global warming. The really inconvenient truth is that it's not about carbon—it's about capitalism. The convenient truth is that we can seize this

existential crisis to transform our failed economic system and build something radically better.[20]

That *is* convenient if you were looking to justify a social change that people had otherwise decisively rejected as a formula for oppression and misery. But it's no way to convince people that claims of climate crisis are honest and data-driven.

President Trump dismisses the storms, droughts, fires, and floods on his watch as a "Chinese hoax." *Nothing is happening, and if anything is happening, it's China's fault.*

That's a reckless message to spread, but some of Trump's opponents are spreading a message only somewhat less reckless. They say that global warming is all the fault of evil energy companies and selfish plutocrats.

"We have got to be super aggressive if we love our children and if we want to leave them a planet that is healthy and is habitable," Senator Bernie Sanders said at the Democratic presidential debate in Detroit in July 2019. "What that means is we got to take on the fossil fuel industry."[21] Progressive Democrats united upon a plan for a Green New Deal that rapidly pivoted away from decarbonization to endorse state ownership of industries, government-guaranteed unionized jobs, and a proliferation of committees of "frontline and vulnerable communities" to "plan, implement, and administer" the spending of government clean-energy money, all while protecting "every business person" from "unfair competition."[22]

Climate is a summons to human reason and problem solving. The rusted-out Marxism that so miserably failed to solve the twentieth-century challenge of housing, clothing, and feeding human beings will *equally miserably* fail to solve the twenty-first-century challenge of preserving a livable environment for human beings. If you tell Americans that saving the planet will raise the pay and benefits of each and every one of them, with the entire cost borne exclusively by the executives and shareholders of the fossil fuel companies, well, you are lying to them as shamelessly and dangerously as President

Trump. Maybe more dangerously, since Trump's lie is more easily detected and rejected.

In the face of wage stagnation and wealth concentration, many Americans express frustration with an economy that feels unfair to them. Some even seek to rehabilitate the ideal of "socialism." If you believe that a more controlled or redistributive economy would lead to better results than a more competitive or incentivized economy—well, you believe it. The evidence may not support you, but some commitments do not depend upon evidence.

To claim, however, that you are supremely committed to reducing greenhouse gases, when in reality you are more concerned with regulating economic competition, dooms your likelihood of achieving either. It is hard enough to achieve the outcomes you actually seek; it is much harder to achieve the outcomes you are only pretending to seek—while actually seeking something very different.

Putting government into the business of busting rent-seeking in the health-care industry—as the leading Democratic candidates for 2020 vowed to do—is already a public administration challenge for a generation. If successful, health-care reform will deliver in itself a big bump to worker pay and alleviate perhaps the single most harrowing anxiety faced by working Americans. Undertaking more social reform than that, in a country where social reform is more fiercely resisted than in almost any other developed democracy, is to risk the failure of everything, and above all, to forfeit any hope of building a congressional majority for climate action in the 2020s. The years 2021–2022 may open a rare window to do one, two, or at most three big and important things. Choose those things wisely.

We will be successful only if we shift the climate debate from accusations to solutions, from conflict to consensus, from identity to policy.

Over hundreds of millions of years, the Earth accumulated vast layers of fossilized plant matter. These plants fed on the carbon dioxide belched forth from the Earth by volcanoes and other titanic earth spasms. They absorbed carbon dioxide into their trunks and stems and leaves, as did algae and kelp. When these prehistoric plants died and were buried, their carbon dioxide intake was buried with them. It fossilized into coal or liquified into oil or vaporized into natural gas. The process went on and on, contributing to the cooling of the Earth from the sultry planet of the dinosaurs and pre-dinosaurs to the more temperate world in which human beings arose to civilization. A little more than two centuries ago, human beings learned to dig and burn this vast accumulated inheritance of ancient plants to generate power, releasing back into the atmosphere in a few decades the carbon dioxide that the planets had sucked out over geologic ages. Now we must slow, stop, and ultimately reverse this process—or else we may find that we have geoengineered a planet on which we cannot live.

On the present trend, the planet will keep warming until the next century at least. The consequences of the warming are showing up much faster than expected. The European heat wave in summer 2019 melted the Greenland ice cap at a rate that was not supposed to occur until 2070. The oceans are warming faster than earlier models predicted too.

Over the whole period 1980 to 2018, the United States averaged six extreme weather events per year. Between 2014 and 2018, the United States has averaged twelve per year. The single worst year was 2017; 2018 was the fourth worst year.[23] If Trump policies continue to drive catastrophic climate change, even heavier costs loom ahead.

The good news is that US emissions peaked in 2005 and have declined since then by more than 850 million tons per year. European Union emissions peaked in 1990.

The bad news is that this decline in the developed world is not happening fast enough. Meanwhile carbon emissions by China, India, and other developing countries are pumping emissions into the atmosphere at a rate that overwhelms anything done by European or American industry in the past.

The same fossil fuels toasting the atmosphere are also choking the oceans. Those oil and gas by-products that cannot be burned as fuel are manufactured into plastic. As Zoë Schlanger reported in *Quartz*, global production of plastics has soared from practically zero in 1950 to almost 350 million metric tons per year by 2020. How fast a change is that? More than one-third of all the plastic ever produced by humanity was produced in the fifteen years since the first appearance of the *World of Warcraft* video game in 2004. The world is on the way to producing a billion tons of plastic a year by 2050. Less than 10 percent of that production is recycled, and because the cost of plastic keeps falling, the economics of recycling are actually becoming more unfavorable all the time.[24]

It's human to assume that the future must look like the immediate past. But that assumption may be unrealistic. Human beings have lived through episodes of climate change before, although in those instances not human-caused. The worrying thing for present-day people facing human-caused change is that those past episodes happened incredibly *fast*.

The most recent change began in the 1590s. After more than half a millennium of benign temperatures, the Northern Hemisphere suddenly cooled. In the generation that followed, China's Ming dynasty collapsed amid the worst slaughter China would suffer until the revolutions and wars of the twentieth century. India and Iran were torn by civil wars. France, Ukraine, and the British Isles disintegrated into civil war. Central Europe plunged into the Thirty Years' War, the most murderous war on that continent between the fall of Rome and the twentieth century. All this human-on-human slaughter was accompanied by pestilence and famines, culminating in the last great bubonic plague epidemic in European history in the 1660s. And then, about 1710, the nightmare ended as suddenly as it had begun.[25]

The climate crisis of the seventeenth century was not human-made of course. But the record of that harsh era should warn modern people that our planet's climate system is prone to tipping points. A human being who lived in the Northern Hemisphere in the thirty years from 1590 to 1620 might have noticed that the winters grew gradually harsher, the summers rather wetter, than when he was young—but nothing so terribly out of the ordinary. Then, very abruptly between 1620 and 1630, the Northern Hemisphere turned frigid. Crops were ruined by rains and hail. Rivers froze; birds died on the branches of trees; summers seemed never to arrive. The Great Canal that carried food from the productive fields of southern China to feed the vast capital of Beijing went dry for the only time in its centuries-long history.

Seventeenth-century human beings struggled desperately to understand what was happening to them. It's probably not a coincidence that the Scientific Revolution of Descartes, Harvey, Leibniz, and Newton begins in this period. Had the climate remained benign, perhaps the founders of modern science might have squandered their genius on theology, as the great minds of the Middle Ages did. Instead, they tried to make sense of the physical universe that had so suddenly turned so inhospitable to humanity.

Of course, there was nothing the scientifically minded people of the seventeenth century could actually *do* about the planet's hostile turn. Modern people are better placed to protect ourselves, or so we must hope and trust. We can do more than slow the rate of carbon emission, more even than stopping it altogether. We can reverse it. We must.

Yet the American political system seems paralyzed. The Trumpist Right denies the climate threat altogether; the progressive Left sees climate not as important in itself but only as a justification for a social transformation otherwise beyond its political grasp. Meanwhile, climate change pushes our world toward crisis, conflict, and even war.

Climate change is implicated in the accelerating movement of people from Africa and the Middle East to Europe. Between 2006 and 2009, drought devastated Syrian agriculture. Hundreds of thousands of farmers left the land for the cities. Unemployed and frustrated, they gathered the grievances that would spark into a civil war that has displaced half that country's prewar population of 22 million.[26]

Some ideas for meeting the climate challenge invite even graver dangers than the climate challenge itself. The Chinese government has launched an ambitious research program to study reversing global warming by what they euphemistically call "solar radiation management."[27] In practice, that means firing millions of tons of tiny particles into the atmosphere to deflect solar radiation back into space. Obviously, this plan carries horrifying risks. The particles could mess with rainfall all over the planet. They could possibly trigger another ice age, if somebody miscalculates and fires off too many of them.

What happens if China's government deems those risks acceptable—while others disagree?

China's rulers incurred extreme environmental risks to develop their country. The Chinese rulers of the next decades may be willing to incur even more risks to protect their country. China's grain production in the arid north has declined for two decades because of water shortages. China's south is ravaged by ever fiercer tropical storms. China's rulers may feel just desperate enough in the 2020s or 2030s to try something reckless. In 2018, Indian scientists modeled the climate effects of injecting 20 million tons of sulfate particles into the atmosphere. Good news: the injection would reduce the earth's average temperature by 1.5 degrees Celsius within two to four years. Bad news: the injection would shift India's monsoons slightly southward into the Indian Ocean, depriving India's hot north of 12 percent of its annual rainfall.[28] It's not hard to imagine China and India plunging into serious conflict over their diverging climate interests. It's not hard to imagine this conflict turning into war, even nuclear war.

Only American leadership can lead all countries together to safety. To preserve a stable, prosperous world, America will need a new environmental policy undertaken with the whole planet in mind. Adopting such policies will demand a new politics: more based on social consensus, more accepting of scientific expertise.

The new policy must be globally minded. We are all in this together, and mutual recrimination achieves nothing.

Trump rose to the presidency by fingering the same culprits for every problem: malignant foreigners and weak American leaders. "We can't continue to allow China to rape our country, and that's what they're doing," he told a rally in Fort Wayne, Indiana, in May 2016.[29] Trump promised that a strong president could stop the metaphorical rape by China and the literal rapes by Mexicans.[30] As he tweeted in November 2017:

> I don't blame China, I blame the incompetence of past Admins for allowing China to take advantage of the U.S. on trade leading up to a point where the U.S. is losing $100's of billions. How can you blame China for taking advantage of people that had no clue? I would've done same![31]

Demagogues not only offer targets for hate. They offer appealing explanations of complex problems—explanations that finger identifiable human culprits. Those explanations are wrong, false, and destructive. But they make intuitive sense to the primordial brain. It's why our ancestors burned witches when a cow unexpectedly died.

Yet mutual recrimination achieves nothing. All the peoples of the planet face the same risks together. The climate debate offers us an opportunity to jolt ourselves out of this useless way of thinking—and toward a healthier US-China relationship.

China builds things and sends them to America. America borrows from China to pay for those things, and then returns the ensuing waste to China to recycle into new things. Until 2018, China received 70 percent of the world's recyclable plastic waste, almost 7 million tons a year. Recycling can be a lucrative business—that's how China's first female billionaire gained her fortune—but it generates many dirty by-products. China was not only "taking" America's jobs, but it was quite literally taking America's pollution. (In 2018, the Chinese government banned the trade in recyclable plastic. Indonesia, Malaysia, and Vietnam have stepped into the gap—and are absorbing the consequences.)[32]

Things should not work this way. The United States is the richer and more mature economy. Instead of China lending to the United States to finance American consumption, the United States should be lending to China to finance Chinese investment—as Britain lent to the United States in the nineteenth century, when Britain was the world's most advanced economy and the United States was faster growing.

This more natural financial relationship has been stunted by three big deformities on either side of the Pacific.

The first deformity is America's habit of running chronic federal budget deficits, in good years and bad. In 2020, the federal government will spend a trillion dollars more than it collects, even assuming no recession. These chronic fiscal deficits summon the world's savings to the United States. As the rest of the world buys American debt, they put foreign cash in American hands with which to buy foreign goods. It's almost an accounting axiom: the bigger the budget deficit, the bigger the trade deficit.

The second deformity is China's closed, corrupt financial system. Why isn't capital flowing into China? Well, would *you* invest there? Property and contracts are insecure. The courts cannot be trusted. The tax system is arbitrary. As much as capital is sucked into the United States, it is repelled from China. And by the same accounting rules as apply to the United States, the bigger the investment deficit, the bigger the trade surplus.

The third deformity is Chinese currency manipulation. All those dollars earned by exports? Sooner or later, somebody in China should want to do something with them: buy American products maybe or else American real estate and other assets. When the dollars were released into the global marketplace, their abundance should cause the value of the dollar to fall relative to China's currency. American products would begin to look cheaper; China's would begin to look more expensive. The balances between the two countries should tend to stabilize. None of that has happened. China's government has been able to lock up those dollars by lending them back to the US government to finance US budget deficits. The dollar stays higher than it should, the Chinese currency cheaper than it should. The trade surpluses keep piling up.

The result of these deformities is a world in which jobs (and especially the jobs of less-skilled men) shift to China from the United States and other developed countries at a faster pace than would happen under other policies. That faster shift in turn empowers demagogues like Trump, destabilizing democracy in the countries losing employment to China.

As production moves, pollution follows. The world loses carbon-soaking forests as Brazil burns the Amazon to grow soybeans for China, as Southeast Asia denudes its jungles to grow rice for China. Carbon suffuses the air from the giant ships carrying products from China: the shipping industry alone accounts for 3 percent of all the planet's carbon emissions, about the same as the entire nation of Germany.[33]

This is not an accusation against China. The rulers of China export to keep their people working, because they fear that a growth slowdown could bring their state crashing down in revolution. But their policy of regime self-preservation is endangering the preservation of the planet.

How do we arrive at a regime that is more sustainable? How do we avoid protectionism that will impoverish us all, hurting the poorest most?

The United States needs to balance its budgets. China needs to open its markets. Everybody needs to emit less. And the lever to do all those things is a carbon tax that will make all fossil fuels—and therefore also all plastics—significantly more expensive than they are today.

An American carbon tax will change behavior not only in this country but around the world. A carbon tax is also a carbon tariff. It can be applied on goods and services as they enter the United States and remitted on goods and services exported from the United States. The tariff would be waived for countries that applied carbon taxes of their own at least equal to the United States.

Unlike Trump's tariffs, carbon tariffs would be legal under existing World Trade Organization rules, which allow tariff barriers to be imposed for environmental reasons. A carbon tax-and-tariff would not upend the world trading system. What it would do is raise the price of Indian and Chinese products until those two countries signed up for carbon taxes of their own.

A carbon tax-and-tariff would endow the United States with a mighty tool for cooperation and friendship with other advanced democracies. The United States will have the means to say to the European Union, Japan, the United Kingdom, South Korea, Canada, Australia, New Zealand, and other like-minded countries: *If you tax your carbon emissions at the same rate as we tax ours, then your goods and services of course can enter our market tariff-free. We'd expect the same courtesy from you. None of us is trying to privilege our industries, only to incentivize everyone to reduce their emissions.*

Better still, the right level of carbon tax could be negotiated in advance between those advanced economies—not in the free-for-all of the multilateral, ineffectual Paris process, but in a more business-like setting of countries with long traditions of cooperation among themselves. Rogue actors like Jair Bolsonaro's Brazil would find themselves in the position of rule takers rather than rule breakers. Even very large countries like India and China will need to make terms with a developed world carbon union. Together, China and India account for more than 27 percent of world output, by the International Monetary Fund's tally,[34] more than either the European Union or the United States. But their economies are not complementary; they do not trade much with each other.[35] Together, they look big, but they cannot act together.

The transition from a carbon-dense economy will not be easy. But I will venture that it will prove way less traumatic than carbon

skeptics fear—and substantially less revolutionary than climate rad-
icals hope.

Claims that carbon taxes will "take away your burger" are absurd. Americans were *already* reducing their red meat consumption.
In the late 1970s, the average American ate more than 140 pounds
of beef and pork per year, down now to under 110 pounds.[36] Worldwide, livestock-raising accounts for 14.5 percent of all greenhouse
gas emissions.[37] In more developed North America, however, agriculture contributes less than 10 percent to emissions in the United
States and Canada; beef production contributes less than 4 percent.[38]
Carbon taxes will add only a little impetus to trends in progress anyway for other reasons: toward eating fewer animals, more humanely
raised. As we reorient from red meat, we'll collect as our reward
the benefits of a less-carnivorous diet: less heart disease, less diabe-
tes, more sex, and fewer antibiotics fed to cows to breed antibiotic-
resistant super bacteria.[39]

More expensive fuel will rebuild our cities in ways that will make
us happier and healthier. After bereavement, divorce, and unemployment, length of commute is the most important predictor of unhappiness in modern life. The most ambitious study—conducted on
twenty-six thousand commuters by a British university—found that
a twenty-minute increase in automobile commute time produces as
much unhappiness as a 19 percent pay cut.[40] People who commute
more by car not only suffer worse health but also face steeper cognitive declines in old age.[41] More expensive fuel will accelerate the
trend—already so strong among the young—toward multipurpose
live-work-play communities. Right now, such communities tend to
be located in old central cities where housing is very expensive: San
Francisco, Manhattan, Brooklyn. But there's no reason that has to
remain true. Crown an old indoor shopping mall with condo towers.
Convert underused stores into bars, restaurants, bowling alleys, and
other forms of fun. Raise low-rise office blocks in the parking lots.
Presto: low-cost live-work-play in former exurbs.

Depressed rural America will find new uses for its land and for its underemployed and alienated people, especially its young men so vulnerable to the fascoid appeal of Donald Trump: wind plantations, solar fields. The employment burst that fracking brought to North Dakota could be replicated on a vaster scale. Already the fastest-growing job category in the United States is solar panel installer. The runner-up: wind turbine technician.[42] (Wind turbine technician is an even more skilled job than solar installer—and pays an average of $10,000 a year more.)

A carbon tax alone will not do the whole job. Between now and the 2070s, we not only have to emit fewer greenhouse gases into the air—we have to pull at least some of them back out.

The Chinese idea of firing particles into the air is a gambler's solution, attractive only because it appears relatively cheap. The United States is a vastly richer and more technologically sophisticated country than China, backed by friends also rich and technologically sophisticated. It can adopt safer, costlier remedies: buying vast tracts of land to plant carbon-fixing tree plantations; growing seaweed forests in coastal waters to slurp carbon dioxide from the seas; and—most ambitious of all—building machines to suck carbon dioxide from the air, compress it into liquid, and then burying it deep underground or beneath the ocean floor where natural pressure will sequester it forever.

Carbon sequestration offers not only an environmental solution but a jobs program for the next generation of Americans, especially those most adrift in the current economy: younger men with less formal education. Now the catch: carbon sequestration will consume enormous amounts of energy. It obviously makes no sense to burn carbon to sequester carbon. Sequestration will require an enormously productive but non-emitting energy source, and at today's level of technology that can only mean nuclear power.

Nuclear energy of course imposes environmental risks of its own. But big problems are solved only by those who can distinguish lesser risks from greater risks—and who will accept the solemn responsibility to choose.

Sequestration will cost a lot of money as well, tens of billions of dollars a year for many, many years. Some of that money can come from carbon taxes, but more will be needed. The one good thing about the incredible wastefulness of American society—spending 18 percent of GDP to buy worse health-care outcomes than most people get for 12 to 14 percent; spending more on defense than the next seven countries combined—is that when Americans really need money for something important, it's obvious where to look for it. The $750 billion a year the United States commits to defense, 3.5 percent of GDP, should be thought of as an insurance premium against external dangers of all kinds, not only classic military threats. The changing climate should be regarded as one of the highest of those threats. James Mattis told the Senate at his 2017 confirmation hearing: "Climate change is impacting stability in areas of the world where our troops are operating today."[43] But under President Trump, the Department of Defense was forbidden to think seriously—or, anyway, publicly—about that threat. The Pentagon's 2019 report on the security effects of climate change considered only an absurdly narrow range of risks, the risk to military facilities and bases from flooding, mudslides, desertification, and so on.[44] So long as Trump is president, this silence will continue. Worse, so long as Trump is president, the US military will invest its resources against the menaces of the past while failing to meet the threats of the future. Trump's adamant refusal to protect the integrity of American elections against foreign cyberattacks may be less a failure of imagination, more a confession of guilt. But his disdain for climate challenges emerges from someplace deep, not only in his own stunted brain but in his party's.

Republicans think of themselves as the party of national security. Yet they are returning to a bad old habit of blinding themselves to contemporary risks. In the 1930s, Republican isolationists insisted that America's mighty battleships would safeguard the nation's coasts, even as Nazi Germany was researching long-range bombers and intercontinental ballistic missiles. Today, Trump-style populists want to build more tanks, aircraft carriers, and fighter-bombers, even as

Russia hacks American elections, China ponders how to blot out the sun, and tens of millions of Africans, Central Americans, and South Asians seek to emigrate from parched farms to the cities of Europe and North America. Building nuclear reactors to sequester carbon is a much more relevant use of defense dollars than building more 1980s-concept weaponry—and people serious about defending the country must say so.

Along the way, they will find they have enhanced American power, not weakened it.

Carbon-taxing America will consume less; carbon-sequestering America will invest more. The two new nuclear reactors being built at Georgia's Vogtle power complex are projected to cost $27.5 billion when complete.[45] The United States will need to build dozens of reactors to power the sequestration project. Granted, a larger, more standardized construction program will have lower unit costs—but the bond issues needed for the energy supply for the future carbon reduction industry will be denominated in the hundreds of billions. Who can even begin to imagine the capital requirements of that future industry itself?

Americans will be induced to consume less, save more. Those two trends together will tend to curtail American imports, especially of consumer products. The trade deficits with Asia will tend to shrink, the currency imbalance with China to right itself. As China pollutes less on behalf of American consumers, China will receive fewer dollars from American consumers. As China is pressured by the carbon tariff to emit less, China's economic activity will turn more inward—and China will find itself spending down its dollar stockpiles to buy food and other necessities from less-polluted and less-polluting countries.

Maybe none of that will alter China's aggressive external behavior. Maybe instead of spending more on its people and its environment, China will continue to build aircraft carriers and fund cyberattacks on US infrastructure and US elections.

If so . . . even shifting as colossal a sum as $100 billion a year from military defense to environmental defense would still leave the United States with a more than 3:1 spending advantage over the Chinese armed forces.[46] And since most Chinese military spending is focused on repressing its own people at home, the American advantage in projectable power would remain that much greater.

A carbon-reversing economy can still be a free-enterprise economy. The Green New Deal's call for more state ownership is perverse. As the grisly history of the Oak Ridge Tennessee nuclear complex should have taught us—thousands of workers left sick and dying from radiation illness—when government acts as an *operator* of potentially hazardous technology, it gives short shrift to its more important role as safety regulator. The public benefits from a slightly adversarial relationship between regulators and regulated. Safety suffers when regulators and regulated both answer to the same boss.

Unlike Ocasio-Cortez, I doubt that very many people who want children really are hesitating because they fear climate apocalypse. But a lot of Americans who want children are finding it difficult to begin because that same indifference to the future at work in the climate debate is also at work in the debate over fertility and child-rearing. The developed world watches the population explosion in the global South as the global North dwindles and wonders, Why should I crimp my lifestyle to preserve a world for others to enjoy after me? Let me live for now; let those others inherit whatever future they inherit. Only when we reconnect Americans and Europeans to posterity will we mobilize them to commit their wealth to preserve this beautiful world for that posterity.

Donald Trump appealed to voters who had lost faith in their country and themselves. "The American dream is dead." Trump is an ill-tempered old man who speaks to and for other ill-tempered old people. For each of us as individual human beings, once we reach a certain age, the future offers us only decline leading to extinction. It's natural for older people to be pessimistic and fearful, especially as families shrink and they have fewer grandchildren to care about. We act for the planet because it will remain home to the people we love even after we are gone.

People who do not feel that love have no tomorrow. Trump loves nobody and has no sense of tomorrow. Like an animal, he lives only in the present. Yet even an animal will avoid fouling the place in which it lives and sleeps. Trump cannot meet even that test. But the rest of us can. We should love our children more, indulge ourselves less. After Trump, that work must begin. That work begins by restoring the world order against which Trump rampaged.

CHAPTER ELEVEN

Great Again

Trump whacked at the world trading system and reviled US alliances. He sought to bust up the European Union and drummed his fingers as South Korea and Japan turned against each other. He betrayed the Kurds and sold out the Ukrainians. North Korea, the Taliban, Russia, and China all stood taller at the end of his presidency, compared to an ever more isolated and distrusted United States. At the beginning of 2020, Trump seemed to be willfully launching a war against Iran.

Trump fantasized that the United States could lead by thuggery. He delighted in narrating imaginary dialogues in which his brute strength forces others into submission. Here's pre-presidential Trump offering insights into how to negotiate with China.

> Somebody said, "What would you do, what can you do?" So easy! I'd drop a 25% tax on China. [Cheers]
>
> I said to somebody that it's really the messenger. The messenger is important. I can have one man say [high effeminate voice], "We're going to tax you 25%"—and I can have another say, [he-man voice; finger pointed like a gun], "Listen you motherfuckers we're going to tax you 25% . . ." [Laughter, loud cheers, applause]
>
> You've said the same exact thing, but it's a different message.[1]

And here he is in July 2018, re-enacting the same fantasy about the European Union, this time at the annual convention of the Veterans of Foreign Wars.

> What the European Union is doing to us is incredible. How bad. They made a $151 billion last year—our trade deficit with the European Union. They sound nice but they're rough. They're all coming in to see me tomorrow. They're all coming to the White House.
>
> I said, "You have to change." They didn't want to change. I said, "Okay. Good. We're going to tariff your cars." They send millions of cars—Mercedes, all of them, BMW. So many cars. I said, "We're going to have to tariff your cars." They said, "When can we show up? When can we be there?"
>
> "Would tomorrow be okay?"
>
> Oh, folks, stick with us. Stick with us. Amazing.[2]

But neither of these performances ended as promised.

Trump's handling of international confrontations is marked by the same consistent approach:

Noisy threats
Preoccupation with image
Maximal goals
Minimal alliances
No apparent strategic plan
No authorization by Congress
Adverse public opinion

It's an approach doomed to failure and humiliation, because its elements contradict each other. Trump would not have had to worry about his lack of public support if he had been willing to act covertly and quietly. *Ooops, the car carrying Iran's top general exploded, how on earth could that have happened?* Trump would not have had to worry about his lack of allies if he had avoided confrontations. Trump's craving for attention would not have done so much harm if he had set more modest goals. But join together Trump's unpopularity, his disdain for Congress, his isolation from allies, his eagerness for "big wins," and his ego needs—and the result was one foreign-policy debacle after another.

Trump's "quarrel with everybody" personality isolated the United States when it needed partners. Thus, Secretary of State Mike Pompeo complained on Fox News about the lack of European endorsement for the targeted killing of General Qassem Soleimani. But after years of anti-European tariffs and tantrums by the Trump administration, the only thing surprising about the European reaction was that Pompeo could be surprised by it.

Trump climbed down from his confrontation with North Korea in 2018, launching himself onto a path of diplomacy as careless as his previous path to war. Trump had ample reasons to climb down from his Iran confrontation, too, including polls that showed 76 percent of Americans (including 63 percent of Republicans) opposed war with Iran.[3] Trump had no plan to change minds, and anyway seems not to have regarded persuasion as part of his job as president. He saw it as his job to issue orders, upon which the army should salute and the public should cheer. But three-quarters opposition frightened even as truculent a personality as Trump's.

Yet there were other powerful forces pulling him forward to conflict. Obama had tilted US policy away from the Sunni Gulf states, toward Iran—so of course Trump had to do the opposite, tilt against Iran and toward the Sunni Gulf states. Many important Trump constituencies favored, if not war against Iran, then at least one more step on the path to war: his Saudi friends, his evangelical voters, his Israeli allies, his most hawkish advisers. Plus, Soleimani had repeatedly taunted Trump personally, in speeches and social media—including posting on his Instagram feed an image of Soleimani standing in front of a burning White House with a walkie-talkie in his hand. After Soleimani ordered an attack on the US embassy in

Baghdad at the end of 2019, Trump tweeted a threat of retaliation. The Ayatollah Khamenei's Twitter account reposted Trump's threat, then superimposed a scornful reply.

> That guy has tweeted that we see Iran responsible for the events in Baghdad & we will respond to Iran. 1st: You can't do anything. 2nd: If you were logical—which you're not—you'd see that your crimes in Iraq, Afghanistan . . . have made nations hate you.[4]

That January 1 tweet seems to have goaded Trump to order the strike on Soleimani. (The Trump administration's claim it acted to thwart an imminent military threat was rapidly exposed as untrue.)

The next president may possibly inherit a Trump war with Iran. What he or she will almost certainly inherit is an Iran that has compared and contrasted Trump's aggression against it—and his deference to North Korea—and has concluded that it must acquire a nuclear bomb. The global coalition against Iran will have slackened under US neglect. The problem faced by Barack Obama in 2009 will re-manifest itself, only now with the US more alone.

But perhaps the worst of Trump's legacy will be not the errors, but the omissions—not the costs, but the lost opportunities.

Trump missed many chances to consolidate the US position in the Islamic world. A remarkable thing happened in the Arab Middle East between 2012 and 2019: an abating of religiosity. The region remains very conservative; prejudice against women, gays, and Jews still seethes. Yet perhaps in reaction to ISIS, perhaps in reaction to the visible corruption of the region's Islamic parties, almost 20 percent of young people from Iraq to Morocco now describe themselves as "not religious," almost double the proportion who said so seven years earlier. An absolute majority of young people in the Arab Middle East would emigrate if they could, according to polls by Arab Barometer, the most ambitious survey of the region.[5] Here was an opportunity to curb extremism and advance modernization. But Trump was the absolute impediment: he was despised in the region. Only 12 percent of Arabs expressed a positive view of him, as compared to a majority who expressed a positive view of Turkish president Recep Erdoğan. Even in countries directly under attack from Iran—Iraq, Jordan, Lebanon, and Yemen—the United States was regarded as virtually equally dangerous as Shiite theocracy. Any chance to redirect the region in more positive directions had been forfeited.

Trump did nothing to help Britain obtain a better deal from the EU. Trump had favored Brexit, and the hardest Brexit possible: not only exit from the Single Market, but from the European Customs Union too. Trump promised a generous US-UK Free Trade Agreement as compensation for a hard Brexit. But Trump did nothing to expedite such a deal. He inveigled a friend into difficulty, then did nothing to help. If anything, Trump seemed intent on exploiting his friend's difficulty for his own advantage: early glimpses of Trump's wish list for the US-UK agreement looked harshly one-sided. Instead of a strong US ally within the EU, Trump idled away the months as the UK staggered into its new status as a midsized economy locked out of the world's trading blocs at a time of rising protectionism.

The Syrian refugee crisis—the biggest since the end of the Second World War—underscored the urgency of coordinated international action to meet migration pressures. The numbers of human beings on the move will only rise in the decades ahead. Many will want to migrate to Europe and North America, but only a comparative few can. Coordinated policy in the developed world offers the best hope for humane but effective policies to settle those allowed to migrate and restrain those who are not allowed. The slowdown in global migration since 2016 offered a respite from crisis, a time to put international institutions and agreements in place. It was squandered by Trump's obnoxious and unsuccessful national egoism.

Perhaps the most spectacular lost opportunity was the opportunity to act cooperatively against transnational corruption. How does the United States urge Ukraine or Pakistan to clean up its act when the US president was kept solvent in the 2000s by the dirty money that flowed into and through his projects? How do we fight nepotism in governments in Africa and the Middle East when the de facto White House chief of staff and de facto secretary of state is the president's son-in-law? How can we speak for integrity in government when the executive branch retaliates against its best employees for refusing to cooperate with the crooked schemes of the president and his so-called personal lawyer? In the words of historian Anne Applebaum:

> Am getting tired of hearing about how "corrupt" Ukraine is. You know which country is corrupt? The United States. We have a president who is using the White House to make money, presidential children who are using their father's prestige to make money.
>
> We have political donors who buy influence, we have legislators who represent private interests, and we have companies who put prominent, unqualified political/military people on their boards to gain credibility. Why was Jim Mattis on the board of Theranos, a scam company?
>
> Also: corruption in places like Ukraine and Russia is facilitated by American banks and by offshore tax havens that exist because the US government tolerates them. And why does the US government tolerate them? Because very wealthy people use them.[6]

Donald Trump supposed US power rested on military hardware and the readiness to use violence. He never understood how much of American power came from other people's idea of America as a land of hope and promise. Secretary of Defense James Mattis told a story of a captured terrorist he had once interrogated. After answering Mattis's questions, the captured terrorist said he had a question in return: If he cooperated with the US forces, could he possibly hope for a visa to the United States? The magnetism is real, even for supposed enemies.

Yet Trump never wanted the United States to lead by example. He never accepted American responsibility for world order. He believed the United States should be a nation among other nations, bigger than most, richer than most, better than none. They kill? We kill. They steal? I steal.

In April 2015, Trump spoke at a conservative political event in Texas. He was still almost two months away from announcing his candidacy for president. The moderator, a prominent local business leader, asked Trump how to restore American exceptionalism. Trump answered (and I'll quote this in full, to show the flow of his thought):

> I don't like the term. I'll be honest with you. People say, "Oh he's not patriotic." Look, if I'm a Russian, or I'm a German, or I'm a person we do business with, why, you know, I don't think it's a very nice term. We're exceptional; you're not. First of all, Germany is eating our lunch. So they say, "Why are you exceptional. We're doing a lot better than you." I never liked the term. And perhaps that's because I don't have a very big ego and I don't need terms like that. Honestly.
>
> When you're doing business—I watch Obama every once in a while saying "American exceptionalism," it's [Trump makes a barf face]. I don't like the term. Because we're dealing— First of all, I want to take everything back from the world that we've given them. We've given them so much. On top of taking it back, I don't want to say, "We're exceptional. We're more exceptional." Because essentially we're saying we're more outstanding than you. "By the way, you've been eating our lunch for the last 20 years, but we're more exceptional than you." I don't like the term. I never liked it.[7]

Trump continued in this vein for some considerable time. It's a fascinating answer. It's an answer that almost conveys a sense of . . . respect for other people. "Because I think you're insulting the world."

Almost. But notice which is the *first* nationality that comes to his mind as one that might be offended by a claim of American exceptionalism: Russia.

And indeed, in a 2014 interview with Jeffrey Lord of the *American Spectator*, Trump clarified the source of his unease with the term *American exceptionalism*. It was, as it is so often, Vladimir Putin.

JL: What does American Exceptionalism mean to you?

DT: Well, I think it's a very dangerous term in one way, because I heard Putin saying, "Who do they think they are, saying they're exceptional?" You can feel you're exceptional, but when you start throwing it in other countries' faces or other people's faces, I actually think it's a very dangerous term to use. Well, I heard that Putin was saying to somebody—you know, I had the Miss Universe contest over in Moscow recently, six months ago, and Putin, by the way, treated us unbelievably well. And it was at that time that Putin said, "Who do they think they are saying they're exceptional?" And I understand that. You know, he said, "Why are they exceptional? They have killings in the streets. Look at what's going on in Chicago and different places. They have all of this turmoil, all of the things that are happening in there."[8]

What Trump was learning from Putin was not humility. It was despair, a gloomy vision of American victimhood that justified American predation: "When I take back the jobs, and when I take back all that money and we get all our stuff . . ."

Trump bequeaths an isolated America. The post-Trump vision must find a way to reintegrate the United States with the world, to inspire the rest of the world without either insulting or humiliating them.

All the democracies together are struggling with the return of illiberal authoritarianism . . . with slowing growth and increasing concentrations of wealth and advantage . . . with the acceleration of global climate change . . . with military threats from rising non-Western powers . . . with migration by tens of millions of people. What the United States, the European Union, the United Kingdom, Japan, Canada, Australia, New Zealand, and other advanced democracies have in common is much more salient and urgent than the different histories that brought them to this point. Even more urgently, their hopes for managing the challenges they face depend on mutual cooperation.

The Chinese economy now very nearly equals that of the United States. China is too big to be bossed about, as Trump discovered to his shock and American national cost. In concert with other like-minded states, however, the United States can write rules of the road that China cannot ignore. That was the point of the Trans-Pacific Partnership negotiated in the Obama years. It is the only hope for managing Chinese power peacefully but effectively in the twenty-first century: cooperation with allies, starting with the world's largest trading bloc, the European Union. Ironically, Trump was correct back in 2015: to insist that America is highest and best only offends partners whose cooperation would help. But Trump was radically wrong in the use he made of his correct observation. He had no interest in gaining friends and allies. He had no interest in winning acceptance of American leadership of a coalition of like-minded democracies. He has weakened America, for all the money he has lavished on weapons of war.

Ironically and perversely, the insistence that the United States is too unique to learn from other countries is becoming one of the greatest impediments to America's continuing leadership of other countries. Because American governments do not heed how other governments control health costs, they squander money and accumulate huge and unnecessary public debts. Because this American administration will not work with others to constrain carbon emissions, it alienates public opinion in the countries that used to admire America most. Because this administration starts simultaneous trade wars not only against China but also against democratic allies, it wrecks the only coalition strong enough to constrain Chinese misconduct. Because this administration yearns for Fortress America, it disregards opportunities to work with partners to speed lawful commerce within the developed world while developing common policies to manage migration from the less-developed world.

Oftentimes in the Bush years, sometimes in the Obama years, you heard people in other countries chafe at American leadership. They expressed many complaints, at least some of them surely valid. In the Trump years, the world has glimpsed its future if and when American leadership fades. It's a terrifying picture. It was not Americans alone who built the better world after World War II. Without Americans, though, it would never have been built at all. Now, as events catch up with Donald Trump, it falls to Americans again—this time working with their friends—to build that world back.

That means reviving trade agreements and recommitting to climate protection, resuming the language of mutual respect, and renewing international cooperation. Wipe the snarl off the American face. Let America be again what its best friends have never given up believing it to be. American generosity, American magnanimity: these are not insignia of suckerhood. These are the resources that have made American leadership acceptable to other strong and rich nations. Looking back on the US-led reconstruction of his country, German chancellor Konrad Adenauer marveled: "Probably for the first time in history, a victorious country held out its hand so that the vanquished might rise again."[9] Sustaining such faith in America has been a high interest of the United States, for reasons both moral and strategic.

Trump renegotiated NAFTA by imposing tariffs on Canada and Mexico and insisting, "Sign here or I blow up your economies." They signed because they had to—and because after all the changes from NAFTA to USMCA were relatively modest: a little more trade protection for American autos; a little less protection for Canadian dairy products (a concession Canada had already made during the negotiation of the Trans-Pacific Partnership). Trump tried the same methods against the more formidable strength of China, this time with even less success.

Republicans accused President Obama of embarking on an international apology tour after his 2009 speech in Cairo attempting to reset the US relationship with the Islamic world.

> I have come here to seek a new beginning between the United States and Muslims around the world; one based upon mutual interest and mutual respect; and one based upon the truth that America and Islam are not exclusive, and need not be in competition. Instead, they overlap, and share common principles—principles of justice and progress; tolerance and the dignity of all human beings.

There was much to question in Obama's approach then, but it sure will be necessary now. Whatever the next president *calls* his or her first round of visits to Canada, Mexico, Germany, and other allies, he or she will most definitely be there to make amends. As new cooperation is required, new modes of cooperation will have to be found. Brazil and Indonesia are potential climate-change superpowers, two nations with the capacity rapidly to entrap carbon by billion-tree reforestation projects: they need to be brought into dialogue at the highest levels with the United States. The US must lead the rewarming of the US-Japan-South Korea triangle after Trump's neglect and worse than neglect. If the US is going to get tough with China, the toughness needs to be embedded in gestures of respect to ensure that inevitable disputes never overwhelm the fundamental message: We are willing to share the planet with you, equal to equal. President Trump announced—and struggled to impose—"a total and complete shutdown of Muslims entering the United States."[10] Some atonement will obviously be necessary after that.

After the fall the Soviet Union, the columnist Charles Krauthammer hailed a "unipolar moment"—a rare opportunity, like that in 1945–1948, for the United States to impose its will on the world:

"The center of world power is the unchallenged superpower, the United States, attended by its Western allies."[11] Krauthammer was wrong then. The US in 1990 produced 25 percent of the planet's output, handsome but nothing like the 50 percent of 1945. Allies like France and reunited Germany were nobody's "attendants." India was already a nuclear power; Pakistan soon would be. An error of observation led to an error of advice: that the most important constraint on the United States was not resistance by objective facts, but a lack of subjective willpower. As Krauthammer also said, "decline is a choice"—the United States could simply *choose* to be as powerful in 1990 as it had been in 1945. Exactly why the British and French had not made this choice after World War II, why the Chinese Empire had not made this choice when barbarians arrived on its shores with opium and guns, why for that matter the Romans had not made it against the Persians, Goths, Huns, and Vandals . . . that was never quite answered.

The claim was all fantasy, and harmful fantasy too. I partook in some elements of the fantasy at the time, and I do not write these words to criticize others more than myself. Yet it is long past time to awake from the fantasy. If nothing else, the Trump experience should have tossed the cold water of reality in the face of even the dreamiest fantasist. The United States can still lead in the twenty-first century, but it must lead by consent—as, in truth, it did in the twentieth century too. It must lead by the glamour and excitement of its example as a country of dynamism, innovation, democracy, and justice. It must lead by demonstrating its capacity for self-renewal.

The faith in America that still inspires America's friends cannot and will not survive a second Trump term. The first term, well, it can be dismissed as a fluke, a mistake, a learning experience. But to do it again? Knowing all that we know? It's on Americans to justify their friends' belief by ensuring that the Trump presidency comes to its deserved crushing end.

CHAPTER TWELVE

Against Revenge

Trump likes to boast of his high approval numbers among Republicans. But the number of such Republicans is shrinking. During the Reagan presidency, about one-third of Americans identified as Republicans. During the Trump presidency, Republican identification has shriveled to between one-fourth and one-fifth of the country.[1] Most of the delegates I met at the 2016 convention expected Trump to lose that election. That was visibly the expectation of the party's donors too. Party conventions are usually awash in lavish celebrations and receptions. Cleveland was the most frugal I have ever attended. The glummest person I met that week was a local lawyer who had served on the host committee that had won the convention for Cleveland. The city had expended tens of millions on security and other improvements to welcome the convention. Local businesses were earning nothing like the hoped-for returns on the city's investment. The restaurants were not crowded, the hotels not sold out.

Nobody likes to lose. But had Trump lost in 2016, his party would have regenerated itself rapidly. Three lost presidential elections in a row—2008, 2012, 2016—concentrate the mind. Something new would have to be tried, and the party could have fruitfully debated what that "something" should be.

During the 2016 campaign, Republicans insisted to each other that a Hillary Clinton presidency would ravage all they held dear. They had to insist it, because otherwise how to justify a vote for a crook like Donald Trump? But once the election lay behind them, they would have noticed that actually President Hillary Clinton would not have been able to do very much they disliked, not with Republicans in control of both houses of Congress and almost two-thirds of the state governments.

As the Clinton administration struggled with the inevitable difficulties of a third consecutive same-party term in the presidency, Republicans could have expanded their coalition among conservative-minded women and members of ethnic minorities. They could have moved forward, expanding their majorities in both houses of Congress in the elections of 2018, readying themselves for a 2020 election where it was the Blue states that were trending Purple.

Most helpfully of all: a Clinton presidency would have spared the party the taint of defending Trump. Republicans could remind new voters born after the year 2000 that their party stalwarts—Ryan and Rubio and Cruz and Graham—had denounced Trump, and either refused to vote for him or voted for him with conspicuous reluctance. The way would have been open to build an ethnically diverse, culturally modern, post-boomer-generation party of markets and enterprise for the twenty-first century.

Under the Trump presidency, instead, the Republican brand has cratered among every group but rural voters, white evangelicals, and white Catholics. Trump won only by a fluke. He won without a popular mandate. He won with clandestine assistance from the Russian intelligence services. He won only after a six-year effort to block African Americans from voting. But win he did—and Republicans for a long time to come will have to reckon with the odium of his presidency.

In the short run, the caper paid off. Under Trump, the Republicans crammed through a gigantic tax cut, bequeathing budget deficits that will constrain any future Democratic administration. They have tightened the conservative grip on the federal judiciary. They have undone environmental regulations and repealed action against climate change.

Then the bill came due, both economic and political.

Democrats won the House of Representatives in 2018 on the strength of the greatest turnout surge in a non–presidential election year since before the First World War. They won because unhappy suburban moderates voted anti-Trump from the top of the ticket to the bottom.

That's how Democrats won congressional districts like Texas's Seventh. This district spans some of the wealthiest areas of Houston. It was won by George H. W. Bush in 1966 and remained Republican through Watergate, through Iran-Contra, through the Clinton impeachment, through the Iraq War, through the 2008 financial crisis—only to go Blue in 2018.

A Democrat won Virginia's Seventh District, formerly held by Eric Cantor, the second-ranking Republican in the House during the Obama administration. Virginia Seventh runs up and down western Richmond, toward Culpeper and Virginia horse country. It voted 53 percent for John McCain despite the crisis in 2008, 57 percent for Romney in 2012, but only 50 percent for Trump in 2016.

Newt Gingrich's former district, Georgia's Sixth, has been Republican since 1978. It delivered 70 percent of its vote to George W. Bush in 2004, 61 percent to Mitt Romney in 2012, a squeaky plurality of 48.3 percent to Trump in 2016. In 2018, the district went Democratic for the first time since 1976. That year, the winning Democrat in Georgia's Sixth had been a staunch segregationist. In 2018, the winning Democrat was a black woman who had lost her son to gun violence.

Indeed, all three of the above winners were women, as were 60 percent of the Democrats who flipped seats from Red to Blue in 2018.[2] In 2017 and 2018, pro-Trump Republicans jeered: "Never Trump is not a political party. It's a dinner party." After 2018, there can be no question that Trump has driven millions of former Republicans to the exits.

Democrats gained seven governorships in 2018. They flipped about 350 state legislative seats. In the elections of 2019, the Republican Party was crushed in Virginia, crushed in suburban and exurban Philadelphia, beaten even in Kentucky.

In 2018, Republicans lost half their US House seats from California. They had fourteen out of fifty-three; they have been reduced to only seven. In that same election, Democrats won sixty of the eighty seats in the state assembly, the biggest majority for any party California has seen in more than a century. And no, this was not the product of some Democratic gerrymander; Democrats won their huge assembly majority by a correspondingly huge margin of the vote: almost 67 percent of all votes cast. They dominate the state senate twenty-seven to thirteen, again on the strength of almost 65 percent of all votes cast. California is more Democratic, as measured by share of the popular vote cast for the state assembly, than Alabama, Nebraska, or South Carolina is Republican. California is the least competitive of the five biggest states, less competitive than Texas or New York, and far less competitive than Florida or Pennsylvania.

But it's not only elections that the Trump Republican Party is losing. The party is losing its place in American culture.

In August 2019, the Trump reelection campaign announced a fundraiser at the East Hampton summer home of New York real estate investor Steve Ross.[3] Ross is an investor in both Equinox gyms and SoulCycle. And both companies were instantly hammered by threats of consumer boycott because of their investor's support for Trump.

Within hours of the announcement of Steve Ross's fundraiser, Equinox and SoulCycle issued statements disavowing the event. "We believe in tolerance and equality, and will always stay true to those values," proclaimed Equinox. "We believe in diversity, inclusion, and equality," read the SoulCycle release. "SoulCycle in no way endorses the political fundraising event being held later this week. SoulCycle has nothing to do with the event and does not support it."

Ross himself felt obliged to release a statement, explaining of President Trump, "While we agree on some issues, we strongly disagree on others, and I have never been bashful about expressing my opinions. I have been, and will continue to be, an outspoken champion of racial equality, inclusion, diversity, public education and environmental sustainability . . ."[4]

Equinox and SoulCycle are prestige brands that sell not only a service but an image: sophisticated, urban, and inclusive. That image is miles away from the Trump image—literally. When I heard the news of the boycotts, I looked up the distance between the nearest Trump rally in 2019 and the nearest Equinox gym. The closest I could find was 148 miles: the distance from Grand Rapids, Michigan, to the posh Detroit suburb of Bloomfield Hills. The runner-up: 178 miles, the distance from Montoursville, Pennsylvania, to Summit, New Jersey.

The imperatives of business in the modern world do not easily accord the message and practice of Trump politics. The 472 counties won by Hillary Clinton in 2016 spanned only a small part of the acreage of the United States, but they produce 64 percent of all US output. The 2,584 counties won by Trump produce only 36 percent of US output. Even in the bright Red state of Texas, Clinton won the counties around Dallas and Houston. Indeed, Clinton won *every* high-output county in the United States except Phoenix's Maricopa County, Tarrant County around Fort Worth, and Suffolk County, the eastern two-thirds of Long Island, New York.[5]

After the election of 2016, Republicans chortled that they now dominated the government of the United States in a way they had not done since the 1920s. But in the 1920s, Republican ascendancy was based in the most dynamic regions of the country. Calvin Coolidge won big in high-technology centers like Rochester, New York, home to the new industry of photography and film development. The Republican ticket in 1924 dominated the centers of the mighty steel industry: Pittsburgh and environs and the vast industrial landscape that stretched from south of Philadelphia up to New York. It won almost North Korean margins of victory in the new automotive belt extending from Detroit up to Flint, Michigan. All told, Coolidge won New York State by 55 percent, Pennsylvania by 65 percent, Michigan by almost 75 percent. The Democrats retreated into their impoverished, reactionary redoubt: the states of the former slaveholding Confederacy.

The Republican map of 2016 could not look more different from the party's map of 1924. Where new products are designed, patents filed, songs composed, science advanced—this is where Republicans are no longer competitive, a weird predicament for a supposed party of enterprise.

The Trump election built political success out of economic failure. A party dependent on the votes of the alienated and the resentful will find itself articulating a message of alienation and resentment. That message will repel the hopeful and optimistic, which in turn will enhance the dependency on the alienated and resentful. The party has become caught in a tightening cycle of self-radicalization— leading ultimately to the Trump presidency. As the Trump party, the GOP becomes even more repulsive to dynamic America.

American political parties are robust beasts. The Democrats bounced back from being on the wrong side of the Civil War, the Republicans from being on the wrong side of the Great Depression. Compared to those epic crises, the Trump presidency would seem an easy thing from which to recover.

But to recover, a party first has to recognize its problems and choose to repair them. That is just what is *not* happening now.

The Trump campaign plan for 2020 is all culture war, all the time. The plan is to leave American elections open to Russian interference, and to suppress minority, youth, and poorer votes wherever possible; it is to raise and spend dark campaign funds on a scale never before seen. It is to hope that a third-party left-wing independent candidacy might cut into the Democratic vote—and so enable Trump to hold on to power via the Electoral College, even in the face of a massive popular-vote defeat. It is a plan that threatens the stability and future of American democracy. Frankly, it's not a plan very likely to work.

Over the course of the Trump presidency, many observers have wondered whether Trump has permanently changed the way politics is done. Won't all politicians rant and rave and shout?

Lie without remorse. Always be polarizing. Speak only to your base. Never admit error. Grab every buck. Conceal every record. Ethics are for schmucks. These are the leadership secrets of Donald J. Trump. The country will not be safe again until these methods are recognized even by Trump's most abject enablers as one-way tickets to political disaster.

The Republican Party carries the nickname "Grand Old Party." It's a strange phrase, since the Republican Party is actually the younger of the two great parties by at least two decades. The title was adopted defiantly at another moment of imminent Republican defeat. The year was 1875, the day was January 14. The speaker was John Logan, one of Grant's favorite generals during the Civil War, now a US senator from Illinois. Republicans had lost badly in the congressional elections of 1874. They were headed to worse trouble in 1876, the election that would restore white supremacy in the former Confederacy. Democrats were in a scornful mood; Republicans, correspondingly downcast. Logan opened by citing a recent report from Louisiana of thirty-five hundred people killed in the state since the end of the war for attempting to exercise their political rights. All were Republicans, most were black. Toward the end of a long speech, Logan said:

> Sir, we have been told that this old craft is rapidly going to pieces; that the angry waves of dissension in the land are lashing against her sides. We are told that she is sinking, sinking, sinking to the bottom of the political ocean. Is that true? Is

it true that this gallant old party, that this gallant old ship that has sailed through troubled seas before is going to be stranded now . . . ?

The speech was applauded at the time, and Logan's phrase soon began to circulate. Along the way, however, it was soon revised from "gallant old party" to "grand old party"—maybe because that second phrase reminded people of the Grand Army of the Republic, an association of Republican-voting war veterans in which Logan also played a great role. The grandeur of the party derived not from its antiquity, but from its association with equal rights and human freedom. That association was sullied and betrayed by the Trump presidency. But as Logan promised, even in dark political trouble, not all is lost.

Even before Donald Trump declared for president, the Republican Party had ceased even to try to represent an American majority. That is why the party was so vulnerable to a Trump. Yet in its ancestry remains much that is precious: enterprise and individuality, markets and freedom, and confidence in American moral purpose and American world leadership.

For forty years, from 1980 to 2020, wealth and power have tended to concentrate in fewer and fewer hands. The United States is probably due for a shift to the left in the 2020s. Whether due or not, the United States is likely to get it—bigger and more enduring than the short spell of united Democratic governance in 2009–2010. Wealth may be taxed more heavily. Labor may be protected more aggressively. Companies and industries may be regulated more intrusively. Social insurance may expand more expensively.

The pendulum of politics always swings, and it usually swings too far. Somebody needs to be there to push it back again. The "conservatism" abused by Donald Trump and his supporters may go out of fashion for a while. But American conservatism contains truths, too, and those truths will in time be rediscovered by people to whom Donald Trump will seem only a sad and squalid figure out of history.

In one term, Trump managed to do immense damage to the world, to the United States, and to his own party—damage that will take a long time to repair, but damage that is not beyond repair. Should there be a second term, however, some things will be wrecked forever—and among those things will be the Republican Party as an institution. The Republican Party enabled Trump's corruption and authoritarianism through four years. It backed him against the most emphatically justified impeachment in US history. Soon it will renominate Trump for president. Its strategy for reelecting him depends on visibly preventing minorities from voting and welcoming foreign interference in US elections. Its most plausible scenario for success is to win the Electoral College against the popular vote for the third time in twenty years. What will be the character of such a political party after such a history? Not a democratic political party, that's for sure. It will have degenerated into a caudillo's personal entourage, a cult of personality that exists to enable and protect the maximum leader. They will not be conservatives; they will be Péronists. And their degradation will degrade the political system in a way that cannot be repaired. No two-party system can remain a democracy unless both parties adhere to democratic values, not just one.

Even the best-intentioned, most public-spirited people had to make deals with the devil to accomplish anything in the Trump years. At first, the compromises might seem modest: some flattery, maybe, or a little lying to cover up some bizarre presidential behavior. Sooner or later, though, the Trump official would find himself or herself in the kind of situation so memorably described by National Security Advisor John Bolton: "I am not part of whatever drug deal Sondland and Mulvaney are cooking up"[6] (referring to EU ambassador Gordon Sondland and chief of staff Mick Mulvaney). But only the very deft or the very lucky will emerge from the Trump administration with altogether clean hands.

Outside the government, many people volunteered to champion Trump's case in the media. They had less power than the insiders.

They will bear even more of the blame because of their greater conspicuousness. Some of them had large personal reputations before they signed up—more or less reluctantly—to the pro-Trump cause. Some of them are—or were—friends of mine.

Why did they do it? Some followed Trump because they saw opportunities for advancement, or because they had families to feed, or because they worried what their friends would think if they did not. Some went along because they did not respect their profession, their audience, or themselves. It was only TV after all, and as presidential adviser Kellyanne Conway self-revealingly remarked in January 2017, "People realize that no one on TV is under oath."[7] The most committed of them volunteered for Trump because—whatever Trump's other faults—he offered them revenge on political or cultural enemies. You don't fight a culture war with the president you want, you fight a culture war with the president you have.

There were Trump defenders in media who tried to preserve some kind of connection to the ethics of journalism. They resolved to tell as much truth as they could, to submit only to the most unavoidable compromises. But they found, as time passed, the compromises accumulated, multiplied, towered, and teetered. Their employers or donors pressed them. Their niche markets rewarded them.

Trump's core supporters were never fooled by him. The DC lobbyists and Beltway operators who profited from the Trump years, the third-tier political hacks who were appointed to top-tier jobs, the Fox News and social media grifters who scammed a living out of cultural resentment, the donors whose taxes dropped by millions: they all accurately perceived Trump's defects as a man and a leader. Trump's defects actually made life easier for them. A more intelligent president would have been harder to manipulate. A more upright president might have calmed the social tensions so lucrative to enflame. Committing to Trump was like investing in Trump henchman Lev Parnas's Fraud Guarantee. What on earth did you expect? They put the warning in writing on the door! And because so many of the core Trump supporters were in on the scam from the start, they will not be troubled to exit the scam when it finally deflates. *I never thought Trump was a real conservative. I always said his tweeting would get him into trouble. I was not pro-Trump; I was anti–media bias.* When support of Trump becomes disadvantageous, his top supporters will erase the memory of their support from their consciousness.[8] Trump keeps faith with nobody, and he has recruited an inner circle as faithless as himself.

But out there in America are tens of millions of people who were not invited into the con. They were duped. Trump duped them by acting on their fears, hatreds, and prejudices. But fear, hatred, and prejudice are innate in almost all human beings. And even if you judge Trump voters negatively, you leave yourself with the question: What to do with them, your fellow Americans?

In the last days of work on this book, I had a long talk with an idealistic and intelligent young Republican—aged only twenty-two—who asked me how I could justify breaking with the most effective party leader since at least Ronald Reagan, and maybe even above and beyond Reagan. He spoke in a tone that I probably had shared at his age: of stark choices between left and right, of certain and eternal doom if the wrong side prevailed even one single time, and of startled surprise that I could not share his perceptions. I answered him only briefly then—I was there to listen, not talk—but here's a longer answer now. The possibilities of the future are shaped always by the decisions of the past. If his elders and leaders succeed now, he will inherit a political system defined not by policy disagreements, but by racial antagonisms. He will inherit a social system from which the idea of "law" means only "jargon we use to get our way and weapons we use to harass our opponents." He will inherit a constitutional system in which that constitution has forfeited its legitimacy because it was abused to impose the wishes of a privileged few upon the permanently disadvantaged many. He will inherit an international system in which the United States wasted trillions of dollars in pursuit of military power—only to discover that its place in the world also depended on the power of the ideals it has jettisoned.

I mentioned before the military extravaganza that Trump summoned to the Washington Mall on the Fourth of July 2019: tanks on the lawn, jets overheard, and a half hour of bluster about America's past victories and present power. Trump's bellicose self-praise reminded me of a caution delivered by the British poet Rudyard Kipling to the strutting military potentates who marched their nations into the apocalypse of the First World War.

> If, drunk with sight of power, we loose
> Wild tongues that have not Thee in awe . . . [9]

No non-American could watch that spectacle at the Lincoln Memorial and feel that America stood for anything good or right or universal. Power worshipped power, for its own sake.

Yet as so often, the bully's boasting betrayed his inner doubts—his haunting fears and midnight worries. Trump insisted on the Mall in 2019:

> We will always be the people who defeated a tyrant, crossed a
> continent, harnessed science, took to the skies, and soared into
> the heavens because we will never forget that we are Americans
> and the future belongs to us.[10]

But of course, that assertion was exactly what has been called into question by Trump's presidency. The people who defeated a tyrant, would they have submitted to a Trump? The people who harnessed science, would they have deferred to Trump's fantasies, conspiracies, and outright lies? The people who crossed a continent, would they sit still for corruption and crime? *Will* Americans always be the people they were? Are Americans that people now?

> For heathen heart that puts her trust
> In reeking tube and iron shard,
> All valiant dust that builds on dust,

And guarding, calls not Thee to guard,
For frantic boast and foolish word—
Thy mercy on Thy People, Lord![11]

The annals of the American role in world history are blotched by errors, hypocrisies, wrongs, and crimes. Power is never wielded innocently in this guilty world. Yet until the advent of Trump, America's strength has again and again extended the shield of protection over the world's freedom and prosperity. By accident of geography, the United States enjoyed a security surplus. It exported that surplus to others, including former enemies like Germany and Japan. With their security provided, other countries could develop along the liberal, democratic, free-trading path consistent with American values and interests.

Trump rejects this generous American tradition. Where brave people stood against authoritarian governments, Trump aligned the United States with the oppressors. He expressed impatience with democratic protesters in Hong Kong, indifference to democratic protesters in China, hatred for Ukrainians building the rule of law in a former Soviet state, outright hostility to civil society groups in Hungary and Poland. Any hope that the United States might stand for something bigger than crass immediate commercial interest faded—and with it faded embattled people's hopes all over the world that somewhere over the horizon their struggles might be reinforced by a power for good.

That hope has sustained people all over this world in dark hours. It has sustained Americans, too, given them faith in themselves at moments of uncertainty. American championing of rights and democracy worldwide sends a moral signal at home, too: *this* is who we are—not the domineering bully as Trump represents us.

It's not possible for anyone who cares for America to accept this. We have to believe this shameful episode will end soon—and that Trump's role in the American story will be to occupy forever the very lowest place on the roster of ex-presidents.

Once he loses his ability to do harm, Trump will be remembered as pathetic and pathological even more than as corrupt and cruel.

Imagine how terrifying it must feel inside the mind of Donald Trump. Throughout his life, he has been tormented by an all-devouring feeling of inadequacy and loneliness. He coped by inventing for himself a personal ideology of his intellect, his success, his sexual irresistibility. He subjected the women and children in his life to the most humiliating dependency, trying to brutalize from them the adulation he craved. He surrounded himself with cringers and toadies. The more they abased themselves to him, the more he despised them. How can he esteem anyone who would be duped by him?

All his rage and resentment spilled from his mouth in hateful speech or was tapped by his fingers into his crazy Twitter feed. But as if under a curse, he could use words only to demean, disparage, defame, and deceive. Pain is all he has, so pain was all he could give.

There's only one thing he trusted: television. He cared about other media, too, especially the front page of the *New York Times*, but he was too distracted to read easily or at any length. Television was his only friend, his only comfort. When his digital friends on Fox News praised him, he felt a rare moment of calm. Some part of him must have remembered that they were only reciting back at him the lies he wrote for them. Ratified by television, his lies seemed true. They comforted him.

But the real world kept inserting itself into his fantasy life. He simply could not do the job of an American president. He did not even understand what the job is. He imagined that a president appears on television, glowers and struts for the cameras, barks orders, and collects adulation. The real job—the grinding work of building coalitions, persuading the public, selecting the least bad option from a menu of grim choices—that job frightened him, when it did not baffle and bore him.

He spent an hour a day trussing himself into a girdle, painting his face like a nineteenth-century canvas, frothing his hair into a fine golden frizz above his head. Then the public day ended, and he returned to his solitary personal quarters to face himself as he is.

Most of his predecessors were comforted in the president's lonely office by the love of a wife and family. Most of them enjoyed the cheerful company of old and trusted friends. Most of them were supported by a faith in God, by a powerful mission, by a bright vision of the future, by a deep emotional connection to the American nation. Some, at the very least, enjoyed the wordless companionship of a cat, a dog, or a horse. Trump relied on none of those things. He loved nobody, and nobody loved him.

Out of office, he will be exposed to the law he defied as president and eluded as a disreputable businessman. His successor will have awkward decisions to make about whether to let the law take its course. Trump's "lock her up" fantasies may prove his own epitaph.

The party that once enabled him will soon disown him. As the sun sets upon him, even his dark shadow will soon fade from sight.

Soon—but not, unfortunately, immediately. Outrage over the Trump presidency has understandably aroused a mood of cultural retaliation in non-Trump America. Non-Trump America is more diffuse than pro-Trump America. Its political strength is discounted by the bias of a political system that weighs some votes more than others. Yet ultimately it is the stronger part of the country, economically and culturally. Non-Trump America can impose its will on Trump America, if non-Trump America pushes hard enough—and post-Trump, there will be those in non-Trump America tempted to try.

Reforms are needed, and this book has tried to suggest some that might make things better. But those reforms will work to stabilize the country only if they are undertaken in the spirit of reconciliation. Agreed, the intentionally bad actors deserve your harshest judgment. But comparatively few of Trump's voters were intentionally bad actors. Most of them were fallible human beings like everybody else. They were deceived by people they trusted. Fox News and Facebook penned them like farmed salmon inside a lagoon of ignorance.

Irresponsible politicians then hauled them flopping into their nets. These Trump voters were not victims, exactly. They could have struggled to overcome their prejudices. They could have sought out better information. They could have made wiser choices. They did grave harm to American democracy. Yet if you are going to hold them accountable for their bad choices, you also should hold yourself accountable for the choices you will make after the political pendulum swings. These are your countrymen. They are not going anywhere.

My very first book, *Dead Right,* published in 1994, warned of the susceptibility of the American conservative movement to someone like Donald Trump.[12] That book observed that the post-Reagan Republican economic message was proving not very popular—and predicted that religiously based social conservatism would fade, as it has. With communism overthrown, nationalism would become the organizing principle of right-of-center politics in the twenty-first century. This tendency was inevitable, it seemed to that younger me, and so a way must be found to manage it. If the cat were not domesticated, it would grow into a tiger.

It's jarring to me now to look back at that book and see endorsements on the back cover from people who would evolve into major figures in both pro- and anti-Trump politics. There's George Will alongside Dinesh D'Souza; Peggy Noonan adjacent to Grover Norquist. The conservative movement of those days combined discordant elements. As conditions changed, those formerly familiar alignments drifted and recombined. Such is the nature of politics and time. Old issues fade; new issues appear. Former allies find themselves at dagger's point; former adversaries forge new alliances.

It's much more likely that George W. Bush and Barack Obama will vote for the same candidate for president in 2020 than it is that George W. Bush and Donald Trump will vote for the same candidate.

The people who most vociferously cheered for Edward Snowden and Julian Assange in the first half of the 2010s made clear they preferred Donald Trump over Hillary Clinton in the second half.

Is anti-vaccination a left-wing or right-wing movement? Hard to say. Who is more anti-Semitic, the far left or the far right? Again, hard to say. Who is more likely to absorb Putin's online propaganda and favor his foreign policy over America's, Bernie bros or MAGA hats? Hard to say once more.

We insist on trying to cram new realities into old categories. The gangster politics of Trump worked in great part because the conservatism that dominated US politics in the 1980s and 1990s lost its relevance to the America of later decades. The inherited political system left a lot of people stranded for meaningful answers at the exact same time that Facebook and YouTube lowered to virtually zero the cost of spreading mass disinformation. Socially disconnected young people, and especially young men, tumbled into their own social anti-knowledge systems, just as their elders were disinformed by Fox and Sinclair. These young men looked online for serious answers to big questions. They, too, often found bigotry and conspiracy theories instead.

Yet even as American conservatism stopped meaning much to people under forty, the need for something *like* conservatism persisted. The psychic impulses that make some "conservative" and others "liberal" arise from the structure of the human brain. Before we are influenced by our environment, we are formed by our nature. These biochemical inclinations predispose us toward "left" or "right," whatever "left" and "right" happen to mean in our society and culture. So long as our local "left" and "right" remain moderate in the substance of their politics—and fair in their methods of competition—our society will bump along the path of progress, sometimes tilting a little that way, sometimes a little this way. But the radicalization of conservative politics after the election of Barack Obama opened a terrifying question. Those brain impulses that incline some of us toward authority and in-group loyalty—what happens to those impulses if they cannot find a decent home? Lacking a responsible, moderate-minded center-right, those inclined to be "conservative" will succumb to more sinister influences. After 2008, the sorcerer's apprentices of the conservative world conjured up demons, intending to control them. But the demons proved too strong for them and knocked them aside, hurling open the door to the sorcerer himself, Donald Trump.

Over the past four years, I have thought and spoken and written about Donald Trump almost more than I can bear. You probably feel the same fatigue. We are all just exhausted with this worthless man: "The worst human being ever to enter the presidency," I tweeted on inauguration day 2017, "and I include all the slaveholders."[13] Andrew Jackson and Andrew Johnson were at least physically brave; James Buchanan, polite and well-informed; John Tyler, an affectionate father; Warren Harding, fun to be around; Richard Nixon, astute and worldly.

We want things to return to normal, back to a world in which we do not have to waste time rebutting demented conspiracy theories and fact-checking farcical lies every single day. We want a government that operates competently and honestly, headed by a president who behaves with dignity and integrity. If we were at risk of under-appreciating the quiet grace of decency, Trump has cured us of that. But after we evict the squatter, we must repair the house he trashed.

Trump became president because millions of fellow Americans felt that a self-satisfied elite had created a pleasant society only for themselves. Millions of other Americans felt disregarded and discarded. They determined to crash their way in, and they wielded Trump as their crowbar to pry open the barriers against them. Trump is a criminal and deserves the penalties of law. Trump's enablers in politics and media are contemptible and deserve the scorn of honest patriots. But Trump's voters are our compatriots. Their fate will determine ours.

You do not beat Trump until you have restored an America that has room for all its people. The resentments that produced Trump will not be assuaged by contempt for the resentful. Reverse prejudice, reverse stereotyping: never mind whether they are right or wrong (they are wrong)—just be aware that they are acids poured upon the connections that bind a democratic society. The social media conversation that taunts men for being men or whites for being white is radicalizing its targets, strengthening the fascoid authoritarianism that the taunters supposedly oppose. Build a world that does not have room for millions of your fellow citizens, and they will burn it down rather than let you enjoy it without them. Maybe you cannot bring everybody along with you—but you still must try, for your own sake as well as theirs.

On the night of his reelection in 1864, President Lincoln received well-wishers on the White House porch. They serenaded him, and he thanked them with a short speech. Who knows what they were expecting to hear, for they cannot have expected what they got. Almost any other human being in that place, on that occasion, would have indulged at least a moment of triumph. Instead, the greatest of presidents, at his pinnacle of success amid the most terrible crisis in American history, issued a plea for forbearance and forgiveness.

What has occurred in this case, must ever recur in similar cases. Human-nature will not change. In any future great national trial, compared with the men of this, we shall have as weak, and as strong; as silly and as wise; as bad and good. Let us, therefore, study the incidents of this, as philosophy to learn wisdom from, and none of them as wrongs to be revenged.

Acknowledgments

My previous book, *Trumpocracy*, erupted in a sudden burst in the first weeks of the Trump administration. This new book was written and rewritten over two years. I long ago lost track of the revisions and rethinkings since Eric Nelson of HarperCollins suggested in the summer of 2018 that I write an "Okay, now what?" book about the world after Trump. I am grateful to his faith and forbearance—and to his tough-love editorial approach: "It's my job to tell you that the chapter didn't work. It's your job to figure out why not and what to do about it."

The other good angel of my authorial career has been my agent at WME, Jay Mandel. I thank him, as does the bursar's office of my youngest daughter's college of choice.

I owe as ever thanks to my colleagues at the *Atlantic*. They built the platform that elevates the voice of all who speak from it. To David Bradley, Jeff Goldberg, Adrienne LaFrance, Don Peck, and Scott Stossel, I am grateful for many kindnesses and much patience. My immediate editor at the magazine, Yoni Appelbaum, has sharpened and clarified my thinking about so many issues through the Trump years.

Geoffrey Kabaservice read an early draft of this book and hauled me out of some dead ends and back onto the main highway. Windsor Mann remembers my work better than I do. He brings the back of the file to the front, while himself sparkling with fresh ideas of his own. He fact-checked the copy and footnotes. If any errors remain, they remain despite his tireless and dedicated efforts. The production team at HarperCollins carefully edited the copy, not an easy job with a writer who habitually types "now" when he means "not" and who amends and revises seemingly finished text until the very final hour.

In many places, this book was improved by the many friends, readers, and journalistic colleagues who share ideas and information on Twitter. Their generous work alerted me to so much that I might otherwise never have seen. I hope I have sometimes returned the favor. Inside this book I have discussed the harm that can be done by social media. They can also enrich our lives and thought.

Finally, and as always: my wife, Danielle. Over ten books, she has inspired, challenged, comforted, delighted, questioned, criticized, and believed. And then after everything, she has applied her fierce and expert editor's pen to perfect a work that would not, could not, exist without her. The first face I see every day has been the last eye on this text. I repeat here the lines Shakespeare wrote with some premonition of what it is like to live in the warmth of the world Danielle makes for those she loves:

> She is mine own,
> And I as rich in having such a jewel
> As twenty seas, if all their sand were pearl,
> The water nectar, and the rocks pure gold.

Endnotes

Introduction

1. Donald Trump, interview with Lester Holt, *NBC Nightly News*, NBC, May 11, 2017. See Ali Vitali and Corky Siemaszko, "Trump Interview with Lester Holt: President Asked Comey If He Was Under Investigation," NBC News, May 11, 2017, https://www .nbcnews.com/news/us-news/trump-reveals-he-asked-comey -whether-he-was-under-investigation-n757821.

2. Donald Trump, interview with George Stephanopoulos, "President Trump: 30 Hours," *20/20*, ABC, June 16, 2019, https://abc.com /shows/2020/episode-guide/2019-06/16-president-trump-30-hours. See "Transcript: ABC News' George Stephanopoulos' Exclusive Interview with President Trump," ABC News, June 16, 2019, https://abcnews.go.com/Politics/transcript-abc-news-george -stephanopoulos-exclusive-interview-president/story?id=63749144.

3. "Trump Talks About His Conversation with Ukraine President, Slams Biden," YouTube video, 8:46, posted by Fox News, September 22, 2019, https://www.youtube.com/watch?v=eltS0vjqGNU.

4. Lauren Fox, "Ryan on Trump's Meetings with Comey: 'He's Just New to This,'" CNN, June 9, 2017, https://edition.cnn.com /2017/06/08/politics/paul-ryan-donald-trump-new-to-this/index .html.

5. David Frum, *Trumpocracy: The Corruption of the American Republic* (New York: HarperCollins, 2018), 206.

6. Brian Tashman, "Tony Perkins Says Gay Rights Advocates Want Anti-Christian Holocaust, Will 'Start Rolling Out the Boxcars,'" Right Wing Watch, June 6, 2014, https://www.rightwingwatch.org /post/tony-perkins-says-gay-rights-advocates-want-anti-christian -holocaust-will-start-rolling-out-the-boxcars/.

Chapter One: The Smash-Up

1. "All Employees, Manufacturing," Federal Reserve Bank of St. Louis, updated November 1, 2019, https://fred.stlouisfed.org/series /MANEMP.

2. "Value Added by Private Industries: Manufacturing as a Percentage of GDP," Federal Reserve Bank of St. Louis, updated October 29, 2019, https://fred.stlouisfed.org/series/VAPGDPMA.

3. Mark Whitehouse, "Trump's Tax Cuts Aren't Doing What They Should," Bloomberg Opinion, April 29, 2019, https://www .bloomberg.com/opinion/articles/2019-04-29/trump-s-tax-cuts -aren-t-leading-to-more-business-investment.

4. Reade Pickert, "U.S. Manufacturing Gauge Contracts for First Time in Three Years," Bloomberg News, September 3, 2019, https://www.bloomberg.com/news/articles/2019-09-03/u-s -manufacturing-contracts-for-first-time-in-three-years.

5. Janet Adamy and Paul Overberg, "Rural America Is the New 'Inner City,'" *Wall Street Journal*, May 26, 2017, https://www.wsj.com /articles/rural-america-is-the-new-inner-city-1495817008.

6. "Highlights from the August 2019 Farm Income Forecast," U.S. Department of Agriculture, last modified August 30, 2019, https:// www.ers.usda.gov/topics/farm-economy/farm-sector-income -finances/highlights-from-the-farm-income-forecast/.

7. Mario Parker and Mike Dorning, "Trump's $28 Billion Bet That Rural America Will Stick with Him," *Bloomberg Businessweek*,

September 19, 2019, https://www.bloomberg.com/news
/articles/2019-09-19/farmers-say-trump-s-28-billion-bailout-isn-t
-a-solution.

8. Mark Muro and Jacob Whiton, "America Has Two Economies—
    and They're Diverging Fast," *Avenue* (blog), Brookings Institution,
    September 19, 2019, https://www.brookings.edu/blog/the
    -avenue/2019/09/10/america-has-two-economies-and-theyre
    -diverging-fast/.

9. Patrick Liu, Ryan Nunn, Jana Parsons, and Jay Shambaugh, "Has
    Job Growth Reached America's Struggling Places?," *Up Front*
    (blog), Brookings Institution, March 7, 2019, https://brookings
    .edu/blog/up-front/2019/03/07/has-job-growth-reached-americas
    -struggling-places.

10. Richard Fry, "For First Time in Modern Era, Living with Parents
    Edges Out Other Living Arrangements for 18- to 34-Year-Olds,"
    Pew Research Center, May 24, 2016, https://www.pewsocialtrends
    .org/2016/05/24/for-first-time-in-modern-era-living-with-parents
    -edges-out-other-living-arrangements-for-18-to-34-year-olds/.

11. Richard Fry, "The Share of Americans Living without a Partner
    Has Increased, Especially among Young Adults," *Fact Tank* (blog),
    Pew Research Center, October 11, 2017, https://www.pewresearch
    .org/fact-tank/2017/10/11/the-share-of-americans-living-without-a
    -partner-has-increased-especially-among-young-adults/.

12. "60% of U.S. Women Say They've Been Sexually Harassed
    Quinnipiac University National Poll Finds; Trump Job Approval
    Still Stuck Below 40%," Quinnipiac University Poll, November 21,
    2017, https://poll.qu.edu/national/release-detail?ReleaseID=2502.

13. Hannah Hartig, "Gender Gap Widens in Views of Government's
    Role—and of Trump," *Fact Tank* (blog), Pew Research Center,
    April 11, 2019, https://www.pewresearch.org/fact-tank/2019/04/11
    /gender-gap-widens-in-views-of-governments-role-and-of-trump/.

14. Robert P. Jones and Daniel Cox, "Hillary Clinton Opens Up a
    Commanding 11-Point Lead over Donald Trump | PRRI/The

Atlantic Survey," Public Religion Research Institute, October 11, 2016, https://www.prri.org/research/prri-atlantic-oct-11-poll -politics-election-clinton-leads-trump/.

15. Robert B. Hudson, "Nostalgia and the Swamp: Aging Politics in the Age of Trump," *Generations*, Winter 2019, https://www.asaging .org/blog/nostalgia-and-swamp-aging-politics-age-trump.

16. David Z. Hambrick and Madeline Marquardt, "Cognitive Ability and Vulnerability to Fake News," *Scientific American*, February 6, 2018, https://www.scientificamerican.com/article/cognitive -ability-and-vulnerability-to-fake-news/; Andrew Guess, Jonathan Nagler, and Joshua Tucker, "Less Than You Think: Prevalence and Predictors of Fake News Dissemination on Facebook," *Science Advances*, January 9, 2019, https://advances.sciencemag.org /content/5/1/eaau4586.

17. Grayson K. Vincent and Victoria A. Velkoff, "The Next Four Decades: The Older Population in the United States: 2010 to 2050," U.S. Census Bureau, May 2010, https://www.census.gov/prod /2010pubs/p25-1138.pdf.

18. Katerina Eva Matsa, "Fewer Americans Rely on TV News; What Type They Watch Varies by Who They Are," *Fact Tank* (blog), Pew Research Center, January 5, 2018, https://www.pewresearch.org /fact-tank/2018/01/05/fewer-americans-rely-on-tv-news-what-type -they-watch-varies-by-who-they-are/.

19. Elisa Shearer and Katerina Eva Matsa, "News Use Across Social Media Platforms 2018," Pew Research Center, September 10, 2018, https://www.journalism.org/2018/09/10/news-use-across-social -media-platforms-2018/.

20. Sean Burch, "Fox News, Ben Shapiro's Daily Wire Dominate Facebook's Most Popular Stories of 2019," the Wrap, March 18, 2019, https://www.thewrap.com/fox-news-ben-shapiro-daily-wire -facebook-most-popular-stories-2019/.

21. Brandy Zadrozny and Ben Collins, "Facebook Bans Ads from the Epoch Times After Huge Pro-Trump Buy," NBC News, August 22,

2019, updated August 26, 2019, https://www.nbcnews.com/tech
/tech-news/epoch-times-begins-hiding-its-connection-huge-pro
-trump-ad-n1045416.

22. Emily Ekins, "The State of Free Speech and Tolerance in America,"
Cato Institute, October 31, 2017, https://www.cato.org/survey
-reports/state-free-speech-tolerance-america.

23. "Bill O'Reilly: The White Establishment Is the Minority—Video,"
Guardian, November 6, 2012, https://www.theguardian.com/world
/video/2012/nov/07/election-2012-bill-oreilly-white-establishment
-minority-video.

24. Robert P. Jones "America's Changing Religious Identity," Public
Religion Research Institute, September 6, 2017, https://www.prri
.org/research/american-religious-landscape-christian-religiously
-unaffiliated/.

25. Daniel Dale, "Fact Check: No, African Americans Are Not Happy
with Trump," CNN, July 30, 2019, https://www.cnn.com/2019/07
/30/politics/fact-check-african-americans-trump-approval/index
.html.

26. "Trump Is Racist, Half of U.S. Voters Say, Quinnipiac University
National Poll Finds; But Voters Say Almost 2-1 Don't Impeach
President," Quinnipiac University Poll, July 30, 2019, https://poll
.qu.edu/national/release-detail?ReleaseID=3636.

27. Megan Brenan, "Americans Feel Generally Positive About Their
Own Finances," Gallup News, April 30, 2019, https://news.gallup
.com/poll/249164/americans-feel-generally-positive-own-finances
.aspx.

28. "Generic Congressional Ballot," Rasmussen Reports, November 5,
2018, http://www.rasmussenreports.com/public_content/politics
/mood_of_america/generic_congressional_ballot_nov05. President
Trump has sometimes tweeted 50 percent numbers generated by
the Rasmussen poll, but Rasmussen habitually screens for "likely"
voters in a way that favors Republicans. This method produces
headlines very appealing to Fox News between elections, but poor

accuracy at elections. Nate Silver has rated Rasmussen consistently the least accurate of the major pollsters.

Rasmussen enjoyed a fleeting triumph in 2016. That year its persistent habit of overestimating white turnout for once paid off. Driven by a surge in voting by white noncollege graduates, white turnout actually increased between 2012 and 2016, something that has not happened in memory: normally the US electorate becomes about slightly less white each election than the election before. Meanwhile, black Americans turned out in unusually low numbers in 2016, 59.6 percent of those eligible, their lowest showing in a presidential election since Gore versus Bush in 2000.

Most pollsters failed to anticipate either the noncollege white voter surge or the black voter drop-off. As a result, almost all of them estimated Hillary Clinton's popular vote margin at anywhere from four to six points ahead of Trump's. Instead, Clinton beat Trump by only two points in the popular vote, which is what Rasmussen almost uniquely predicted.

That sole success allowed Rasmussen (and Trump) two years of bragging rights. But in 2018, past patterns reasserted themselves, and Rasmussen returned to its record of dramatic wrongness.

In their last report before the 2018 midterm election, Rasmussen predicted a generic congressional vote of 46 percent Republican to 45 percent Democrat.

Actual result: 53.1 percent Democrat versus 45.2 percent Republican.

29. Philip Bump, "About 1 in 8 Voters Say Trump Acts in an Unpresidential Way—and Also Approve of His Presidency," *Washington Post*, July 8, 2019, https://www.washingtonpost.com /politics/2019/07/08/about-voters-say-trump-acts-an-unpresidential -way-also-approve-his-presidency/.

30. Donald Trump (@realDonaldTrump), Twitter, January 19, 2019, 7:11 a.m., https://twitter.com/realdonaldtrump/status /1086597047229300737.

31. Trump, Twitter, February 17, 2019, 7:52 a.m., https://twitter.com /realdonaldtrump/status/1097116612279316480.

32. Trump, Twitter, February 24, 2019, 10:02 a.m., https://twitter.com /realdonaldtrump/status/1099685950077222913.

33. Trump, Twitter, June 5, 2019, 4:17 a.m., https://twitter.com/real donaldtrump/status/1136185163971407873.

34. V. S. Naipaul, *The Writer and the World: Essays* (New York: Knopf, 2002; New York: Vintage, 2003), 398.

35. Jonathan Chait, "Trump Is a Snob Who Secretly Despises His Own Supporters," *New York*, August 30, 2018, http://nymag.com /intelligencer/2018/08/coastal-snob-trump-mocks-sessions -alabama-accent-degree.html.

36. Sasha Savitsky, "Melania Trump's Rep Dismisses Anna Wintour Vogue Diss: 'She's Been There, Done That,'" Fox News, April 12, 2019, https://www.foxnews.com/entertainment/melania-trump -anna-wintour-vogue-cnn-first-lady.

37. Evan Sayet, "He Fights," Townhall, July 13, 2017, https://townhall .com/columnists/evansayet/2017/07/13/he-fights-n2354580.

38. Adam Serwer, "The Cruelty Is the Point," *Atlantic*, October 3, 2018, https://www.theatlantic.com/ideas/archive/2018/10/the-cruelty-is -the-point/572104/.

39. U.S. Immigration and Customs Enforcement, "Fiscal Year 2018 ICE Enforcement and Removal Operations Report," https://www.ice .gov/doclib/about/offices/ero/pdf/eroFY2018Report.pdf.

40. Lisa Riordan Seville and Hannah Rappleye, "Trump Admin Ran 'Pilot Program' for Separating Migrant Families in 2017," NBC News, June 29, 2018, https://www.nbcnews.com/storyline /immigration-border-crisis/trump-admin-ran-pilot-program -separating-migrant-families-2017-n887616.

41. Lauren Pearle, "Trump Administration Admits Thousands More Migrant Families May Have Been Separated Than Estimated," ABC News, February 4, 2019, https://abcnews.go.com/US/trump

-administration-unsure-thousands-migrant-families-separated
-originally/story?id=60797633.

42. Nicole Acevedo, "Why Are Migrant Children Dying in U.S. Custody?," NBC News, May 29, 2019, https://www.nbcnews.com /news/latino/why-are-migrant-children-dying-u-s-custody-n1010316.

43. *Meet the Press*, NBC, June 23, 2019. See "President Trump's Full, Unedited Interview with Meet the Press," NBC News, June 23, 2019, https://www.nbcnews.com/politics/meet-the-press/president -trump-s-full-unedited-interview-meet-press-n1020731.

44. Oscar Wilde, *Children in Prison and Other Cruelties of Prison Life* (London, 1898; Project Gutenberg, 2013), http://www.gutenberg .org/files/42104/42104-h/42104-h.htm.

45. William D. Cohen, "'There Is Definite Hanky-Panky Going On': The Fantastically Profitable Mystery of the Trump-Chaos Trades," *Vanity Fair*, October 16, 2019, https://www.vanityfair.com/news /2019/10/the-mystery-of-the-trump-chaos-trades.

46. Robert Frank, "Mar-a-Lago Membership Fee Doubles to $200,000," CNBC, January 25, 2017, https://www.cnbc.com/2017/01/25/mar-a -lago-membership-fee-doubles-to-200000.html.

47. Justin Rohrlich and Dan Kopf, "Republicans Have Spent at Least $4.7 Million at Trump Properties Since He Took Office," Quartz, April 20, 2019, https://qz.com/1597139/republicans-have-spent-at -least-4-7-million-at-trump-properties-since-he-took-office/.

Chapter Two: The Wall of Impunity

1. Kathleen Parker, "Whoever Wins, We'll Be Fine," *Washington Post,* November 6, 2016, https://www.washingtonpost.com /opinions/calm-down-well-be-fine-no-matter-who-wins /2016/11/04/e5ca3c32-a2d3-11e6-a44d-cc2898cfab06_story.html.

2. David Frum, "What the Mueller Report Actually Said," *Atlantic*, May 29, 2019, https://www.theatlantic.com/ideas/archive/2019/05 /mueller/590467/.

3. David Frum, "A Special Prosecutor Is Not the Answer," *Atlantic*, May 14, 2017, https://www.theatlantic.com/politics/archive/2017/05 /a-special-prosecutor-is-not-the-answer/526662/.

4. Robbie Gramer and Amy Mackinnon, "U.S. Ambassador to Ukraine Recalled in 'Political Hit Job,' Lawmakers Say," *Foreign Policy*, May 7, 2019, https://foreignpolicy.com/2019/05/07/us -ambassador-to-ukraine-recalled-in-political-hit-job-lawmakers -say-marie-yovanovitch-lutsenko-right-wing-media-accusations -congress-diplomats-diplomacy/.

5. "Fractured Nation: Widening Partisan Polarization and Key Issues in 2020 Presidential Elections," Public Religion Research Institute, October 20, 2019, https://www.prri.org/research/fractured -nation-widening-partisan-polarization-and-key-issues-in-2020 -presidential-elections/.

6. Andrew Kaczynski, Chris Massie, and Nate McDermott, "Donald Trump to Howard Stern: It's Okay to Call My Daughter a 'Piece of Ass,'" CNN, October 9, 2016, https://www.cnn.com/2016/10/08 /politics/trump-on-howard-stern/index.html.

7. Jason Miller, "Judge Sentences Former GSA Official Jeff Neely to 3 Months in Jail," Federal News Network, July 1, 2015, https:// federalnewsnetwork.com/management/2015/07/judge-sentences -former-gsa-official-neely-3-months-jail/.

8. Eric Lipton and Annie Karni, "Checking In at Trump Hotels, for Kinship (and Maybe Some Sway)," *New York Times*, September 7, 2019, updated October 25, 2019, https://www.nytimes.com/2019 /09/07/us/politics/trump-hotel.html.

9. U.S. Office of Special Counsel, "Report to the President Re Kellyanne Conway Hatch Act," June 13, 2019, https://assets .documentcloud.org/documents/6152218/Report-to-the-President -Re-Kellyanne-Conway.pdf.

10. Peter Baker, "Trump Is Urged to Fire Kellyanne Conway for Hatch Act Violations," *New York Times*, June 13, 2019, https://www .nytimes.com/2019/06/13/us/politics/kellyanne-conway-hatch

-act.html. See "Kellyanne Conway Remarks to Reporters," C-SPAN video, 21:42, May 29, 2019, https://www.c-span.org/video/?461193-1 /kellyanne-conway-defends-president-trumps-criticism-joe-biden.

11. Todd Garvey, "Congress's Contempt Power and the Enforcement of Congressional Subpoenas: Law, History, Practice, and Procedure," Congressional Research Service, May 12, 2017, https://fas.org/sgp /crs/misc/RL34097.pdf.

12. P. J. Meitel, "The Perjury Paradox: The Amazing Under-Enforcement of the Laws Regarding Lying to Congress," Quinnipiac Law Review 25, no. 3 (2007).

13. Todd Ruger, "Cohen Among Select Few Charged with Lying to Congress," Roll Call, November 30, 2018, https://www.rollcall.com /news/politics/cohen-among-select-charged-lying-congress.

14. Nolan D. McCaskill, "Spokesman: Yoho 'Misspoke' When He Said Nunes 'Works for the President,'" Politico, March 30, 2017, https:// www.politico.com/story/2017/03/ted-yoho-misspoke-devin-nunes -works-for-the-president-236705.

Chapter Three: World War Trump

1. David Corn, "Donald Trump Is Completely Obsessed with Revenge," Mother Jones, October 19, 2016, https://www .motherjones.com/politics/2016/10/donald-trump-obsessed-with -revenge/.

2. Donald J. Trump and Bill Zanker, Think BIG and Kick Ass in Business and Life (New York: HarperCollins, 2007), 30.

3. Jonathan Swan, "Axios Sneak Peak," Axios, November 25, 2018, https://www.axios.com/newsletters/axios-sneak-peek-3d9cd027 -b3bb-4276-aaba-6e75c5c5aeee.html.

4. Mark Landler and James Risen, "Trump Finds Reason for the U.S. to Remain in Afghanistan: Minerals," New York Times, July 25, 2017, https://www.nytimes.com/2017/07/25/world/asia/afghanistan -trump-mineral-deposits.html.

5. Dwight D. Eisenhower, "First Inaugural Address," January 20, 1953, Miller Center of Public Affairs, University of Virginia, https://millercenter.org/the-presidency/presidential-speeches /january-20-1953-first-inaugural-address.

6. Bill Clinton, "Remarks by the President to Multinational Audience of Future Leaders of Europe," Brussels, Belgium, January 9, 1994, https://clintonwhitehouse6.archives.gov/1994/01/1994-01-09 -presidents-speech-to-future-european-leaders.html.

7. Cristiano Lima, "Trump Calls Trade Deal 'a Rape of Our Country,'" Politico, June 28, 2016, https://www.politico.com /story/2016/06/donald-trump-trans-pacific-partnership-224916.

8. Donald Trump (@realDonaldTrump), Twitter, March 2, 2018, 5:50 a.m., https://twitter.com/realdonaldtrump/status/9695 25362580484098.

9. Trump, Twitter, June 1, 2019, 6:20 p.m., https://twitter.com /realdonaldtrump/status/1134947966320553986.

10. Niraj Chokshi, "The 100-Plus Times Donald Trump Assured Us That America Is a Laughingstock," *Washington Post*, January 27, 2016, https://www.washingtonpost.com/news/the-fix/wp/2016 /01/27/the-100-plus-times-donald-trump-has-assured-us-the -united-states-is-a-laughingstock/.

11. "Trump: 'The World Laughs at Us,'" YouTube video, 0:25, posted by TPM TV, June 27, 2017, https://www.youtube.com/watch?v=PrTs 8bdVT78.

12. Tamara Keith, "Trump and First Lady Make Secret Trip to Iraq to Visit U.S. Troops," NPR, December 26, 2018, https://www.npr .org/2018/12/26/680057009/trump-and-first-lady-make-secret-trip -to-iraq-to-visit-u-s-troops.

13. Jonathan O'Connell, Joshua Partlow, and David A. Fahrenthold, "Trump Pledged Not to Use His Office to Help His Business. Then He Pitched His Florida Club for the Next G-7," *Washington Post*, August 31, 2019, https://www.washingtonpost.com/politics

/trump-pledged-not-to-use-his-office-to-help-his-business-then
-he-pitched-his-florida-club-for-the-next-g-7/2019/08/30/98b353c0
-ca7b-11e9-be05-f76ac4ec618c_story.html.

14. John Shanahan, "Trump: U.S. Should Stop Paying to Defend Countries
    That Can Protect Selves," Associated Press, September 2, 1987, https://
    apnews.com/05133dbe63ace98766527ec7d16ede08; Donald Trump,
    "There's Nothing Wrong with America's Foreign Defense Policy
    That a Little Backbone Can't Cure," *Washington Post*, September 2,
    1987, A9, https://assets.documentcloud.org/documents/4404425/Ad
    -in-The-Washington-Post-from-Donald-Trump.pdf.

15. "Transcript: Donald Trump Expounds on His Foreign Policy
    Views," *New York Times*, March 26, 2016, https://www.nytimes
    .com/2016/03/27/us/politics/donald-trump-transcript.html.

16. Richard Wike, Bruce Stokes, Jacob Poushter, Laura Silver,
    Janell Fetterolf, and Kat Devlin, "Trump's International Ratings
    Remain Low, Especially among Key Allies," Pew Research Center,
    October 1, 2018, http://www.pewglobal.org/2018/10/01/2-faith-in
    -the-u-s-president-remains-low/.

17. Matthias Gebauer, Christiane Hoffmann, René Pfister, and Gerald
    Traufetter, "German-U.S. Ties Are Breaking Down," Spiegel
    Online, August 21, 2019, https://www.spiegel.de/international
    /germany/inside-the-breakdown-of-ties-between-germany-and-the
    -u-s-a-1282295.html.

18. Trump, Twitter, May 25, 2019, 9:32 p.m., https://twitter.com
    /realdonaldtrump/status/1132459370816708608. This was the
    breathtakingly awful tweet that also approvingly quoted Kim
    Jong-un's as purportedly slurring the intelligence of former Vice
    President Joe "Bidan."

19. See Greg Miller, *The Apprentice: Trump, Russia and the Subversion
    of American Democracy* (New York: Custom House, 2018).

20. Scott Lincicome (@scottlincicome), Twitter, June 12, 2019, 3:12
    p.m., https://twitter.com/scottlincicome/status/113888687775
    3352192.

21. "Transcript: Donald Trump's Foreign Policy Speech," *New York Times*, April 27, 2016, https://www.nytimes.com/2016/04/28/us /politics/transcript-trump-foreign-policy.html.

22. Steve Holland, "Exclusive: Trump Says Clinton Policy on Syria Would Lead to World War Three," Reuters, October 25, 2016, https://www.reuters.com/article/us-usa-election-trump-exclusive /exclusive-trump-says-clinton-policy-on-syria-would-lead-to -world-war-three-idUSKCN12P2PZ.

23. Jill Colvin, "10 Moments from Trump's Iowa Speech," Associated Press, November 13, 2015, https://apnews.com/0b285a3d58c54716 ac8bb8201b14e8ee.

24. "Transcript of the New Hampshire GOP Debate, Annotated," *Washington Post*, February 6, 2016, https://www.washingtonpost .com/news/the-fix/wp/2016/02/06/transcript-of-the-feb-6-gop -debate-annotated/.

25. Tim Hains, "Donald Trump's ISIS Policy: 'Cut Them Off Where They Are Getting Their Wealth . . . Take the Oil,'" RealClearPolitics .com, August 11, 2015, https://www.realclearpolitics.com/video /2015/08/11/donald_trumps_isis_policy_cut_them_off_where _theyre_getting_their_wealth_take_the_oil.html.

26. Peter Baker and Choe Sang-Hun, "Trump Threatens 'Fire and Fury' Against North Korea If It Endangers U.S.," *New York Times*, August 8, 2017, https://www.nytimes.com/2017/08/08/world/asia /north-korea-un-sanctions-nuclear-missile-united-nations.html.

27. Trump, Twitter, May 19, 2019, 4:25 p.m., https://twitter.com /realdonaldtrump/status/1130207891049332737.

28. Trump, Twitter, March 29, 2019, 11:37 a.m., https://twitter.com /realdonaldtrump/status/1111653530316746752; Trump, Twitter, March 29, 2019, 11:43 a.m., https://twitter.com/realdonaldtrump /status/1111655194658508800.

29. Mary Beth Sheridan and Kevin Sieff, "Trump Plans to Cut U.S. Aid to 3 Central American Countries in Fight Over U.S.-Bound

Migrants," *Washington Post*, March 30, 2019, https://www
.washingtonpost.com/world/the_americas/trump-plans
-us-aid-cut-to-3-central-american-countries-as-fight-widens
-over-us-bound-migrants/2019/03/30/d6814b42-52ff-11e9-bdb7
-44f948cc0605_story.html.

30. Katie Rogers, "Trump, Seeking to Put Pressure on Maduro,
Threatens a Full Embargo on Cuba," *New York Times*, April 30,
2019, https://www.nytimes.com/2019/04/30/us/politics/trump
-maduro-cuba.html.

31. Maureen Dowd, "Donald the Dove, Hillary the Hawk," *New York
Times*, April 30, 2016, https://www.nytimes.com/2016/05/01
/opinion/sunday/donald-the-dove-hillary-the-hawk.html.

32. Donald Trump, "Remarks by President Trump to the 73rd
Session of the United Nations General Assembly | New York, NY,"
September 25, 2018, https://www.whitehouse.gov/briefings
-statements/remarks-president-trump-73rd-session-united-nations
-general-assembly-new-york-ny/.

33. Michael R. Pompeo, "Restoring the Role of the Nation-State in the
Liberal International Order," Brussels, Belgium, December 4, 2018,
https://www.state.gov/restoring-the-role-of-the-nation-state-in-the
-liberal-international-order-2/.

34. Cordell Hull, "What America Is Fighting For," Washington, DC,
July 23, 1942, American Rhetoric, https://americanrhetoric.com
/speeches/cordellhullwhatamericaisfightingforspeech.htm.

35. *Larry King Live*, CNN, May 17, 1989. See Andrew Kaczynski and
Jon Sarlin, "Trump in 1989 Central Park Five Interview: 'Maybe
Hate Is What We Need,'" CNN, October 10, 2016, https://www
.cnn.com/2016/10/07/politics/trump-larry-king-central-park-five
/index.html. The interview concerned the full-page ads Trump
had bought in New York newspapers to demand the death penalty
for five black youths arrested for the brutal rape of a white woman
jogging in Central Park. The story of the Central Park Five, as
they became known, is a complicated one. Their sentences would
ultimately be vacated. Another man confessed to the crime,

and DNA evidence supported him. The youths' sentences were vacated, and in 2014 the city would pay $41 million to settle their claims. But a 2002 independent investigation by the city produced strong evidence that the youths were part of a group of thirty boys and men who had committed a series of robberies and assaults in the park in the evening of April 19, 1989. The independent investigation concluded that if the convicted young men had not committed the rape, they were accessories to it. The 2014 settlement remains very controversial with city officials convinced that they would have won the case had it gone to trial.

36. Alex Pappas, "Trump, in Fox News Interview, Says of Kim Jong Un: 'We Understand Each Other,'" Fox News, June 13, 2018, https:// www.foxnews.com/politics/trump-in-fox-news-interview-says-of -kim-jong-un-we-understand-each-other.

37. Josh Dawsey, "In Post Interview, Trump Calls Saudi Crown Prince Mohammed a 'Strong Person' Who 'Truly Loves His Country,'" *Washington Post*, October 20, 2018, https://www.washington post.com/politics/in-post-interview-trump-calls-saudi-crown -prince-mohammed-a-strong-person-who-truly-loves-his -country/2018/10/20/1eda48c0-d4d5-11e8-b2d2-f397227b43f0 _story.html.

38. "Transcript: Donald Trump on NATO, Turkey's Coup Attempt and the World," *New York Times*, July 21, 2016, https://www.nytimes .com/2016/07/22/us/politics/donald-trump-foreign-policy -interview.html.

39. Donald Trump, interview with Bill O'Reilly, *The O'Reilly Factor*, Fox News, September 29, 2015.

40. Abby Phillip, "O'Reilly Told Trump That Putin Is a Killer. Trump's Reply: 'You Think Our Country Is So Innocent?,'" *Washington Post*, February 4, 2017, https://www.washingtonpost.com/news /post-politics/wp/2017/02/04/oreilly-told-trump-that-putin-is-a -killer-trumps-reply-you-think-our-countrys-so-innocent/.

41. Pappas, "Trump, in a Fox News Interview."

42. Jeremy Diamond, "Trump Praises Saddam Hussein's Efficient Killing of 'Terrorists,' Calls Today's Iraq 'Harvard for Terrorism,'" CNN, July 6, 2016, https://www.cnn.com/2016/07/05/politics /donald-trump-saddam-hussein-iraq-terrorism/index.html.

43. "Playboy Interview: Donald Trump," *Playboy*, March 1990, https:// www.playboy.com/read/playboy-interview-donald-trump-1990.

44. Donald Trump, "Remarks by President Trump to the People of Poland," July 6, 2017, https://www.whitehouse.gov/briefings -statements/remarks-president-trump-people-poland/.

45. Ronald Reagan, "Radio Address to the Nation on the Canadian Elections and Free Trade," November 26, 1988, Ronald Reagan Presidential Library, https://www.reaganlibrary.gov/research /speeches/112688a.

Chapter Four: White Terror

1. Jenna Johnson, "Donald Trump Seems to Connect President Obama to Orlando Shooting," *Washington Post*, June 13, 2016, https://www .washingtonpost.com/news/post-politics/wp/2016/06/13/donald-trump -suggests-president-obama-was-involved-with-orlando-shooting/.

2. Ibid.

3. Lisa Marie Pane, "US Mass Killings Hit New High in 2019, Most Were Shootings," Associated Press, December 23, 2019, https:// apnews.com/4441ae68d14e61b64110db44f906af92.

4. Alex Amend, "Analyzing a Terrorist's Social Media Manifesto: The Pittsburgh Synagogue Shooter's Posts on Gab," Southern Poverty Law Center, October 28, 2018, https://www.splcenter.org /hatewatch/2018/10/28/analyzing-terrorists-social-media -manifesto-pittsburgh-synagogue-shooters-posts-gab.

5. Jessica McBride, "Robert Bowers: See Squirrel Hill Suspect's Social Media," Heavy.com, October 27, 2018, https://heavy.com /news/2018/10/robert-bowers-social-media-rob-gab/.

6. Anti-Defamation League, "Murder and Extremism in the United States in 2018," January 2019, https://www.adl.org/murder-and -extremism-2018.

7. Donald Trump (@realDonaldTrump), Twitter, August 11, 2018, 9:26 a.m., https://twitter.com/realdonaldtrump/status/102827 1447632957441.

8. Trump, Twitter, September 29, 2019, 9:11 p.m., https://twitter.com /realdonaldtrump/status/1178477539653771264.

9. @Oathkeepers, Twitter, September 30, 2019, 1:59 a.m., https:// twitter.com/oathkeepers/status/1178549790847590400.

10. Alexander Marlow, Matthew Boyle, Amanda House, and Charlie Spiering, "Exclusive—President Donald Trump: Paul Ryan Blocked Subpoenas of Democrats," Breitbart, March 13, 2019, https://www .breitbart.com/politics/2019/03/12/exclusive-trump-on-campus -free-speech-executive-order-were-going-to-do-a-very-big-number -probably-next-week/.

11. "Trump: 'They're So Lucky That We're Peaceful,'" YouTube video, 2:47, posted by AP Archive, September 26, 2018, https:// www.youtube.com/watch?v=XfgwfCNOqfY. For full speech, see "President Trump Rally in Missouri," C-SPAN video, 1:14:37, September 21, 2018, https://www.c-span.org/video/?451691-1 /president-trump-campaigns-missouri-senate-candidate-josh -hawley.

12. Cydney Hargis, "New NRA Ad Warns Trump Opponents 'Will Perish in the Political Flames of Their Own Fires,'" Media Matters for America, October 20, 2017, https://www.mediamatters.org /blog/2017/10/20/new-nra-ad-warns-trump-opponents-will-perish -political-flames-their-own-fires/218283.

13. William S. Smith, "The Civil War on America's Horizon," *American Conservative*, September 11, 2018, https://www.the americanconservative.com/articles/the-civil-war-on-americas -horizon/.

14. David Neiwert, "Milo Announces His Intent to Lead the Next Civil War," Crooks and Liars, May 21, 2019, https://crooksandliars.com /2019/05/milo-announces-his-intent-lead-next-civil.

15. "Dana Loesch: We're Coming for You New York Times," YouTube video, 0:53, posted by NRATV, https://www.youtube.com/watch ?v=AGa-GoILV9Y.

16. Steve Holland, "Trump Says Media Uses Bomb Case to Score Political Points Against Him," Reuters, October 26, 2018, https:// www.reuters.com/article/us-usa-packages-trump-rally/trump-says -media-uses-pipe-bomb-case-to-score-political-points-against-him -idUSKCN1N02Y3.

17. John Wagner, "Trump Says He 'Wouldn't Be Surprised' If Unfounded Conspiracy Theory about George Soros Funding Caravan Is True," *Washington Post*, November 1, 2018, https:// www.washingtonpost.com/politics/trump-wouldnt-be-surprised-if -democratic-megadonor-george-soros-is-funding-the-migrant-cara van/2018/11/01/9ea196a0-ddcf-11e8-85df-7a6b4d25cfbb_story.html.

18. John E. Lewis, "Animal Rights Extremism and Ecoterrorism," Testimony Before the Senate Judiciary Committee, May 18, 2004, https://archives.fbi.gov/archives/news/testimony/animal-rights -extremism-and-ecoterrorism.

19. Federal Bureau of Investigation, *Hate Crime Statistics, 2002* (Washington, DC: U.S. Department of Justice, 2003), https://ucr .fbi.gov/hate-crime/2002.

20. "Tucker: Why Question US Obligations to Montenegro," YouTube video, 4:38, posted by Fox News, July 18, 2018, https://www.youtube .com/watch?v=OXoVv2cGRoI.

21. "Tucker: Russian Collusion Is Not a Real Story," YouTube video, 9:54, posted by Fox News, December 2, 2019, https://www.youtube .com/watch?v=Dfc_QEY4NQg.

22. Trudy Ring, "Evangelist Franklin Graham Loves Putin's Antigay Policies," *Advocate*, November 3, 2015, https://www.advocate.com

/world/2015/11/03/evangelist-franklin-graham-loves-putins
-antigay-policies.

23. Christopher Caldwell, "How to Think about Vladimir Putin,"
    Imprimis, March 2017, https://imprimis.hillsdale.edu/how-to
    -think-about-vladimir-putin/4/.

24. Eugene Scott, "One of Trump's Most Vocal Black Supporters
    Seemed to Defend Hitler in a Recent Speech," *Washington Post*,
    February 8, 2019, https://www.washingtonpost.com/politics
    /2019/02/08/one-trumps-most-vocal-black-supporters-seemed
    -defend-hitler-recent-speech/.

25. Anthony Faiola and Marina Lopes, "How Jair Bolsonaro Entranced
    Brazil's Minorities—While Also Insulting Them," *Washington Post*,
    October 24, 2018, https://www.washingtonpost.com/world/the
    _americas/how-jair-bolsonaro-entranced-brazils-minorities
    --while-also-insulting-them/2018/10/23/a44485a4-d3b6-11e8-a4db
    -184311d27129_story.html.

26. Weiyi Cai and Simone Landon, "Attacks by White Extremists Are
    Growing. So Are Their Connections," *New York Times*, April 3,
    2019, https://www.nytimes.com/interactive/2019/04/03/world
    /white-extremist-terrorism-christchurch.html.

27. Catherine Thompson, "Trump Lets His Followers Know 'Hillary
    Clinton Can't Satisfy Her Husband,'" Talking Points Memo, April
    17, 2015, https://talkingpointsmemo.com/livewire/donald-trump
    -hillary-cant-satisfy-america.

28. Glenn Kessler, "Trump's Claim That Clinton Lacks the 'Physical
    Stamina' to Be President," *Washington Post*, August 18, 2016,
    https://www.washingtonpost.com/news/fact-checker/wp/2016
    /08/18/trumps-claim-that-clinton-lacks-the-physical-stamina-to
    -be-president/.

29. Angela Giuffrida, "Italy May Scrap Vaccine Certificates for Young
    Children," *Guardian*, April 1, 2019, https://www.theguardian.com
    /world/2019/apr/01/italy-may-scrap-vaccine-certificates-for-young
    -children-five-star-matteo-salvini.

30. Harald Franzen, "Are Right-Wing Populists a Threat to European Climate Policy?," DW, May 16, 2019, https://www.dw.com/en/are -right-wing-populists-a-threat-to-european-climate-policy /a-48764969.

31. Jason Samenow, "Trump Taps AccuWeather CEO to Head NOAA, Breaking with Precedent of Nominating Scientists," *Washington Post*, October 12, 2017, https://www.washingtonpost.com/news /capital-weather-gang/wp/2017/10/12/trump-taps-barry-myers -accuweather-ceo-to-head-noaa-choice-seen-as-controversial/.

32. Chia-Yi Hou, "Trump Issues Executive Order That Could Reduce Scientific Advice," *Scientist*, July 17, 2019, https://www.the-scientist .com/news-opinion/trump-issues-executive-order-that-could -reduce-scientific-advice-66015.

33. Milan Kundera, *The Book of Laughter and Forgetting*, trans. Aaron Asher (New York: Perennial Classics, 1999), 4.

34. Donald Trump, "Remarks by President Trump at the Veterans of Foreign Wars of the United States National Convention | Kansas City, MO," July 24, 2018, https://www.whitehouse.gov/briefings -statements/remarks-president-trump-veterans-foreign-wars -united-states-national-convention-kansas-city-mo/.

35. Caitlin Oprysko, "Trump on Russia Dispute: 'Ultimately I'm Always Right,'" Politico, June 12, 2019, https://www.politico.com /story/2019/06/12/trump-russia-venezuela-1362383.

36. Tom Balmforth, "Putin Backs Venezuela Talks Rejected by Opposition Leader," Reuters, September 25, 2019, https://www .reuters.com/places/russia/article/us-russia-venezuela-dialogue /putin-backs-venezuela-talks-rejected-by-opposition-leader -idUSKBN1WA0ZE.

37. Brittany Shammas, Seung Min Kim, and Mike DeBonis, "Trump Allies Attack Loyalty of Impeachment Inquiry Witness Because He Was Born in Ukraine," *Washington Post*, October 29, 2019, https:// www.washingtonpost.com/politics/2019/10/29/trump-allies-attack -loyalty-impeachment-inquiry-witness-because-he-was-born-ukraine/.

38. Michael Kruse, "'I Need Loyalty,'" *Politico Magazine*, March/April 2018, https://www.politico.com/magazine/story/2018/03/06/donald -trump-loyalty-staff-217227.

39. Andrew Kirell, "White House Press Secretary: Those 'Against' Trump Deserve to Be Called 'Human Scum,'" Daily Beast, October 24, 2019, https://www.thedailybeast.com/white-house-press-secretary-grisham -those-against-trump-deserve-to-be-called-human-scum.

40. "German Pro-Immigration Mayors Get Death Threats," BBC News, June 20, 2019, https://www.bbc.com/news/world-europe -48703302.

41. Franklin D. Roosevelt, "Fireside Chat," April 14, 1938, American Presidency Project, https://www.presidency.ucsb.edu/documents /fireside-chat-15.

Chapter Five: "Real" versus "Unreal" Americans

1. In 2004, I shared a TV panel with Gore Vidal, who asserted that elections in the nineteenth century were more honest than those today. I replied that I could not fathom an American historical novelist knowing so little of American history.

2. Donald Trump, interview with Chris Wallace, *Fox News Sunday*, Fox News, December 11, 2016.

3. Donald Trump (@realDonaldTrump), Twitter, November 27, 2016, 3:30 p.m., https://twitter.com/realdonaldtrump/status/802972944 532209664.

4. Dan Crenshaw (@DanCrenshawTX), August 31, 2019, 3:30 p.m., https://twitter.com/DanCrenshawTX/status/1167882388380123137.

5. Paul Ryan, "The Path to Prosperity," American Enterprise Institute, Washington, DC, April 5, 2011, https://www.aei.org/research -products/speech/the-path-to-prosperity/.

6. David Bahnsen, "Every Single Thing Is Now Different: The Kavanaugh Moment Is Not Done. It Is Just Beginning," October 8,

2018, https://www.davidbahnsen.com/index.php/2018/10/08
/every-single-thing-is-now-different-the-kavanaugh-moment
-is-not-done-it-is-just-beginning/, cited by Rush Limbaugh, *Rush
Limbaugh Show*, October 9, 2018, https://www.rushlimbaugh.com
/daily/2018/10/09/we-must-understand-what-were-up-against
-because-this-is-new/; "Rush Limbaugh Cites David Bahnsen—
October 9, 2018," YouTube video, 4:55, posted by "The Bahnsen
Group—Your elite financial concierge," October 9, 2018, https://
www.youtube.com/watch?v=_wPnMz9T_sw.

7. Mollie Hemingway, "GOP Has a Choice: Fight Anti-Trump Coup
    Effort or Surrender Government to Democrats," Federalist,
    October 25, 2019, https://thefederalist.com/2019/10/25/gop-has
    -a-choice-fight-anti-trump-coup-effort-or-surrender
    -government-to-democrats/.

8. Joshua Caplan, "Glenn Beck: 'We Are Officially at the End of the
    Country' If Trump Loses 2020," Breitbart, March 19, 2019, https://
    www.breitbart.com/the-media/2019/03/19/glenn-beck-we-are
    -officially-at-the-end-of-the-country-if-trump-loses-2020/

9. Sarah Sanders, "Press Briefing by Press Secretary Sarah Sanders,"
    October 29, 2018, https://www.whitehouse.gov/briefings
    -statements/press-briefing-press-secretary-sarah-sanders-102918/.

10. Peter Thiel, "The Education of a Libertarian," Cato Unbound, April 13,
    2009, https://www.cato-unbound.org/2009/04/13/peter-thiel
    /education-libertarian.

11. Ari Berman, "The Courts Won't End Gerrymandering. Eric Holder
    Has a Plan to Fix It Without Them," *Mother Jones*, July/August 2019,
    https://www.motherjones.com/politics/2019/07/the-courts-wont
    -end-gerrymandering-eric-holder-has-a-plan-to-fix-it-without-them/.

12. Scott Walker (@ScottWalker), Twitter, June 27, 2019, 5:03 p.m.,
    https://twitter.com/ScottWalker/status/1144350611506438144.

13. Ben Nadler, "Voting Rights Become a Flashpoint in Georgia
    Governor's Race," Associated Press, October 9, 2018, https://
    apnews.com/fb011f39af3b40518b572c8cce6e906c.

14. George W. Bush, "President Bush Signs Voting Rights Act Reauthorization and Amendments Act of 2006," July 27, 2006, https://georgewbush-whitehouse.archives.gov/news/releases /2006/07/20060727.html.

15. Rob Arthur, "EXCLUSIVE: Trump's Justice Department Is Investigating 60% Fewer Civil Rights Cases Than Obama's," *Vice News*, March 6, 2019, https://news.vice.com/en_us/article/bjq37m /exclusive-trumps-justice-department-is-investigating-60-fewer -civil-rights-cases-than-obamas.

16. Katie Benner, "Trump's Justice Department Redefines Whose Civil Rights to Protect," *New York Times*, September 3, 2018, https://www .nytimes.com/2018/09/03/us/politics/civil-rights-justice-department.html.

17. Kelli Ward (@kelliwardaz), Twitter, November 6, 2019, 10:14 p.m., https://twitter.com/kelliwardaz/status/1192279093909192704.

18. Harvey C. Mansfield, "Why Donald Trump Is No Gentleman," *Wall Street Journal*, July 29, 2016, https://www.wsj.com/articles /why-donald-trump-is-no-gentleman-1469831003.

19. Thomas Gibbons-Neff, "'Nobody Really Cares': In This Ohio Town, Trump and Russia Aren't Really on the Radar," *Washington Post*, March 8, 2017, https://www.washingtonpost.com/news/post-nation /wp/2017/03/08/nobody-really-cares-in-this-ohio-town-trump-and -russia-arent-really-on-the-radar/.

20. Trip Gabriel, "In Iowa, Trump Voters Are Unfazed by Controversies," *New York Times*, January 12, 2017, https://www .nytimes.com/2017/01/12/us/donald-trump-iowa-conservatives.html.

21. Jessica Glenza, "Trump Supporters in the Heartland Fear Being Left Behind by GOP Health Plan," *Guardian*, March 12, 2017, https://www.theguardian.com/us-news/2017/mar/12/republican -healthcare-trump-pence-medicaid-indiana.

22. Tim Reid, "In Trump's Ohio Bastion, Supporters Dismiss Uproar over Donald Jr.," Reuters, July 12, 2017, https://www.reuters.com /article/us-usa-trump-russia-ohio-idUSKBN19X2TN.

23. Martin Savidge, Tristan Smith, and Emanuella Grinberg, "What Trump Supporters Think of Family Separations at the Border," CNN, June 19, 2018, https://www.cnn.com/2018/06/19/us/trump -voters-family-separation/index.html.

24. Ashton Pittman, "'It's All Fake': In Trump's Heartland, Talk of White House Chaos Rings Hollow," *Guardian*, September 9, 2018, https://www.theguardian.com/us-news/2018/sep/09/trump -supporters-mississippi-white-house-op-ed-woodward.

25. Peggy Lee, "Luzerne County Voters React to Impeachment Inquiry Launched Against President Trump," WNEP, September 25, 2019, https://wnep.com/2019/09/25/luzerne-county-voters-react-to -impeachment-inquiry-launched-against-president-trump/.

26. Glenn Beck, "We Surround Them," April 2, 2009, https://www .glennbeck.com/content/articles/article/198/21018/.

27. Rick Newman, "Some Republicans Approve of Russia's Help in Elections," Yahoo Finance, July 31, 2018, https://finance.yahoo.com /news/republicans-want-russia-influence-us-elections-202847050 .html.

28. "Support for Impeachment Grows Quinnipiac University National Poll Finds; Majority of Voters Approve of Impeachment Inquiry," Quinnipiac University Poll, September 30, 2019, https://poll.qu.edu /national/release-detail?ReleaseID=3642.

29. Tim Alberta, *American Carnage: On the Front Lines of the Republican Civil War and the Rise of President Trump* (New York: HarperCollins, 2019), 350.

Chapter Six: The Deep State Lie

1. Byron Tau and Natalie Andrews, "Comey Tells House Panel He Suspected Giuliani Was Leaking FBI Information to Media," *Wall Street Journal*, December 8, 2018, https://www.wsj.com/articles /comey-tells-house-panel-he-suspected-giuliani-was-leaking-fbi -information-to-media-1544322346.

2. Hillary Rodham Clinton, *What Happened* (New York: Simon & Schuster, 2017), 406.

3. Robert O'Harrow Jr., "Trump's Ties to an Informant and FBI Agent Reveal His Mode of Operation," *Washington Post*, September 17, 2016, https://www.washingtonpost.com/investigations /trumps-ties-to-an-informant-and-fbi-agent-reveal-his-modes -of-operation/2016/09/16/6e65522e-6f9f-11e6-9705-23e51a2f424d _story.html.

4. Bob Woodward, *Fear: Trump in the White House* (New York: Simon & Schuster, 2018), 147.

5. Michael D. Shear and Julie Hirschfeld Davis, "Shoot Migrants' Legs, Build Alligator Moat: Behind Trump's Ideas for Border," *New York Times*, October 1, 2019, updated October 2, 2019, https://www .nytimes.com/2019/10/01/us/politics/trump-border-wars.html.

6. Angelique Chrisafis, "Macron Pulls Out All the Stops on Bastille Day as Trump Leaves Satisfied," *Guardian*, July 14, 2017, https:// www.theguardian.com/world/2017/jul/14/macron-pulls-out-all -stops-bastille-day-parade-trump-france.

7. Amanda Macias, "Trump's Military Parade Is Now Estimated to Cost $92 Million—$80 Million More Than Earlier Estimate," CNBC, August 16, 2018, updated July 3, 2019, https://www.cnbc .com/2018/08/16/trump-military-parade-expected-to-cost-80 -million-more-than-estimated.html.

8. Leo Shane III, "Military Times Poll: What You Really Think About Trump," *Military Times*, October 23, 2017, https://www .militarytimes.com/news/pentagon-congress/2017/10/23/military -times-poll-what-you-really-think-about-trump/.

9. @USNavyCNO, Twitter, August 12, 2017, 8:31 p.m., https://twitter .com/USNavyCNO/status/896529683508015104.

10. @CMC_MarineCorps, Twitter, August 15, 2017, 6:51 p.m., https:// twitter.com/CMC_MarineCorps/status/897591648007446529.

11. @ArmyChiefStaff, Twitter, August 16, 2017, 4:50 a.m., https://
twitter.com/ArmyChiefStaff/status/897742317897093121.

12. Dave Goldfein (@GenDaveGoldfein), Twitter, August 16, 2017,
10:01 a.m., https://twitter.com/GenDaveGoldfein/status
/897820707727577089.

13. Joseph Lengyel (@ChiefNGB), Twitter, August 16, 2017, 11:27 a.m.,
https://twitter.com/ChiefNGB/status/897842312704917505.

14. "U.S Army W.T.F! moments" (usawtfm), "Defense Secretary Mattis
Impromptu Speech," Facebook, August 24, 2017, https://www
.facebook.com/usawtfm/videos/10155815797353606.

15. Leo Shane III, "Half of Active-Duty Service Members Are Unhappy
with Trump, New Military Times Poll Shows," *Military Times*,
December 17, 2019, https://www.militarytimes.com/news
/pentagon-congress/2019/12/17/half-of-active-duty-service
-members-are-unhappy-with-trump-new-military-times-poll
-shows/.

16. Nicole Gaouette, "Trump Hikes Price Tag for US Forces in Korea
Almost 400% as Seoul Questions Alliance," CNN, updated
November 15, 2019, https://www.cnn.com/2019/11/14/politics
/trump-south-korea-troops-price-hike/index.html.

17. Merrit Kennedy, "Pentagon Says U.S. Troop Position in Syria
Came Under Fire from Turkish Incursion," NPR, October 11, 2019,
https://www.npr.org/2019/10/11/769293935/u-s-officials-slam
-turkish-incursion-into-syria-that-has-displaced-70-000-people.

18. Joseph Votel and Elizabeth Dent, "The Danger of Abandoning Our
Partners," *Atlantic*, October 8, 2019, https://www.theatlantic.com
/politics/archive/2019/10/danger-abandoning-our-partners/599632/.

19. Karen DeYoung, Dan Lamothe, Missy Ryan, and Michael
Birnbaum, "Trump Decided to Leave Troops in Syria After
Conversations About Oil, Officials Say," *Washington Post*,
October 25, 2019, https://www.washingtonpost.com/world
/us-defense-secretary-mark-esper-says-us-will-leave-forces-in

-syria-to-defend-oil-fields-from-islamic-state/2019/10/25/fd131f1a
-f723-11e9-829d-87b12c2f85dd_story.html.

20. Eric Schmitt and Helene Cooper, "Hundreds of U.S. Troops
Leaving, and Also Arriving in, Syria," *New York Times*, October 30,
2019, https://www.nytimes.com/2019/10/30/world/middleeast/us
-troops-syria-trump.html.

21. Eric Schmitt, Helene Cooper, and Julian E. Barnes, "Trump's Syria
Troop Withdrawal Complicated Plans for al-Baghdadi Raid," *New
York Times*, October 27, 2019, https://www.nytimes.com/2019
/10/27/us/politics/baghdadi-isis-leader-trump.html.

22. Wesley Morgan, "General Won't Confirm Trump's Description of
Baghdadi's Death," Politico, October 30, 2019, https://www.politico
.com/news/2019/10/30/mckenzie-baghdadi-death-062318.

23. Greg Jaffe, John Hudson, and Philip Rucker, "Trump, a Reluctant
Hawk, Has Battled His Top Aides on Russia and Lost," *Washington
Post*, April 15, 2018, https://www.washingtonpost.com/world
/national-security/trump-a-reluctant-hawk-has-battled-his-top
-aides-on-russia-and-lost/2018/04/15/a91e850a-3f1b-11e8-974f
-aacd97698cef_story.html.

24. "Mattis Mocks Trump's Bone Spurs During Al Smith Dinner
Speech," YouTube video, 16:44, posted by CNN, October 17, 2019,
https://www.youtube.com/watch?v=g_sG7N7pJ6g.

25. "Sebastian Gorka: Gen. James Mattis Is 'Un-American' for
Criticizing Trump and He Should 'Act Like a Bloody Marine,'"
Media Matters for America, October 18, 2019, https://www
.mediamatters.org/sebastian-gorka/sebastian-gorka-gen-james
-mattis-un-american-criticizing-trump-and-he-should-act.

26. See Thomas Philippon, *The Great Reversal: How America Gave Up
on Free Markets* (Cambridge: Belknap Press), 2019.

27. Aaron Flaaen and Justin Pierce, "Disentangling the Effects of the
2018-2019 Tariffs on a Globally Connected U.S. Manufacturing
Sector," Finance and Economics Discussion Series 2019-086

(Washington: Board of Governors of the Federal Reserve System, 2019), https://www.federalreserve.gov/econres/feds/files/2019086 pap.pdf.

28. Jesse Drucker and Jim Tankersley, "How Big Companies Won New Tax Breaks from the Trump Administration," *New York Times*, December 30, 2019, https://www.nytimes.com/2019/12/30 /business/trump-tax-cuts-beat-gilti.html.

Chapter Seven: How to Lose to Trump

1. Barack Obama, *The Audacity of Hope: Thoughts on Reclaiming the American Dream* (New York: Crown, 2006), 266.

2. Katharine Q. Seelye, "Clinton Now Against Licenses for Illegal Immigrants," *Caucus* (blog), *New York Times*, November 14, 2007, https://thecaucus.blogs.nytimes.com/2007/11/14/clinton-now -against-licenses-for-illegal-immigrants/.

3. Jack Crowe, "Every Dem on Debate Stage Endorses Publicly Funded Health Care for Illegal Immigrants," National Review Online, June 28, 2019, https://www.nationalreview.com/news /every-dem-on-debate-stage-endorses-publicly-funded-health-care -for-illegal-immigrants/.

4. Donald Trump (@realDonaldTrump), Twitter, June 27, 2019, 9:37 p.m., https://twitter.com/realdonaldtrump/status/11444194107292 42625.

5. "NPR/PBS NewsHour/Marist Poll Results & Analysis," Marist Poll, July 23, 2019, http://maristpoll.marist.edu/npr-pbs-newshour -marist-poll-results-analysis-6/.

6. Zach Goldberg, "America's White Saviors," *Tablet*, June 5, 2019, https://www.tabletmag.com/jewish-news-and-politics/284875 /americas-white-saviors.

7. Elizabeth Warren (@ewarren), Twitter, August 29, 2019, 12:50 p.m., https://twitter.com/ewarren/status/1167117415857238016.

8. "Biden Bounces Back as Harris Slumps among U.S. Dems, Quinnipiac University National Poll Finds; 54 Percent of All U.S. Voters Say Never Trump," Quinnipiac University Poll, July 29, 2019, https://poll.qu.edu/national/release-detail?ReleaseID=3635.

9. "American Voters Still Want to See Trump's Tax Returns, Quinnipiac University National Poll Finds; Approval Dips Back Below 40 Percent," Quinnipiac University Poll, February 21, 2018, https://poll.qu.edu/national/release-detail?ReleaseID=2522.

10. "Exit Polls," CNN, accessed November 9, 2019, https://www.cnn.com/election/2018/exit-polls.

11. Hannah Hartig, "Gender Gap Widens in Views of Government's Role—and of Trump," *Fact Tank* (blog), Pew Research Center, April 11, 2019, https://www.pewresearch.org/fact-tank/2019/04/11/gender-gap-widens-in-views-of-governments-role-and-of-trump/.

12. Domenico Montanaro, "Poll: Most Americans Want to See Congress Pass Gun Restrictions," NPR, September 10, 2019, https://www.npr.org/2019/09/10/759193047/poll-most-americans-want-to-see-congress-pass-gun-restrictions.

13. Kathy Frankovic, "After Kavanaugh Hearings, Americans Believe Blasey Ford," YouGov, October 3, 2018, https://today.yougov.com/topics/politics/articles-reports/2018/10/03/after-kavanaugh-hearings-americans-believe-blasey-.

14. Julie Baumgold, "Fighting Back," *New York*, November 9, 1992, 43.

15. Reuters/Ipsos/UVA Center for Politics Race Poll, August 8, 2018, http://www.centerforpolitics.org/crystalball/wp-content/uploads/2018/08/2018_Reuters_UVA_Ipsos_Race_Poll_8_8_2018.pdf.

16. NPR/PBS NewsHour/Marist Poll, December 19, 2018, http://maristpoll.marist.edu/wp-content/uploads/2018/12/NPR_PBS-NewsHour_Marist-Poll_USA-NOS-and-Tables_Civility_1812051719.pdf#page=3. See also Yascha Mounk, "Americans Strongly Dislike PC Culture," *Atlantic*, October 10,

2018, https://www.theatlantic.com/ideas/archive/2018/10/large-majorities-dislike-political-correctness/572581/.

17. NPR/PBS NewsHour/Marist Poll, December 19, 2018.

18. "Winthrop Poll Southern Focus Survey Reveals Black and White Divide," Winthrop Poll, January 24, 2019, https://www.winthrop.edu/news-events/winthrop-poll-southern-focus-survey-reveals-black-and-white-divide.aspx.

19. Nate Cohn, "Huge Turnout Is Expected in 2020. So Which Party Would Benefit?," *New York Times*, July 15, 2019, https://www.nytimes.com/2019/07/15/upshot/2020-election-turnout-analysis.html.

20. Sally Goldenberg and Alex Thompson, "Warren, in NYC Rally, Casts Campaign as Successor to Other Women-Led Movements," Politico, September 16, 2019, https://www.politico.com/story/2019/09/16/warren-women-new-york-1499570.

21. Jim Tankersley, "Trump's Washing Machine Tariffs Stung Consumers While Lifting Corporate Profits," *New York Times*, April 21, 2019, https://www.nytimes.com/2019/04/21/business/trump-tariffs-washing-machines.html.

22. Deena Shanker, "Del Monte CEO Says Tariffs Driving Up Price of Canned Fruits, Vegetables," Bloomberg News, May 16, 2019, https://www.bloomberg.com/news/articles/2019-05-16/tariffs-spark-an-inflationary-environment-del-monte-ceo-says.

23. Danielle Kurtzleben, "Here's How Many Bernie Sanders Supporters Ultimately Voted for Trump," NPR, August 24, 2017, https://www.npr.org/2017/08/24/545812242/1-in-10-sanders-primary-voters-ended-up-supporting-trump-survey-finds.

Chapter Eight: Unrigging the System

1. Alyssa Milano (@alyssa_milano), Twitter, October 15, 2017, 4:21 p.m., https://twitter.com/alyssa_milano/status/919659438700670976.

2. "Attitudes on Same-Sex Marriage," Pew Research Center, May 14, 2019, https://www.pewforum.org/fact-sheet/changing-attitudes-on -gay-marriage/.

3. Alexander Burns, "Warren Leads Tight Iowa Race as Biden Fades, Poll Finds," *New York Times*, November 1, 2019, https://www .nytimes.com/2019/11/01/us/politics/iowa-poll-warren-biden.html.

4. Mitch McConnell, "The Filibuster Plays a Crucial Role in Our Constitutional Order," *New York Times*, August 22, 2019, https:// www.nytimes.com/2019/08/22/opinion/mitch-mcconnell-senate -filibuster.html.

5. Richard Borean, "Monday Map: Federal Aid as a Percentage of State General Revenue," Tax Foundation, June 18, 2013, https:// taxfoundation.org/monday-map-federal-aid-percentage-state -general-revenue.

6. Devlin Barrett, Matt Zapotosky, Carol D. Leonnig, and Shane Harris, "Trump Offered Ukrainian President Justice Dept. Help in an Investigation of Biden, Memo Shows," *Washington Post*, September 26, 2019, https://www.washingtonpost.com/national -security/transcript-of-trumps-call-with-ukrainian-president -shows-him-offering-us-assistance-for-biden-investigation /2019/09/25/16aa36ca-df0f-11e9-8dc8-498eabc129a0_story.html.

7. David Shortell and Jeremy Herb, "Senate Confirms Justice Department Nominee with Ties to Russian Bank," CNN, July 11, 2018, https://www.cnn.com/2018/07/11/politics/brian-benczkowski -confirmed-senate-justice-department/index.html.

8. Charlie Savage and Adam Goldman, "Justice Dept. Nominee Says He Once Represented Russian Bank," *New York Times*, July 24, 2017, https://www.nytimes.com/2017/07/24/us/politics/brian -benczkowski-justice-alfa-bank.html.

Chapter Nine: Uniting "Us" and "Them"

1. Frank Newport, "Top Issues for Voters: Healthcare, Economy, Immigration," Gallup News, November 2, 2018, https://news.gallup

.com/poll/244367/top-issues-voters-healthcare-economy
-immigration.aspx.

2. Megan Brenan, "American Pride Hits New Low; Few Proud of
    Political System," Gallup News, July 2, 2019, https://news.gallup
    .com/poll/259841/american-pride-hits-new-low-few-proud
    -political-system.aspx.

3. Rob Picheta, "Spain to Lead Japan in Global Life Expectancy, US
    Continues to Slide," CNN, October 18, 2018, https://www.cnn
    .com/2018/10/17/health/life-expectancy-forecasts-study-intl/index
    .html.

4. Tom Miles, "China Overtakes U.S. for Healthy Lifespan: WHO
    Data," Reuters, March 30, 2018, https://www.reuters.com/article
    /us-health-lifespan/china-overtakes-u-s-for-healthy-lifespan-who
    -data-idUSKCN1IV15L.

5. Anna Wilde Mathews, "Cost of Employer-Provided Health
    Coverage Passes $20,000 a Year," Wall Street Journal, September 25,
    2019, https://www.wsj.com/articles/cost-of-employer-provided
    -health-coverage-passes-20-000-a-year-11569429000.

6. Organization for Economic Cooperation and Development, "Self-
    Employment Rate," September 18, 2019, accessed November 12,
    2019, https://data.oecd.org/emp/self employment-rate.htm.

7. Douglas Webber, "Higher Ed, Lower Spending," Education Next 18,
    no. 3 (Summer 2018), https://www.educationnext.org/higher-ed
    -lower-spending-as-states-cut-back-where-has-money-gone/.

8. Kim Christensen, "Is UC Spending Too Little on Teaching, Too
    Much on Administration?," Los Angeles Times, October 17, 2015,
    https://www.latimes.com/local/education/la-me-uc-spending
    -20151011-story.html.

9. Steven A. Camarota, "Facts on Immigration and Health
    Insurance," Center for Immigration Studies, August 30, 2009,
    https://cis.org/Fact-Sheet/Facts-Immigration-and-Health
    -Insurance.

10. The discussion in the previous four paragraphs recapitulates material previously presented in *Trumpocracy*.

11. Daniel J. Willis, John Fensterwald, Yuxuan Xie, Matt Levin, and John Osborn D'Agostino, "States in Motion," EdSource, updated November 14, 2018, https://edsource.org/2015/states-in-motion -school-finance-naep-child-poverty/83303.

12. "Public School Enrollment, by Race/Ethnicity," Kidsdata, accessed November 10, 2019, https://www.kidsdata.org/topic/36/public schoolenrollment-race/table.

13. Willis et al., "States in Motion."

14. Ibid.

15. Winston S. Churchill, "A Tribute to the Physicians," Royal College of Physicians, London, England, March 2, 1944, in Winston S. Churchill, *The Dawn of Liberation* (Boston: Little, Brown, and Company, 1945), 31.

16. Foundation for a Healthy Kentucky and Interact for Health, "More Kentucky Adults Feel Favorable Rather Than Unfavorable about ACA," Kentucky Health Issues Poll 2018, December 2018, https:// www.healthy-ky.org/res/images/resources/KHIPACA_FINAL.pdf.

17. Matt Broaddus, "Research Note: Medicaid Enrollment Decline Among Adults and Children Too Large to Be Explained by Falling Unemployment," Center on Budget and Policy Priorities, July 17, 2019, https://www.cbpp.org/research/health/medicaid-enrollment -decline-among-adults-and-children-too-large-to-be-explained-by.

18. Jordan Misra, "Voter Turnout Rates Among All Voting Age and Major Racial and Ethnic Groups Were Higher Than in 2014," U.S. Census Bureau, April 23, 2019, last modified July 16, 2019, https:// www.census.gov/library/stories/2019/04/behind-2018-united -states-midterm-election-turnout.html.

19. Grace Sparks, "Majority Say Migrants in Caravan Should Be Given the Opportunity to Enter the Country," CNN, November 19, 2018,

https://www.cnn.com/2018/11/19/politics/migrants-poll/index
.html.

20. Luther Gulick, "Memorandum on Conference with FDR
Concerning Social Security Taxation, Summer, 1941," FDR
Presidential Library, as reproduced in Larry DeWitt, "Luther
Gulick Memorandum re: Famous FDR Quote," Research Note #23,
Social Security History, July 21, 2005, https://www.ssa.gov/history
/Gulick.html.

21. William H. Frey, "The US Will Become 'Minority White' in 2045,
Census Projects," *Avenue* (blog), Brookings Institution, March 14,
2018, updated September 10, 2018, https://www.brookings.edu
/blog/the-avenue/2018/03/14/the-us-will-become-minority-white
-in-2045-census-projects/.

22. Jefferson Cowie, *The Great Exception: The New Deal and the Limits
of American Politics* (Princeton, NJ: Princeton University Press,
2016), 9.

23. Jeffrey S. Passel and D'Vera Cohn, "Mexicans Decline to Less
Than Half the U.S. Unauthorized Immigrant Population for the
First Time," *Fact Tank* (blog), Pew Research Center, June 12, 2019,
https://www.pewresearch.org/fact-tank/2019/06/12/us
-unauthorized-immigrant-population-2017/; Jynnah Radford,
"Key Findings about U.S. Immigrants," *Fact Tank* (blog), Pew
Research Center, June 17, 2019, https://www.pewresearch.org/fact
-tank/2019/06/17/key-findings-about-u-s-immigrants/; Mohammad M.
Fazel-Zarandi, Jonathan S. Feinstein, and Edward H. Kaplan,
"The Number of Undocumented Immigrants in the United States:
Estimates Based on Demographic Modeling with Data from
1990 to 2016," *PLOS One* 13, no. 9 (September 21, 2018), https://
doi.org/10.1371/journal.pone.0201193; Office of Immigration
Statistics, *Population Estimates: Illegal Alien Population Residing
in the United States: January 2015*, U.S. Department of Homeland
Security, December 2018, 3, https://www.dhs.gov/sites/default/files
/publications/18_1214_PLCY_pops-est-report.pdf.

24. Shannon McConville, Laura Hill, Iwunze Ugo, and Joseph Hayes,
"Health Coverage and Care for Undocumented Immigrants,"

Public Policy Institute of California, November 2015, https://www
.ppic.org/publication/health-coverage-and-care-for-undocumented
-immigrants/.

25. Theodore Roosevelt, speech, Cairo, Illinois, October 3, 1907, in
Theodore Roosevelt, *Presidential Addresses and State Papers:
January 16, 1907 to October 25, 1907*, vol. 6 (New York: Review of
Reviews Company, 1910), 321.

Chapter Ten: Greener Planet, Better Jobs

1. Hannah Arendt, *The Origins of Totalitarianism* (Orlando, FL:
Harcourt, 1973), 446.

2. Nicole Goodkind, "Alexandria Ocasio-Cortez Asks: Is It Still OK
to Have Kids in Face of Climate Change?," *Newsweek*, February 25,
2019, https://www.newsweek.com/alexandria-ocasio-cortez-aoc
-climate-change-have-kids-children-1342853.

3. Lyman Stone, "How Big Is the Fertility Gap in America?," Medium,
October 5, 2017, https://medium.com/migration-issues/how-big-is
-the-fertility-gap-in-america-fd205e9d1a35.

4. OECD Family Database, "Ideal and Actual Number of Children,"
updated December 17, 2016, http://www.oecd.org/els/family
/SF_2_2-Ideal-actual-number-children.pdf.

5. Eunjung Jee, Joya Misra, and Marta Murray-Close, "Motherhood
Penalties in the U.S., 1986–2014," Washington Center for
Equitable Growth, March 2018, http://equitablegrowth.org
/wp-content/uploads/2018/03/0313018-WP-motherhood-penalties
.pdf.

6. Dennis Prager, "If You Can't Sell Your Hysteria to Adults, Try
Kids," National Review Online, September 24, 2019, https://www
.nationalreview.com/2019/09/american-left-climate-change
-hysteria-kids/.

7. John Nolte (@NolteNC), Twitter, September 23, 2019, 1:22 p.m.,
https://twitter.com/noltenc/status/1176185011776761857.

8. Erick Erickson, "The Left's Abusive Use of Greta Thunberg," Resurgent, August 30, 2019, https://theresurgent.com/2019/08/30/the-lefts-abusive-use-of-greta-thunberg/.

9. Josh Hammer, "HAMMER: Using Children to Advance Your Political Agenda Isn't Just Wrong. It's Evil," Daily Wire, September 24, 2019, https://www.dailywire.com/news/hammer-using-children-advance-your-political-josh-hammer.

10. Brendan O'Neill, "The Cult of Greta Thunberg," Spiked, April 22, 2019, https://www.spiked-online.com/2019/04/22/the-cult-of-greta-thunberg/.

11. Donald Trump (@realDonaldTrump), Twitter, September 23, 2019, 11:36 p.m., https://twitter.com/realdonaldtrump/status/1176339522113679360.

12. "Glenn Beck: From Nudge to Shove," Fox News, September 28, 2010, updated January 14, 2015, https://www.foxnews.com/story/glenn-beck-from-nudge-to-shove.

13. W. E. B. Du Bois, *The Souls of Black Folk* (Chicago: A.C. McClurg, 1903), 1.

14. Charlie Nash, "Rep. Matt Gaetz Mocks Media as 'Kale and Quinoa' Eaters Who Look Down Upon 'Fried Food' Eating 'Real America,'" *Mediate*, November 7, 2019, https://www.mediaite.com/tv/rep-matt-gaetz-mocks-media-as-kale-and-quinoa-eaters-who-look-down-upon-fried-food-eating-real-americans/.

15. See Charles Moore, "From Blue to Green," chap. 13 in *Margaret Thatcher: Herself Alone; The Authorized Biography* (New York: Knopf, 2019).

16. Eric Pianin and Amy Goldstein, "Bush Drops a Call for Emissions Cuts," *Washington Post*, March 14, 2001, https://www.washingtonpost.com/archive/politics/2001/03/14/bush-drops-a-call-for-emissions-cuts/cbfe9644-0586-4cff-93a9-66446e4c07bd/.

17. I wrote some of the speeches they unsuccessfully pressed President Bush to deliver on the subject

18. Zeke Hausfather, "Analysis: Global CO2 Emissions Set to Rise 2% in 2017 After Three-Year 'Plateau,'" Carbon Brief, November 13, 2017, https://www.carbonbrief.org/analysis-global-co2 -emissions-set-to-rise-2-percent-in-2017-following-three-year -plateau.

19. Paul Gilding, *Climate Emergency Defined: What Is a Climate Emergency and Does the Evidence Justify One?* (Melbourne, Australia: Breakthrough, September 2019), 26, https://52a87f3e -7945-4bb1-abbf-9aa66cd4e93e.filesusr.com/ugd/148cb0_3be3bfab 3f3a489cb9bd69e42ce22e7c.pdf.

20. "This Changes Everything—The Book," This Changes Everything, accessed November 13, 2019, https://thischangeseverything.org /book/.

21. "Transcript: The First Night of the Second Democratic Debate," *Washington Post*, July 30, 2019, https://www.washingtonpost.com /politics/2019/07/31/transcript-first-night-second-democratic -debate/.

22. Recognizing the duty of the federal government to create a Green New Deal, H. Res. 109, 116th Cong. (2019), https://www.congress .gov/bill/116th-congress/house-resolution/109/text.

23. "Billion-Dollar Weather and Climate Disasters: Overview," NOAA National Centers for Environmental Information, accessed November 13, 2019, https://www.ncdc.noaa.gov/billions/.

24. Zoë Schlanger, "The World Is Stuck with Decades of New Plastic It Can't Recycle," *Quartz*, November 4, 2019, https://qz.com/1738706 /the-futility-of-recycling-most-plastic/.

25. See Geoffrey Parker, *Global Crisis: War, Climate Change and Catastrophe in the Seventeenth Century* (New Haven, CT: Yale University Press, 2013).

26. Joshua Hammer, "Is a Lack of Water to Blame for the Conflict in Syria?," *Smithsonian Magazine*, June 2013, https://www .smithsonianmag.com/innovation/is-a-lack-of-water-to-blame-for -the-conflict-in-syria-72513729/.

27. Mechanism and Impacts of Geoengineering, accessed November 13, 2019, http://www.china-geoengineering.org.

28. Aditya Nalam, Govindasamy Bala, and Angshuman Modak, "Effects of Arctic Geoengineering on Precipitation in the Tropical Monsoon Regions," *Climate Dynamics* 50, nos. 9 and 10 (May 2018): 3375–95, https://doi.org/10.1007/s00382-017-3810-y.

29. Jeremy Diamond, "Trump: 'We Can't Continue to Allow China to Rape Our Country,'" CNN, May 2, 2016, https://www.cnn .com/2016/05/01/politics/donald-trump-china-rape/index.html.

30. "Donald Trump: 'Somebody's Doing the Raping' (CNN Interview with Don Lemon)," YouTube video, 1:59, posted by CNN, July 1, 2015, https://www.youtube.com/watch?v=2O6Nmx _kZMQ.

31. Trump, Twitter, November 9, 2017, 6:39 p.m., https://twitter.com /realdonaldtrump/status/928769154345324544.

32. Christopher Joyce, "Where Will Your Plastic Trash Go Now That China Doesn't Want It?," NPR, March 13, 2019, https://www.npr .org/sections/goatsandsoda/2019/03/13/702501726/where-will-your -plastic-trash-go-now-that-china-doesnt-want-it.

33. Henrik Selin and Rebecca Cowing, "Cargo Ships Are Emitting Boatloads of Carbon, and Nobody Wants to Take the Blame," Conversation, December 18, 2018, https://theconversation.com /cargo-ships-are-emitting-boatloads-of-carbon-and-nobody-wants -to-take-the-blame-108731.

34. "GDP Based on PPP, Share of World," IMF Data Mapper, World Economic Outlook (October 2019), accessed November 12, 2019, https://www.imf.org/external/datamapper/PPPSH@WEO /WEOWORLD/IND/CHN.

35. World Integrated Trade Solution, accessed November 22, 2019, https://wits.worldbank.org/Default.aspx.

36. National Chicken Council, "Per Capita Consumption of Poultry and Livestock, 1960 to Forecast 2020, in Pounds," updated September 24, 2019, https://www.nationalchickencouncil.org /about-the-industry/statistics/per-capita-consumption-of-poultry -and-livestock-1965-to-estimated-2012-in-pounds/.

37. Food and Agriculture Organization of the United Nations, *Tackling Climate Change Through Livestock: A Global Assessment of Emissions and Mitigation Opportunities*, Rome, 2013, xii, http:// www.fao.org/3/i3437e/i3437e.pdf.

38. Georgina Gustin, "As Beef Comes Under Fire for Climate Impacts, the Industry Fights Back," *Inside Climate News*, October 21, 2019, https://insideclimatenews.org/news/17102019/climate-change -meat-beef-dairy-methane-emissions-california.

39. See Michael Pollan, *The Omnivore's Dilemma: A Natural History of Four Meals* (New York: Penguin, 2006), 72–84.

40. Ben Clark, Kiron Chatterjee, Adam Martin, and Adrian Davis, "How Commuting Affects Subjective Wellbeing," *Transportation*, March 11, 2019, https://doi.org/10.1007/s11116-019-09983-9.

41. Kishan Bakrania, Charlotte L. Edwardson, Kamlesh Khunti, Stephan Bandelow, Melanie J. Davies, and Thomas Yates, "Associations Between Sedentary Behaviors and Cognitive Function: Cross-Sectional and Prospective Findings from the UK Biobank," *American Journal of Epidemiology* 187, no. 3 (March 2018): 441–54, https://doi.org/10.1093/aje/kwx273.

42. Bureau of Labor Statistics, "Fastest Growing Occupations," Occupational Outlook Handbook, U.S. Department of Labor, last modified September 4, 2019, accessed November 13, 2019, https:// www.bls.gov/ooh/fastest-growing.htm.

43. Andrew Revkin, "Trump's Defense Secretary Cites Climate Change as National Security Challenge," ProPublica, March 14, 2017,

https://www.propublica.org/article/trumps-defense-secretary-cites
-climate-change-national-security-challenge.

44. Office of the Under Secretary for Acquisition and Sustainment, *Report on Effects of a Changing Climate to the Department of Defense*, U.S. Department of Defense, January 2019, https://media .defense.gov/2019/Jan/29/2002084200/-1/-1/1/CLIMATE-CHANGE -REPORT-2019.PDF.

45. Darrell Proctor, "Georgia PSC Backs Additional Costs for Vogtle Nuclear Project," *POWER Magazine*, February 19, 2019, https:// www.powermag.com/georgia-psc-backs-additional-costs-for -vogtle-nuclear-project/.

46. Center for Strategic and International Studies, "What Does China Really Spend on Its Military?" ChinaPower, accessed November 13, 2019, https://chinapower.csis.org/military-spending/.

Chapter Eleven: Great Again

1. Donald Trump, speech to Clark County (NV) Republican Party, Las Vegas, NV, April 28, 2011. See "Donald Trump Speech in Las Vegas," C-SPAN video, 37:24, https://www.c-span.org/video /?299259-1/donald-trump-speech-las-vegas.

2. Donald Trump, "Remarks by President Trump at the Veterans of Foreign Wars of the United States National Convention | Kansas City, MO," July 24, 2018, https://www.whitehouse.gov/briefings -statements/remarks-president-trump-veterans-foreign-wars -united-states-national-convention-kansas-city-mo/.

3. "American Attitudes toward the Middle East," Critical Issues Poll, University of Maryland, October 2019, https://criticalissues.umd .edu/sites/criticalissues.umd.edu/files/UMCIP%20Middle%20 East%20Questionnaire.pdf.

4. Ali Khamenei (@khamenei_ir), Twitter, January 1, 2020, 4:14 a.m., https://twitter.com/khamenei_ir/status/1212301034 871279616.

5. "The Arab World in Seven Charts: Are Arabs Turning Their Backs on Religion?," BBC News, June 24, 2019, https://www.bbc.com /news/world-middle-east-48703377.

6. Anne Applebaum (@anneapplebaum), Twitter, October 3, 2019, 10:32 a.m., https://twitter.com/anneapplebaum/status/117976 6267965624320; Applebaum, Twitter, 10:35 a.m., https://twitter .com/anneapplebaum/status/1179766835538825216; Applebaum, Twitter, 10:37 a.m., https://twitter.com/anneapplebaum/status /1179767333411155970.

7. "The Trump Files: Donald Doesn't Believe in 'American Exceptionalism,'" YouTube video, April 30, 2015, 2:00, posted by *Mother Jones*, June 7, 2016, https://www.youtube.com/watch ?v=72wM6cqPS-c.

8. Jeffrey Lord, "A Trump Card," *American Spectator*, June 20, 2014, https://spectator.org/a-trump-card/.

9. Konrad Adenauer, interview by Philip C. Brooks, Bonn, Germany, June 10, 1964, Harry S. Truman Library, https://www.truman library.gov/library/oral-histories/adenauer.

10. "Presidential Candidate Donald Trump Rally in Mount Pleasant, South Carolina," C-SPAN video, 57:30, December 7, 2015, https:// www.c-span.org/video/?401762-1/presidential-candidate-donald -trump-rally-mount-pleasant-south-carolina.

11. Charles Krauthammer, "The Unipolar Moment," *Foreign Affairs* 70, no. 1 (1990/1991): 23-33, https://www.foreignaffairs.com/articles /1991-02-01/unipolar-moment.

Chapter Twelve: Against Revenge

1. Elaine Kamarck, Alexander R. Podkul, and Nicholas W. Zeppos, "Trump Owns a Shrinking Republican Party," *FixGov* (blog), Brookings Institution, June 14, 2018, https://www.brookings.edu /blog/fixgov/2018/06/14/trump-owns-a-shrinking-republican -party/.

2. Catie Edmondson and Jasmine C. Lee, "Meet the New Freshmen in Congress," *New York Times*, updated January 3, 2019, https://www.nytimes.com/interactive/2018/11/28/us/politics/congress-freshman-class.html.

3. Ross is a second cousin of mine. His last name and my mother's maiden name of Rosberg were both shortened from the original "Wronsberg." The Wronsberg clan traveled together to Quebec City from Tsarist Russia in 1913. On the voyage, the clan bitterly quarreled, and they went their separate ways as soon as they landed.

4. Lauren Frias, "SoulCycle, Equinox Owner Stephen Ross Responds after Trump Fundraiser Backlash," Business Insider, August 7, 2019, https://www.businessinsider.com/soulcycle-equinox-owner-stephen-ross-issues-response-trump-fundraiser-backlash-2019-8.

5. Jim Tankersley, "Donald Trump Lost Most of the American Economy in This Election," *Washington Post*, November 22, 2016, https://www.washingtonpost.com/news/wonk/wp/2016/11/22/donald-trump-lost-most-of-the-american-economy-in-this-election/.

6. Peter Baker and Nicholas Fandos, "Bolton Objected to Ukraine Pressure Campaign, Calling Giuliani 'a Hand Grenade,'" *New York Times*, October 14, 2019, https://www.nytimes.com/2019/10/14/us/politics/bolton-giuliani-fiona-hill-testimony.html.

7. Joe Helm, "'They Never Saw This Coming': A Q&A with Kellyanne Conway," *Washington Post Magazine*, January 26, 2017, https://www.washingtonpost.com/lifestyle/magazine/they-never-saw-this-coming-a-qanda-with-kellyanne-conway-on-trumps-victory/2017/01/26/2bf64c10-da96-11e6-9a36-1d296534b31e_story.html.

8. I witnessed such erasure in real time in the case of Fox News personality Greg Gutfeld. We got into a Twitter exchange in November 2019 over his justifications of President Trump's extortion of Ukraine. After telling me that I was an irrelevant, unemployed loser, Gutfeld threw his master accusation: "but at

least my comments never contributed to the deaths of hundreds of thousands. May your axis of evil keep you warm at night!" It took just a few minutes of googling to pull up multiple instances of Gutfeld not only praising the axis of evil speech, but supporting the Iraq war, saluting President Bush, and even endorsing waterboarding—and not in the bygone days immediately after September 11, but as recently as the spring of 2018. When I pointed out this sudden and unexplained self-reversal, Gutfeld was not even slightly chagrined. His words about Bush no longer served his advantage in the moment, and so they vanished from his consciousness. The same will very soon be true about his service of Trump. Gutfeld boasted of his TV success, then invited me to valet his car for him. I replied that I would prefer to valet his conscience; it seemed small, nimble, and easy to park. You can read the main points of the exchange here: David Frum (@davidfrum), Twitter, November 16, 2019, 4:28 p.m., https://twitter.com/davidfrum/status/1195815847517921281; and here: Frum, Twitter, November 16, 2019, 4:29 p.m., https://twitter.com/davidfrum/status/1195816247541276672.

9. Rudyard Kipling, "Recessional," in Rudyard Kipling, *Kipling: Poems*, ed. Peter Washington (New York: Everyman's Library, 2007), 95. See David Frum, "Trump's Recessional," *Atlantic*, July 5, 2019, https://www.theatlantic.com/ideas/archive/2019/07/trumps-july-fourth-speech-had-no-purpose/593401/.

10. Donald Trump, "Salute to America."

11. Kipling, "Recessional," 96.

12. David Frum, *Dead Right* (New York: Basic Books), 1994.

13. Frum, Twitter, January 20, 2017, 8:06 a.m., https://twitter.com/davidfrum/status/822430065208291328.

Index

About the Author

David Frum is a staff writer at the *Atlantic*. He has written or cowritten nine previous books, three of them *New York Times* bestsellers. In 2001 and 2002, he served as speechwriter and special assistant to President George W. Bush. From 2014 through 2017, he chaired Policy Exchange, Britain's leading center-right think tank. He and his wife, Danielle Crittenden Frum, live in Washington, DC, and Wellington, Ontario. They have three children.